Archibald Clavering Gunter

A Princess of Paris

A Novel

Archibald Clavering Gunter

A Princess of Paris
A Novel

ISBN/EAN: 9783337026325

Printed in Europe, USA, Canada, Australia, Japan

Cover: Foto ©Thomas Meinert / pixelio.de

More available books at **www.hansebooks.com**

A PRINCESS OF PARIS

A Novel

BY

ARCHIBALD CLAVERING GUNTER

AUTHOR OF

"MR. BARNES OF NEW YORK," "MR. POTTER OF TEXAS,"
"THAT FRENCHMAN," "MISS NOBODY OF NOWHERE,"
"MISS DIVIDENDS," "BARON MONTEZ," ETC., ETC.

NEW YORK
THE HOME PUBLISHING CO.
3 EAST FOURTEENTH STREET
1894.

THE WINTHROP PRESS,
52-54 LAFAYETTE PLACE,
NEW YORK.

CONTENTS.

BOOK I.

COMRADES OF THE SWORD

BOOK II.

THE SPECULATION IN BEAUTY.

BOOK III.

A PRINCESS OF PARIS.

A PRINCESS OF PARIS

BOOK I.

COMRADES OF THE SWORD.

CHAPTER I.

THE LONE BASTION AT FRIBURG.

"Monsieur le Comte, how many of us will come back?" whispers Lieutenant d'Essais.

"About our usual proportion—one out of two. The regiment of Laval is always lucky," laughs Raymond d'Arnac, as he looks into the blindness of a night opaque as chaos.

But in this darkness, he knows straight in front of him lie the fortifications and strong works of the little town of Friburg, manned by the German, crowned with cannon and laden with death.

These works consist of walls of unusual thickness, pierced by four sortie-gates, eight heavy bastions with *demi-lunes* protecting their curtains, and the usual covered-ways, escarpments and glacis peculiar to the method of fortification invented by that first great master of artillery attack and defense, Monsieur Vauban, the French Engineer.

Beyond the walls are the mediæval streets of the little town of Friburg, and half a mile away, back of these, the great mountain of Schlossberg, upon whose terraces, and dominating all below them, stand four great forts; first, the Castle, which commands the whole town; above it, the Eagle Fort, which dominates the Castle; higher up, the Star Fort, which commands the Eagle, and crowning the summit, the Fort of St. Peter, which dominates them all. On the terraces of this mountain are military works contrived after the best possible manner to resist the escalade and bombardment of that epoch —the year of our Lord 1713.

Within this series of strongholds is a garrison of fifteen battalions of stout Austrian infantry and five hundred semi-barbarous Hungarian horse. The whole commanded by Baron de Arsch, one of the sturdiest commanders of that stout time—the entire affair making one of the hardest military nuts M. le Duc de Villars, the Commander in Chief of his most Christian Majesty Louis XIVth's armies on the Rhine and in Flanders, ever had to crack.

Above all the thing must be done quickly, for just in the distance are the mountains of the Black Forest, famous in legend and story, and beyond them lies Prince Eugene, Generalissimo of the German armies, biting his nails with rage, and sending courier after courier to ride their horses to death, imploring his Imperial Master of Austria to hurry the troops en route from Italy to re-inforce him; and post after post to the States General and the Princes of the German Empire, begging and beseeching they will keep their promises of men and money so he can take open field against his old enemy De Villars, and not see pass from him by forced inactivity and lack of men, the conquests he had so gloriously made in succeeding campaigns together with Church-hill, Duke of Marlborough, and the English Army at Blenheim, Ramillies and Oudenarde over the French.

This town of Friburg DeVillars has been attempting for the last thirty days, carrying his trenches forward, establishing his batteries and *places d'armes*, and battering with siege artillery the stout walls in front of him, until this evening, the breach of Fort Escargo, the first bastion, is reported practical, the assault ordered and the Forlorn Hope detailed and ready—one hundred and fifty of the sturdy Grenadiers of Laval, at their head the two boys, whose whispers are so low that they are unintelligible to their men ten feet to their rear.

For a moment these two boys—Lieutenant d'Essais is but seventeen, and his captain, Raymond, le Comte d'Arnac, scarce twenty—peer into the darkness.

Then Raymond tosses his blonde curls about and laughs: "But if we come back, you will return a *captain*, and I a *major*, my little D'Essais!"

"But so few of us come back!" mutters the boy lieutenant. "Our regiment always gets the hottest places now. Our Colonel, Le Marquis Laval, is disabled by a broken jawbone, and a hundred and fifty is all that's left of us. It was not so before you, D'Arnac, joined us from Paris. Two months ago we lost no more than the others; at that time Clancarthy's Irish Regiment was getting the places nearest to Heaven or Hell. There's very few of them left also."

But here the Captain stops further remark by a hastily muttered "Quiet! I want to place the location of the works in my mind, D'Essais, so I'll know our route in the dark when we make the assault!"

And Raymond d'Arnac peers out into the darkness again, and seeing nothing, imagines Friburg as he saw it at sunset—the last he may ever look on.

In front of him are the low works of the old town; beyond, its hill covered with forts; about him the pretty valley with its low green fields and stately mathematic poplars with faded October leaves, through which the river Dreisam winds, its waters washing the walls of Friburg. Back of all this is the French Army of the siege; in advance, their trenches and batteries, and behind their tents, camp equipage and camp followers, women of pleasure, mummers, acrobats, and wandering musicians who play the soft melodies of Luilli, that bring back to the boy Captain's remembrance the laughing eyes and dancing feet of the beauties of courtly Versailles and joyous Paris.

But his revery is broken in upon. In the darkness he distinguishes a military salute.

A moment after he hears a voice with the soft brogue of an Irish gentleman, whisper in his ear: "Captain d'Arnac, I belave? Permit me to introduce O'Brien Dillon, Major of Clancarthy's Regiment of the Irish Brigade. It's too dark to see, so I hope you'll do me the honor to remember me by me voice, which is a very purty one."

"I have heard of Major Dillon," remarks Raymond, saluting.

"Ah, from whom?"

"The whole army! That affair of outposts."

"Thank you, Captain d'Arnac," interrupts the Irish Major, "though by St. Patrick I don't think you should have told me. I've just been absolved for to-night's bloody work. You make me vain. Vanity, the priests say, is a mortal sin, so perhaps your light words will send the soul of O'Brien Dillon the wrong way to-night. But to business! The order to move is by word of mouth—no rockets or fireworks to give the German gentlemen over there a hint of our visit this evening. They might be *too* hospitable. You and *your* command (you lead the Forlorn Hope, I belave) form the advance. You will be supported by the Regiment Clancarthy as a storming party, which will be followed by two regiments of Swiss, the worst attacking troops in the world. They always stand and shoot, and never charge and stab, which is fatal in assaults on strong places. But I digress. You are to pass to the right of our advance battery, then straight for the main breach of the fort. Ye'll know its position by bringing the lantern of the Gineral's headquarters in line with the torch on our advance battery. Then up the breach—and God help ye, for I think it is about as difficult a place as I ever saw in the way of warfare."

"These are General du Bourg's orders?" mutters D'Arnac, his lips compressed, but his eyes very bright, for he knows how desperate the affair must be.

"Yes," answers the Irishman, shortly. "You will start in five minutes after I lave you. Five minutes after that the supporting columns will move, so what is left of ye will have company Now, good-bye, and the Virgin protect ye," and he silently wrings the hand of the young Frenchman.

As he does so, their interview is broken in upon by a peculiar melodious, yet whining voice, which says plaintively: "Maister!"

"Ah! what the divil do you want, Lanty?"

"Maister, I was just thinkin'"——

"By the soul of Moses, if you think for me again, I'll break ivery bone in your body!" whispers the Irish Major. "Six times in the month have you taken the liberty of thinking for me, and ivery time some devil's luck has come upon me!"

"Maister, I was just thinkin' that I heard a noise in the Escargo Fort, as if the Germans, bad 'cess to them! were marching out of it."

"Ye suspect a sortie?" asks the Irish officer hurriedly, curiosity getting the better of superstition.

"No! Faith I thought they were going back."

"Deserting the fort? Impossible! Lanty, never before did I say you were a fool, but now, mark me, you're brainless!"

"I have been yer Honor's servant for eight years, and it's a pity if I haven't grown like ye!"

"Obey me, or by me soul, you'll not be my servant eight hours! Back to your company!"

"Faith! what does discharging me matter? We're in the storming party, and both of us'll have the divil for our master to-morrow!" mutters Lanty, who saunters back, his gait indicating, as far as darkness permits Raymond to notice, great length of awkward limb.

"Ah, the liberty of an old family servant, I presume, Major Dillon!" remarks the young Frenchman.

"No, all my old family servants died at Limerick," mutters the Irish officer.

"Do you think your servant heard correctly?" asks Raymond eagerly.

"That the Germans left the fort and went back into the town? Impossible! It's against all the rules of war, and I've fought in twenty-two pitched battles. But it is time for you to move, Captain, and for me to marshal the storming party that follows you."

So with a stiff military salute, the Irishman disappears in the darkness, as Raymond d'Arnac whispers to little D'Essais, and each one of his sergeants: "Tell the men to get ready to move! Musketeers in the front and on the flanks! Grenadiers handle your pouches, and light port fires. Forward by column of fours!"

Then the French Forlorn Hope disappears into the darkness of the night, and two minutes after passing the advance breaching battery, makes straight for the glacis and covered-way of the Fort Escargo.

All this is done very quietly—very silently. The blackness of this October night is so great that were it

not for the touch of his file to the right or left of him,
and the muffled tramp of his comrades about him, each
man of that storming party might have thought himself
alone.

The silence is unbroken even by muttered curse of
soldier stumbling in the darkness, for the officers have
sworn to pass sword through the body of any man who
gives tongue even in whisper till the wild rush up the
breach of the German fort.

So, after five minutes of slow and cautious marching,
Raymond, who heads the Forlorn Hope, pauses, and
with his hand keeps back the first four grenadiers
marching behind him, and they in their turn stay the
next line and so on, till all the party have halted.

Then D'Arnac commences to grope about; he thinks
they must be very near the glacis of the Escargo
battery. Creeping forward for some twenty yards, he
comes to the commencement of the fortifications, out-
lined by a small ditch. Carefully crawling until the
two lights that have been pointed out to him in the
French camp are in line, Raymond knows he is exactly
opposite the practicable breach in the walls of the
bastion.

Still creeping he returns to his men, and they, following him very cautiously and very slowly now, soon find
themselves upon the glacis, at the point of attack.

All this time the German fort is very quiet. No
noise of ordering officers. No rattle of accoutrements—
no clank of sabre—no creek of gun carriage comes
down the breach of the slumbering fortress.

Noiselessly the Forlorn Hope commences to mount
the glacis.

Still silence!

A second after, the leading files stumble into the
covered-way.

Silence no longer!

Musketry crackles in the breach above them, hand
grenades explode amongst them—but not many.

There is a hoarse roar from the Forlorn Hope, and
D'Arnac, crying: "Give them the steel!" scrambles
up the broken stonework and rubbish of the breach,
and though sabres flash around him, and muskets are
fired almost in his face, death misses him. The next

second his men are around him, the Germans in full
flight; and Raymond and his one hundred and forty
grenadiers are masters of the Escargo battery, for they
have lost only ten men, killed and wounded, in their
quick rush up the breach.

"Protect the work!" the Captain cries to D'Essais,
who stands beside him. "We have taken it easily—
now to hold it!"

And D'Essais, under his orders, deploys his men so
as to check any return of the Germans, while his
Captain, looking around the deserted ruins of this
strong work, is astounded at the ease of his victory,
for stout German soldiers are not wont to fight in this
half-hearted way, and acute German officers are not apt
to be taken by surprise.

Even as D'Arnac thinks this, and examines what is
beyond him, telling the men to barricade the military
lane that runs to the next fortification (which he knows
is but fifty yards away), and to prepare for a counter
attack—some one, unheeding a musket which is fired at
him by one of the men on guard at the breach, crawls
up into the fort, and giving the password "Malplaquet!"
O'Brien Dillon stands beside D'Arnac.

"*Sapristi!* Major, your supports are soon after me!"
exclaims the young man.

"Faith! I'm the only support ye have at present.
I came ahead of me men, unless it is that fellow Lanty,
but I have outrun him!" gasps the Irishman, who has
apparently come at an awful speed, and still is in a
hurry, for even while he is speaking, Dillon is making
a hasty examination of the fort.

A second after he speaks again: "From the lack of
noise, I discovered you took this too aisey, and I feared
for you."

He is still looking about, examining the embrasures
and guns in them, as Mr. Lanty, crying, "Malplaquet!" the word of the night, before the sentries shoot
at him, stands beside them.

"Examine the cannon in those embrasures, Lanty!"
cries his master. "You know everything. How old
are they?"

"By me soul! they are bombards—culverins and
spiroles—out of date a century ago!"

"As I thought," mutters the Major. "Out of use
since the Thirty Years War. The Germans' real
service guns have all been withdrawn and carried into
the town."

"What does it mean?" gasps Raymond, astounded.

"It means they let you take the fort, but left
nothing in it worth taking. *It means that they've fired a
mine under it!* THE SLOW MATCH IS NOW LIGHTED!"

"And in three minutes we'll all be blown in little
paices to the other world!" cries Lanty with a shriek.

Excitement makes the Irish Major's voice high and
strident, and some of the men hearing him give a little
shudder, veterans as they are, one muttering, "Back,
or we're dead!"—Another second and the French will
be in flight!

But Dillon cries, "Not *back*, but FORWARD! The
Germans don't expect us on the other side of that wall!"

And Raymond yells, "Two bastions instead of *one*.
Masters of these we're masters of Friburg!"

Rushing to D'Essais they throw down the barricade
he is about erecting, and spring out into the military
cause-way—one hundred and forty to attack a garrison
of eight thousand.

In the darkness, not knowing the fortifications
exactly, they soon find themselves, to their wonder,
in a cross trench, and there pause, groping which way
to go.

A second after, they have the light of Hell to point
their path. With a mighty roar, the Fort Escargo leaps
into the air, killing some of the advance of Clancarthy's
Irish Regiment that are even now climbing its breach.

Now Dillon and Raymond see where they are.

The straight military lane they have wandered out of
leads from a second German bastion. Down this some
five hundred stout Walloon infantry have rushed to
overpower any of the French left alive in the Escargo
after the explosion.

In their excitement, these Walloons, not knowing the unexpected movement of Raymond's Forlorn
Hope, rush past them as they stand secreted in the cross
trench.

Then, with a muttered "We have them!" O'Brien
Dillon springs into the main military lane again, and he

and Raymond, followed by their grenadiers, rush into the second bastion, the possession of which gives pass to the streets of the town, if they can hold it.

It is practically a detached fort, a deep fosse or moat filled with water from the river cutting it off from the neighboring walls—but has a gate leading to the town.

There are but few Germans in this work; these, unexpecting attack, are now bayoneted to a man. Then D'Arnac shuts the gates on the town side, just in the face of some Austrian infantry that are going down to the assistance of the Walloon Regiment, which is even now in the ruins of the Fort Escargo, engaging the Irish Regiment of Clancarthy, and its Swiss supports, who are by this time crowding up the ruined glacis.

Thus, sandwiched between Germans in the town and Germans outside the town, who keep succor and support from coming to them, the grenadiers of Raymond find they have two desperate duties—one to keep the German garrison of the town from entering this second bastion they have seized by audacious luck ; the other, to prevent the return of the five hundred Walloons that are now slowly giving back before the Irish regiment. Some of these now turn to re-enter the town, but find themselves, to their dismay, barred out, and lighted hand grenades thrown upon them, and musketry assaulting them, from the fort they have just sallied out of.

The plight of these Walloons is now terrible. On one side, walls they cannot scale, and a gate they cannot force, and on the other, the wild yells and cold steel of the Irish regiment and the cold lead of the Swiss Reserves.

But these Walloon infantry, worthy descendants of Wallenstien's stout cutthroats of the Thirty Years War—die-hards and devil-may-cares—hold themselves well together, and intrenching themselves in the cross road into which Raymond and his followers had wandered by mistake some five minutes before, hold this, like veterans in a trap, against the repeated efforts of the French to dislodge them, until morning comes, some two hours afterwards.

The desperate resistance of the Walloons prevents the French supports reaching Raymond, Dillon, and their devoted band, who are now attacked from the town.

Leaving a few men under D'Essais to keep any struggling Walloons from forcing the outer gates, they now turn their attention to defending the inner wall against the assaults from the garrison, for Baron de Arsch, the German Governor, is thoroughly awake by this time, and very much astounded, and his drums beat a general alarm.

A moment after, one thousand Bavarian infantry headed by Ratzow, come to drive out and destroy these few French dare-devil lunatics, for the position of D'Arnac and Dillon is rather that of insanity than military method.

But assaulted as they are all this night, the Frenchman and the Irishman and their grenadiers—who gradually become fewer and fewer—hold that wall against the repeated attacks of the Austrian infantry.

These would assuredly succeed were they able to use their full force against the French; but a narrow mediæval street leads up to the fortification, and only a narrow front of stout German infantry can be brought to bear against it.

So battling side by side, the Irish veteran and the boyish French Captain grow into each other's love and friendship.   Thirty minutes makes them comrades—an hour devoted friends.

They fight on till after a time, plied by French musketry and exploding hand grenades, the Austrians despair of taking the work by ordinary assault.   De Arsch, who has come to the scene in person, orders cannon to be brought up and sappers and miners to clear away the few houses at the end of the street.

At this the pioneers go to levelling the dwellings of the affrighted townsmen, who with their women and children, run shrieking out of their homes, crying: "Sac!" "Rapine!" "Holy Virgin preserve us!"   For a Sac in those days was as cruel as the torture chamber, and as ruthless as an earthquake.

Gazing at these preparations, the Irish Major mutters: "They're going for artillery.   When they've cleared away the houses, we're doomed!"

To this Lanty, who has been fighting like a devil all night, mutters: "Maister—I've been thinkin'."

"Thinking be d—ned! Keep fighting! It's your infernal thinking that brought us here!"

"Maister, I've been thinkin' the guns on the outer walls are loaded to the muzzle with bullets and slugs for our benefit to-night. Couldn't we bring some of 'em round to this side and feed the German beggars with their own food?"

"Yes! Fight artillery with artillery!" cries D'Arnac.

"Better than that!" chuckles Dillon. "We'll drive them from the street. Then sally out and butcher the sappers in the houses."

While they are speaking they are acting!

In a jiffy they have seized two short twelve-pounders loaded to the muzzle with slugs and dragged them from the outer wall towards the gate opening on the town, against which the German infantry, profiting by the French inaction, are now thundering harder than ever.

A moment after, little D'Essais, his blonde curls waving in the torchlight that illumines their labors, brings up two long nine-pounders, each charged with a round shot and bag of bullets. So four cannon face the gate.

All this is done with desperate rapidity, for the French are working not only for the blood of their enemies, but their own lives.

"Now then—throw open the gates!" cries the Major, the fire of battle in his eyes. "We'll give them first their bellies full of slugs, and through the lanes in them pour the two nine-pounder round shots. D'Arnac, attack with your column before the Austrians recover their senses! Into the houses and cut off the sappers. Hold! first depress the guns until they hit the front rank knee high. Are ye ready?"

"Yes!" answers Raymond from the head of his grenadiers—only one hundred of them now."

"Then throw open the gates!"

As the heavy iron doors clank out the Germans, who are swarming in front of them, give shout of triumph, and rush towards the portals. They think it is surrender.

Then four short, heavy reports—four lanes of fire and death through masses of living men—shrieks of agony from the dying in front—cries of horror from the affrighted in the rear.

"Charge!" yells D'Arnac, and, pouring out into the street, his men give one sharp deadly volley, then use cold steel, trampling over the dead and bayonetting the wounded, for there is little of quarter and none of mercy this desperate night.

The Germans give hurriedly back, thinking the whole French army outside have forced the Walloons, and are coming upon them. For a short five minutes the French have their own way.

"Quick! Into the houses and butcher the working parties!" cries Dillon.

The French swarm into the dwellings, which the sappers are still demolishing, and taking them unawares slaughter them *ad libitum.*

In the dust and darkness of this house-fight Raymond, as he cuts down his foes, hears from the next room a girlish cry. His opponents vanquished, the soldier flies to aid beauty and distress.

He finds both.

Two of his grenadiers are quarreling over a girl of fourteen they have found cowering from fright in the darkness.

"Here's beauty!" laughs one, and seizes the child.

"And booty!" yells the other, dragging a heavy gold chain from her white neck, for the girl is only clothed in the garments of night.

"I buy both!" cries Raymond, stepping beside her. "Ten *louis d'or* for the child—two *louis* for the chain!"

"They're yours, Captain! Settle in camp!" answer the men, fortunately giving their boy commander no trouble, for he would have saved the girl by his sword could he not save her by his purse.

"Quick! or we won't get back!" orders Raymond, who sees through a window the Germans coming on again, and hears Dillon crying: "Retreat! or they'll get in the gate with us!"

Then the child having fainted, Raymond hurriedly picks her up, though somehow her round white arms close round his neck, as if she knew she had found protection. So the French draw off—but not all of them!

Some wretches, **forgetting peril in** love **of** plunder, stay to loot the houses, **and are** hemmed in and slaughtered, for the Germans, savage **at** their losses, have now discovered their foes **are** few, and are advancing rapidly, pouring **out musketry fire as** they come on.

Through **a storm of** bullets D'Arnac, shielding his charge by holding her in front of him, makes his way—he **and** what is left of his band—now but fifty grenadiers.

Some of these are so wounded that, waiting for them, the Austrians almost come up to the French. Hindered by his burden, Raymond is for a moment surrounded, and would be lost, did not the Irish Major, whose arms are bloody to the shoulder, sally **forth** and cut him out.

But this keeps the gates open, and they would be forced now and the work carried had not little D'Essais, who has been left in charge of the fortification, brought up another muzzle loaded cannon.

With it he rakes another line in the advancing columns

Then **the gates close.**

As the **iron bars fall into place,** Dillon gives a low laugh and says : "Ye're a lucky fellow, D'Arnac ! Ye're the only man **who took a prisoner** to-night—and she's a beauty !"

Coming **to** him, he clasps his hand and mutters: "I'm glad ye've taken care of the poor little girl !" and pats her head and strokes her curls. Next he says suddenly: "But we must go to fighting again, me boy, or both of us will be dallying with angels to-morrow—not flesh and blood darlings."

So Raymond takes his little charge, who is still unconscious, and putting her in an out-of-the-way embrasure, where flying bullets will not be apt to find her, girds up his loins for another grapple with his foes.

This has now become almost a death struggle, for the Austrian sappers are working again, and Austrian cannon make their appearance at the end of **the** street, and the attack is pressed more fiercely **than** ever. Grenades and small bombs are thrown by hand from the roofs **of** neighboring houses upon the few Frenchmen who still stand and fight, **and fight** and die, cheered by the gallant Irishman and the French Captain.

At each flight of hand grenades, and each discharge
of Austrian bullets, there are fewer Frenchmen to fight
—fewer Frenchmen to kill. As the last houses that
protect the French work from general assault are
levelled and the German artillery opens fire, Raymond,
his arm cut open by a sabre stroke in the street fight,
clasps the hand of O'Brien Dillon, who is bleeding from
a scalp wound, and mutters: " Thank you for trying to
save my life!"

To this the Irish Major answers through clenched
teeth: "We'll send a few more to Kingdom Come ahead
of us yet. Good-bye, me boy, till the other world! We
go together!"

" *Together !* " echoes D'Arnac.

They know their time has come—for their enemies
have now made temporary bridges and are preparing to
cross the moat and attack them on the flanks, which
they cannot defend—and the Austrians are in no mood
to give quarter.

Even as they speak, a lighted carcass filled with
burning sulphur, to illuminate the work of death, is
thrown into the bastion held by the French, and De
Arsch, the German Commandant, smiling to himself,
says: "We'll have these few Frenchmen!" for he sees
there are now only ten.

But he doesn't!

For now there is a sudden discharge of cannon from
the other side of the bastion, and Lanty, giving shrieks
of joy, comes running to Dillon, crying: "It's me
thinking that's saved ye, ungrateful maister!"

"What the divil have you done?"

"I jest found two cannon that raked the little lane
the cursed Walloons outside were holding. They were
both loaded to the muzzle. So I turned 'em loose on
the bastes that were keepin' succor from coming to us.
I killed a hundred and they've fled. Begorra! Isn't
that a swate Irish yell?"

And so it is!

The Irish regiment, swarming to their aid, stands
beside them, and the Swiss sharpshooters are being
deployed upon the walls. There is the rattle of a
French battery that is being dragged by hand through
the breach of the Escargo and up the military lane, the

whole Irish Brigade is following after it, and the town of Friburg is lost to the Austrians, and stout De Arsch is uttering German curses and withdrawing his garrison into the four great forts upon the Schlossberg that stands half a mile away.

Then Raymond, wiping the blood from his arm, clasps hands with O'Brien Dillon, Major of Clancarthy's Regiment of Irish troops in the French service. Next going in search of the one thing this night has given him save wounds and glory—the little girl he has rescued from the town of Friburg—he takes her tenderly up.

And she, recognizing him, puts her arms round his neck and says: "Brave gentleman! You have saved me! I love you!"

So, clasping her by the hand, and to the word of command and tap of drum, and beside him O'Brien Dillon, followed by Lanty, Raymond marches his storming party—*four* grenadiers of the Regiment Laval now—all that remain alive of this night's death frolic—out of the fort they have given to the King of France, and with it the fair City of Friburg.

But he leaves behind little D'Essais, his blonde curls stained with blood, lying dead upon the lone bastion, and one thousand more brave men, Germans and French, food for the crows, in the broken embrasures and battered walls of the Escargo Fort and narrow streets of the town. All because his Most Christian Majesty of France and his cousin, the Emperor of Austria, had had a little dispute as to who should be King of Spain.

CHAPTER II.

THE ANNALS OF A SOLDIER OF MISFORTUNE.

So THEY march down over the ruins of the exploded bastion, a melancholy but glorious procession, greeted with the *bravas* of the French troops and the wild yells of the Irish Brigade, who line the road to the little bridge over the Dreisam.

Here some columns, marching to the further assault and occupation of the town, open their ranks and cheer them as they pass through, though there is little time for ceremony, for the French are following up their successes of the night, and the rattle of musketry from Friburg now shows they are driving the last of the Austrians out of the streets of the place into their fortresses on the Schlossberg.

At last the heroes of the night stand before Raymond's tent with the grime of battle still on them; their uniforms are rags, their limbs trembling with the wear and tear, both mental and physical, of fighting without hope of victory—without hope of life. The four grenadiers, veterans as they are, look at each other as if astounded they still live, until dismissed to their quarters.

Notwithstanding offers of hospitality the Irish Major says: "Good-bye, my lad. I want a little sleep, and Lanty, as usual, wants his breakfast. I presume this afternoon will see you at least a major."

" And you, I presume, a colonel," answers Raymond, pressing the hand of his friend of a night.

"Faith, I hope so," mutters Dillon, "but the divil's own luck has been upon me ever since I was—" He checks himself suddenly, biting his lip, then goes on— "for the last year. If I was anybody else they might make me a gineral, but, bedad! when you've given up hoping it's best to stop guessing."

Then casting his eyes over the tents of the surrounding army, he says suddenly: "Lanty, they must have moved the headquarters of our regiment."

"Begorra! the Rigiment Clancarthy can get along without headquarters after last night."

" What do you mean ? "

" Why, I mane that I counted 'em on the bastion before we left and I could only find twenty-five of 'em, all tould. The colonel's dead and there's divil another officer in the rigiment, save yourself. Shure, yer Honor 'll be the colonel and perhaps they'll make me the next in command."

But this prophecy does not seem to affect Dillon with joy. He mutters to himself these curious words: "It's the second regiment my bad luck has destroyed." A moment after, as if trying to throw something from his mind, he laughs a little shortly, and patting Raymond on the shoulder, says: "Good-bye. I leave you to yòur luck. Faith, you've captured a little beauty. Every man in the camp will envy you."

But Raymond, who has been too short a time a soldier to have acquired the vices peculiar to the camps of those rough-and-tumble days, replies curtly: "No one will envy me, Major Dillon. Until I can restore her to her friends, my capture of last night rests there," and points up the valley of St. Peters, towards the spires of the Carthusian monastery and convent that pierce the blue sky a couple of miles away.

"Ah! God bless you for a good-hearted and an honest boy!" cries Dillon. "Couldn't you tell I was only testing you, to find out if you were as bad as all the rest of the young bloods, and now that I find you're better, it's the joy of my heart to have saved your life. Good-bye until ——"

"Until this afternoon," answers Raymond, "The friendship of last night shall last till you wish it to cease."

"Faith, an' it will be a long one, then," replies Dillon Then, looking at the child, whose loveliness is heightened by her little bare feet made rosy by the cold and made picturesque by Raymond's blue infantry coat in which he has wrapped her to keep her white limbs from the fresh October breeze, the Major remarks: "I hope she'll bring you more happiness than the one I saved. Always dread beauty."

"An Irishman a woman-hater!" ejaculates Raymond.

"Not a woman-hater, but a woman-*fearer*," replies Dillon. Then he gives a gloomy sigh, wrings Raymond's hand and strides away, followed by Mr. Lanty, who has taken advantage of this colloquy to borrow from D'Arnac's servant enough wine and provisions to make a very comfortable meal for himself and master, laughingly remarking, "Excuse the liberty, Captain, but we've not been foraging for a week."

Left alone, Raymond turns to the child, who has been looking at him eagerly—perhaps almost timidly— and her beauty interests him more than ever. He asks, reassuringly, "What is your name, little one?"

"Jeanne," she replies.

"Jeanne? No other?"

"Oh, yes. Jeanne Françoise Quinault."

"And your father and mother?"

"My father is dead."

"Oh! Killed during the siege?"

"No, doing a triple somersault."

"A what?"

"A triple somersault. My father was an acrobat—my mother is an actress. I have two brothers, Abraham and Maurice. I am an actress, too. I play children's parts, and dance and sing. Would you like me to recite? I know some of Moliere's lines."

"Oh, strolling players!" ejaculates the young man, perhaps looking with slightly less reverence at the pretty little goddess who stands in bare feet beside him.

Then a struggle comes into his mind. Her family dispersed, perhaps destroyed. Why should he not take what has been given into his hands? He will be kinder to her than others. It will be a better life than that she has been following, for strolling players in the year 1713 were not considered of any great account in the social life of this world.

But even as he thinks this, trusting blue eyes are turned upon him. The child says: "You have saved my life. You are as noble as the hero of the play. I trust you."

D'Arnac feels two soft lips pressed upon his hand, and mutters to himself: "She shall not trust in vain."

Calling to his servant he says: "Get one of the laundresses of the regiment—one of the soldier's wives—and let her get some clothes for this little girl, and see she has enough to eat, and at one o'clock have my horse ready," then goes in and writes a report of last night's affair to his commanding officer, tumbles upon his cot, and goes to sleep like Morpheus himself.

Five hours after he takes breakfast with his protegé, and finds the girl so fascinating that, horses being brought, he takes personal charge of her journey to the Carthusian Convent, for the lanes about an army of those days were filled with camp followers who were little better than banditti.

Arriving at the Convent, Raymond places his little protegé in charge of the good nuns, upon which she bursts into tears, and sobs: "Don't leave me here *forever!*"

And he, looking at the bright face, and thinking it is too sunny to become that of a nun, says: "No, only till I can place you in your mother's arms!"

"Pooh! I love you much better!" At this Raymond laughs merrily, and the mother superior gives a gasp of horror.

"My mother gets drunk!" continues little Jeanne.

"Does she? Then I'll forward you to my relatives in France!" says this young gentleman, who does not do things by halves.

Having made up his mind on this point, D'Arnac hastily bids her adieu, and rides back to his quarters, where he finds an orderly from his brigade general bearing a packet marked "*Colonel d'Arnac, on Service,*" and opening it, finds a most complimentary epistle, thanking him for the town he has given to the French Arms, and notifying him of his appointment as Acting Colonel of his regiment, a rank that the writer states there is no doubt will be confirmed by the King at Versailles, as soon as he hears of Raymond's marvelous achievement.

Filled with joy and pride, this boy Colonel of twenty thinks: "Egad! had it not been for the noble Irishman, I would have been buried under the débris of the Escargo Fort, and not a colonel. I will ride over and congratulate Dillon. He at least must be a colonel also!"

With the impetuosity of youth, Raymond throws himself upon his steed once more, and gallops to the tent occupied by O'Brien Dillon, to find that veteran very gloomy and morose.

"Let me congratulate you!" he cries.

"Congratulate me on what?" answers the Irishman, savagely. "On being arrested?"

"Arrested!" gasps Raymond. "They've made me a colonel."

"And, begorra, put O'Brien Dillon under arrest, and poor Lanty is in the guard tent."

"*Impossible!*"

"Divil doubt it! Look at that letter!" and the Major hands Raymond one in the same handwriting that had brought joy to D'Arnac, but which curtly orders Major O'Brien Dillon, of Clancarthy's Regiment of Foot, to deliver up his sword to the officer bearing the note, and hold himself under arrest in his tent, until a court martial can be called together to try him on the following charge, viz: "Conduct unbecoming an officer, on the evening of the 13th of October, 1713, in deserting his command in the presence of the enemy, during active service on an attack upon the Escargo Fort, and not being with his regiment during the night in question."

"Why, you were the hero of the attack! Deserting your command! You were *in front* of it!"

"Yes, too far in front of it; I presume that's what they mean," sneers the Major. "And then, poor Lanty, they talk about making him run the gauntlet. There are only twenty five men in the regiment, and it will be a very short, though not a merry run Mr. Lanty will have."

"This outrage I will prevent with my life—with my sword—with my honor!" cries Raymond, and impulsively runs out to mount his horse again.

"Where are you going?" calls O'Brien after him.

"To the Duc de Villars, Maréchal of France!"

"Then, for God's sake, don't leave till I speak to you! I'm under arrest and can't leave me tent, or I would pull you off that horse myself!"

Thus adjured, Raymond, stifling his indignation, though his cheeks are flushed, his eyes flashing and his lips trembling, unhorses himself again, and re-enters the tent of the Irish Major.

"Now sit down on that corn-beef keg, and promise not to get up from it until I tell you."

"But I can arrange this affair—I can do justice to you!" urges Raymond. "Maréchal de Villars is my father's friend, and was my granduncle, the great Turenne's pupil in arms. He will believe me. I will destroy your cowardly enemies——"

"Enemies—that's what it is! That's what I want to talk to you about, before you go to the Duke, so you may know how to meet them. Listen to me! I think it is enemies we both have!"

"Pooh! I haven't an enemy in the world!" sneers Raymond, "unless it is the Austrians over there, as a matter of business."

"Haven't you—my poor confidin' babe—Colonel though ye are? I think ye have a very deadly and

a most secret one! But light a pipe with me. I've got
some rare Virginia tobacco—some of the last that
my—— But we won't think of that!" he says, with a
sigh. "Present evils take precedence of past ones.
Now, you smoke, and I'll talk. What—you won't
light up? You haven't learned the fashionable amusement. Bedad! it's the only thing that's kept me from
going crazy. Sometimes in the last year, when I think
of my——!"

He checks himself suddenly again, but a fearful
expression, sterner than even that of battle, has come
into the Irishman's blue eyes.

Next he says: "I can smoke and talk too. You
listen, and answer my questions straight as a lunge *en
carte*—for perhaps your life depends on it. Have ye
ever noticed, since you joined it two months ago, what
has been happening to your regiment?"

"I hardly think I understand you," returns Raymond.
"The Regiment of Laval has had the usual chances of
war. Our losses have been——"

"Enormous! Unheard of!" interrupts the Major.
"When you joined your regiment you were about eight
hundred strong. To-day you're *four*, rank and file, and
you, its Colonel, have had a cat's lives or you'd have
been in the burial trench a hundred times. Before
you came your regiment averaged about the same death
rate as the rest of the army, barring my regiment,
which was always in bad luck ever since I joined it.
We always had the most desperate places, and before
that the regiment I belonged to, that of De Crissey, was
equally unfortunate. They were always put into the
deadly place in the fight. Why did the Headquarters'
staff do it? It wasn't luck that *always* gave my regiment the worst of it. Neither was it luck that has
always put your regiment—since you joined—at the
point of massacre. There must be some reason for it."

"The chances of war."

"This is no chance, it's design I am talking about!
My regiment, De Crissey's, lost four hundred men in
the escalade and fight in the swamp at Landau, and four
hundred more in the attack upon the ravelin at that
place. Then there was no more regiment of De Crissey,
and I was transferred to as fine an Irish one as ever

carried the colors of France, only three weeks ago,
and we have now got twenty-five men left, according
to Lanty, and a major under arrest. You join your
regiment, and in less than two months, from eight
hundred, you come down to four men, all told, and
a colonel, not under arrest, thank God! Now, there
is some reason for this. Who do you think your
enemy is?"

"Great Heaven! you don't imagine Du Bourg, the
General in command of our division?"

"Oh no! He is simply a soldier. It is his Chief-of-
Staff, I think—that little snivelling dandy who has just
come from the Court at Versailles, that little sycophant
to the powers that be."

"Lenoir?"

"The man! Gaston Lenoir!"

"Why should he hate us?"

"He don't hate us. He's simply doing the dirty
work of some one in the French Court. Perhaps two,
my enemy and thy enemy. Raymond le Comte
d'Arnac, who is the lady who hates you?"

"No one!" replies the young Frenchman. Then he
asks suddenly: "Who is your fair enemy?"

"Divil if I know. There is only one, and she—
sometimes I think she must be dead, and sometimes,
God knows I don't know what I think!" and tears
stand in the Irish officer's eyes, which make him look
very tender, and very handsome, for he is as yet under
thirty, and though he has the strong yet graceful
figure of a soldier, his face has a genial and kindly
look, and his eyes would be laughing ones had not some
incident of his military life made them seem almost
sad. Then he says solemnly: "Last night made you
my friend, the only friend I have got in the world now.
All the officers of my regiment are killed, and Lanty in
the guard-tent, poor divil! Sometimes I feel as if
I must tell somebody about my sore heart, and you're
the only man this side of Ireland that I would tell, and
perhaps it may help you to fight my battle a little for
me, and may be it may help you to fight your battle for
yourself. Would you like to hear the annals of a soldier
of misfortune, before you go to see, on his behalf, the
Maréchal of France?"

"If it will please you to tell me!" mutters Raymond, noting the agitation of his Irish friend.

"Very well, then. My father was killed some twenty-five years ago, fighting for his King, James the Second, of the Holy Catholic faith, at the siege of Limerick, and with him the most of my relatives, save my cousin, Arthur Dillon, who, they tell me, is coming over here to take the French service, like myself. I was educated by the Priests of Tralee, and there picked up Lanty, who was a lay brother, and knew more than all the rest of the monastery. He was a great student—he could read Latin and Greek, and was experimenting with what he called the forces of nature, and what the monks thought was unholy, and meant dealings with the divil. So one night, after he had illuminated the whole monastery with some candles he made of nothing by a whirling machine he had invented, they accused him, on account of the great *light* he produced, of having dealings with the Prince of *Darkness*, and put him into a cell for life. And I, God forgive me for my sin, if I committed one! thought his was a hard fate, as he told me he had only got the idea of the light by stroking a cat's back the wrong way, and gitting a spark out of her. So, as he'd been very kind to me when I ran away from the monastery to be a soldier, I slipped down into the vaults, and released him. And from that day to this, if it wasn't for his infernal thinking all the time, he'd be the best servant and most faithful creature that ever followed a man through the bad luck and good luck, through the famine and plenty, through the poverty and riches that always come to a dashing soldier of fortune.

"With Mr. Lanty following after me, by hook and by crook we evaded the priests and made our way to the Cove of Cork, and from there got passage in a trading lugger to Ostend, which was then, as luck would have it, in possession of the French, where I enlisted as a gintleman volunteer, and fought my way up in three pitch battles to that of a lieutenant of De Crissey's Regiment of Horse. Lanty, to give me a genteel appearance, acting as my servant, and swearing my family was the oldest in Ireland, which I supported with my sword in three bloody duels, until no one doubted the good

blood of O'Brien Dillon.   Then, with a little luck at
gaming, I bought my captain's commission, and became
Captain O'Brien Dillon of De Crissey's Dragoons, and
thought myself a very fine gintleman, and a very lucky
one.   That was three years ago.   Two more years of
battle, and I became a major, and then came—but a
little over a year ago—the greatest joy of my life, and
the greatest misery as well.   One evening, just after
De Villars had forced Prince Eugene at Denain, and
Du Bourg had captured Marchiennes with all the
German supplies and most of their ammunition, and had
settled down very comfortably to the siege of Douay,
for we were having rather easy work of it now, Queen
Anne having made peace with his Majesty of France,
and Marlborough and his British guards, infantry and
cavalry, that were always killing us, and making themselves disagreeable to us, having sailed away across the
water,———

"Well, one night De Crissey, our Colonel, sent for
me to his tent, and says: 'Major, do you want desperate
duty?'

"I says: 'If there's anything in it in the way of
glory or honor.'

"He says: 'More!   There's money!'

"'Where is it?' whispered I, very eager.   Then he
detailed me with two squadrons of dragoons to join
Colonel Pasteur in his great raid on Dutch Brabant,
that was to make things even for General Grovestein's
outrageous treatment of the French peasantry about
Metz.   It was to be a foray of blood, a foray of fire,
and a foray of robbery, for which they had picked out
nearly a thousand of the most desperate riders in the
French army.

"Leaving   camp   that   night,   we   skirted   and
flanked Prince Eugene's entrenchments and got
safely into Namur by the morning.   We were there
reinforced by a detachment from the garrison, which
made in all about fifteen hundred as wild and reckless
recruits as ever the divil enlisted, that were to be let
loose like a pack of mad dogs on the peaceful peasantry
and rich burghers of the Low Countries.

"And what a foray it was!

"We left Namur early in the morning and crossing

the Schelde at Langdorp, we pushed up right through the heart of Flanders, into Holland, swimming dykes, burning villages, and traveling with fire and blood, but taking no plunder—being in too much of a hurry. So in twenty-four hours we were at Bergen-op-Zoon—ninety full long English miles from Namur. Then we started back—and this time it was fire and blood and *plunder* also. We harried the country between the Schelde and the Meuse. Lanty was in his element. He had three burgomasters under ransom himself, in one day, and the whole of us had taken some sixty of them, and bailiffs and magistrates as hostages. Oh, the richness of the country! Bedad the men got so much silver, they almost turned up their noses at gold, and as for jewelry it was nothin' less than diamonds they'd look at towards the end. But word being brought to the States General of our diviltries, they had detachments from the garrisons of Antwerp, and Ghent, and Leige, and Brussels, and every other place in Flanders, Brabant and Holland looking after us.

"One time we were surrounded, and divil a man of us would have gotten away alive, let alone carryin' off any booty, but our Colonel Pasteur was the man for the emergency, and he asked for volunteers to disguise themselves as peasants and give the surrounding detachments wrong information of our route. I would have volunteered myself for this duty, but they stopped me on account of my brogue, which would have betrayed me and been the ruin of us. In the excitement I had forgotten my Irish accent.

"So our volunteers, disguised as Dutch peasants, were questioned by the enemy as to our line of travel, and gave 'em such true information they missed us entirely. So we, coming down by the way of Lilo, crossed the Schelde by boat, and passing within five miles of Brussels, harrying, burning, plundering and ravaging, at last got deep into the recesses of Sonien forest.

"There we camped, after three blessed days of the hardest work that mortal man ever endured, for one or two of the troopers had died from fatigue in the saddle; and as for the horses, if we had not remounted ourselves from the Dutch farmers, we would have all been foot soldiers by this time. But our flesh and blood was weak and hungry, and must have rest and food.

"We were compelled to encamp for a few hours, I taking up my quarters in a little farmhouse along with Captain Ducroc and some other officers of Pasteur's own regiment. There my adventure came upon me, that changed me from a soldier of fortune to a soldier of *misfortune.*

"Sometimes I think it was judgment upon me for confiscating a gold communion service; but that was from a Lutheran church, so it can hardly count against me. Anyhow, the Virgin help me! there's been a curse on me from that day to this. Sometimes I think it's God's doings, and sometimes I feel it is a man sneaking behind my back and plotting my despair and death." And the Major's eyes glow as he tosses his long hair back from his forehead, like a lion looking for the sulking savage whose arrow is in his hide.

CHAPTER III.

THE DUEL BY THE CAMP FIRE.

AFTER a moment O'Brien Dillon overcomes his emotion and goes hurriedly on, as if hoping by narrative to destroy sentiment.

"So I came up to the house followed by Lanty and his burgomaster captives—who had been tied on horses to keep them from running away—myself laden down with the gold I had gathered up in the way of cups and plates and doubloons from many a rich Flemish village, to say nothing of jewelry, till I felt myself more like a *fermier général* than a soldier of fortune.

"In front of the gate leading to the little orchard stood a coach with four horses, one of those grand equipages that people of quality travel in.

"'Is that some of our plunder, Lanty?' says I, for by this time I thought the whole world entirely was mine, spoils were so piling up on me.

"Lanty answers, 'No, yer honor, that's Captain Ducroc's capture, and he's mighty proud of it, and more proud of what's inside of it.'

"Just then-Ducroc stepped out of the coach, carrying a bag of plunder also, to prevent any one else robbing him of it, for the whole command had gotten so in the way of confiscation that a priest three days in our company would have become a thafe from very force of example. After the Captain stepped out a little snivelling maid servant, but, notwithstanding the tears in her eyes, very pretty in a peasant way.

"I was just turning away to mind my own business when Ducroc's voice caught me. He was standing by the side of the carriage, his handsome, wicked face blazing with anger, and saying very much after the manner of the Sultan of Turkey to an odalisque: 'Step out of the carriage at once, madame! Obey me!'

"Then, deeply veiled, I saw the figure of a female Venus leave the equipage and follow him into the farmhouse.

"'They killed the postilions and captured the lady and the coach, and it's full o' jewels and lots o' fine things, only half an hour ago, just off the road leading from Brussels!' says Lanty, who always seems to know other people's business as well as his own. 'That Ducroc,' he whispers in me ear, 'is a great brute!'

"Though I myself didn't like the Captain's manner, still, if it had been a peasant girl, or perchance, a burgomaster's daughter, I should not have interfered; but something in the style of the lady's walk, something in her haughty carriage, told me Ducroc's captive was more like to be a princess than anything else.

"However, I stepped into the farmhouse and found an empty room, the other officers not having come in yet, being busied about the proper care of their booty.

"In the next room was Ducroc and the lady, from which I heard these words, in a voice so swate it went to me heart of hearts: 'One thousand crowns for my safe conveyance into France!'

"Then I heard Ducroc's nasty, dirty, mean, rascally laugh.

"Again the voice pleadingly: '*Five* thousand crowns for my safe conduct into France—and my blessing—and my prayers.'

"Still Ducroc's jeering laugh.

"'TEN THOUSAND!'

"But her captor'sneers: 'I have so much plunder already, mademoiselle, that I care nothing for money— only for beauty!'

"At this the lady's voice grew very sad and very desperate, as I heard her gasp in tones that broke my heart: 'Then I kill myself!'

"At which I burst into the room, calling out: 'Ducroc, come to dinner, me boy! Ye've only three hours before we march again. Our scouts say Prince Eugene has despatched thirty squadroons to capture us, dead or alive.' Then, appearing to be astonished, I said: 'Excuse me—a lady! Oh, naughty Captain!' and looked at her.

"Oh, Raymond! the form of a Greek Venus! Eyes blue as the Irish Sea! Hair with sunset in it!

"As I gazed at her I put my hand on Ducroc's shoulder. 'Come to dinner, dear boy,' I said laughingly. 'Appetite first—love afterwards! Come—to dinner!'

"But I didn't mean dinner, I meant death, because I had made up my mind to save that poor despairing girl, or kill him before we broke camp.

"So coming out, we sat down to a very hasty and impromptu meal that was served in the little orchard by the Flemish farmer and his trembling *frau*. It was a pretty piece of greensward with a couple of apple trees stuck in it for ornament. A camp fire was blazing as the sunset was coming on. This, as the night was cold, was surrounded by us officers, each with his plunder, for safe keeping, behind him, and his servant sitting at his hand and helping him to wine and food. Each man taking his master's leavings for himself— Lanty doing the same by me.

"There were some eight or ten of us now, and the wine flowed fast, and all the time I kept my eye on Ducroc to see he didn't leave us.

"Then eating being finished and only drinking going on, I proposed dice, for I knew Ducroc's weakness. He had *all* the vices, but he loved gambling *the most*.

"The stakes were very high, for every man of us thought himself a Crœsus, and as the bottle passed and repassed, they grew higher and higher.

"I wagered two golden goblets for me first throw, and won. Lanty grabbed up me winnings mighty quick and piled them up behind me for safety. Soon the game grew desperate, and by the blessing of Heaven I was very lucky, and in a couple of hours, by continuous throwing, I had won from the rest enough to make them drop out, and from Ducroc every bit of plunder he had stolen in our three days' foray, and he had done more than his share.

"'Have ye anything else ye'd like to lose, Captain?' said I, easily, with a little laugh, which made him angry.

"'That coach and four horses!' cried he desperately, pointing to the equipage. Then he muttered to himself: 'She can ride behind me!'

"'Five hundred crowns agin' them, if ye like!'

"Up they went!

"Again I won!

"He looked around for more to stake, for he'd have played for his life by this time, if any one had valued it save himself. After an instant he muttered, 'The trunks containing her dresses. The clothes she has on now will last her my time.'

"'Faith! ye're about right, thinks I, Captain Ducroc. But I only remarked, 'Two diamond rings and a couple of hundred crowns against them.'

"'All right,' said he.

"Then, a flambeau being brought, for it was very dark now, and the only light we had was from the camp fire, the game went on.

"'Three sixes and a deuce,' said he.

"'Four fives!' cried I, and Lanty gave a yell of joy and gathered in the stakes.

"'Have ye anything else?' I said.

"'My horse and accoutrements,' he groaned. 'She can walk as well as I.'

"'Against this diamond ring?'

"'If you add one hundred crowns to it.'

"'Done!' says I, 'but you like more than the worth of your money.'

"Agin I won.

"'Have ye anything else ye'd like to lose very quick?' I laughed. I was bantering him and he was growing savage and desperate. Finally he says 'YES.'

"'What?'

"'The girl in the house.'

"'The servant maid? Lanty might gamble with you for her.'

"'No! the mistress.'

"'She's not worth much. She will only bother me to get her away. She's too delicate a piece of merchandise,' says I, trying to appear unconcerned.

"'You've seen her. You know how beautiful she is,' he answered. 'What will you put against her?'

"I was going to say 'everything I have in the world,' but I restrained myself and laughed. 'Would one hundred crowns please ye?'

"'One hundred crowns!' he cried. 'Bring her out. Let him look on her beauty She is worth ten thousand.'

"The other officers applauded this idea.

"I said nothing. I had a guess she'd like to see me kill him, and I was pretty sure the sword would follow the dice box, Ducroc was in such a divilish humor.

"So they led her out, she looking like an old picture I had seen in a monastery in Ghent of Bordicea when the Romans captured her. If glances would have stabbed, her eyes would have been the death of every man of us round the camp fire. But after one fierce look she gave a sigh and stood before us having the beauty of a despairing goddess. Then the flickering fire lit up her face, and there was a cry of admiration from every man of them.

"'Gintlemen,' said I, 'I intind to win this lady, but I won't shame her by valuing charms that are inestimable.'

"At this she muttered, wringing her hands, 'Diced for as a slave,' and, growing cold and haughty as a martyred saint, drooped her lovely eyes, and the roses on her cheeks became lillies.

"So I said hurriedly, 'Make my bet for me, gintlemen, and *put it high.*'

"They decided that I must risk all I had won against her.

"'Murdher! she's not worth that much,' shrieked Lanty.

"'Shut your lying mouth, ye scoundrel!' cried I. 'She's worth the earth to me.'

"So we prepared to throw. My heart was in my mouth

as Ducroc handled the dice, but Lanty whispered in my ear: 'Look out! he's chatin'! he's changin' the bones on ye!'

"Then I knew I had him.

" Even as he made his throw—four infernal sixes—I put my hands on the dice and said: 'Captain Ducroc, ye're a chate and a scoundrel!'

"With that he sprung, not for my throat, but for the dice that would prove my words; but I held him off with one hand on his gizzard, and tossed the cubes to the officers gathered round, and they, testing them, gave a gasp of horror. Robbers that they were, they could not stomach a gintleman's chatin' at the gambling table; so they declared me the man of honor —the victor!

" 'Not yet!' gasps Ducroc, and in a second his sword was out. But mine was out, too, and parried his first wild lunge.

"In a moment our blades were knocked up by the others; but after a little consultation they decided it best for us to fight it out.

"I might have stood on me honor, for he had been caught chatin', but we didn't care very much for etiquette when on a foray in Flanders. Besides, I thought for her sake that he had better be out of the way.

"As we threw off our cuirasses and cavalry jackets my second, as he handed me my sword, whispered: "Dillon, beware his lunge over the arm. Ducroc is the deadliest swordsman in the army of the Rhine.'

"And Lanty hearing this commenced to wring his hands and groan. But just before we engaged he said to my ear: 'Play him quiet, Major dear, for God's sake, till I flash the blaze in his face!'

"I couldn't understand his hint, for divil a blaze could I see as Ducroc and I faced each other! The camp fire had smouldered down to ashes and embers.

"Then in the half darkness our blades crossed. Never had I faced such a fencer! Time after time I tried each trick of the sword I knew—*and it was parried!* Before me was a wrist of steel springs, an arm of iron and *riposte* quicker than lightning and every time his point came straight for my heart.

"It was like fighting with a ghost, as we moved about in the dim glow of the camp fire.

"I was growing tired. Ducroc was smiling a deadly, cold, victorious smile. The perspiration of despair was on me as I thought of the girl's fate with me dead.

"The glare of the flickering camp fire scarcely flashes on our dancing blades. Then Lanty whispers: 'Get the wind at your back, Major dear, before he finishes ye!'

"With a last effort I circled round the fire till I felt the breeze cool the back of my burning neck.

"Suddenly Lanty throws a heavy branch of wood on to the embers. Up flashes the blaze blown by the wind into Ducroc's triumphant eyes!

"With that flash I lunge—my one last trick *en tierce;* for one second the glimmer dazes him, and in that second I run Ducroc through the body up to my sword hilt, as dead a man as ever died in uniform.

"Disengaging my blade the warrior became the courtier. I stepped to the captive of me dice box and me sword, who had looked on, her beautiful eyes dazed with horror, and making her a bow in my neatest style, said: 'Madam, honor me by considering me your brother till I have the pleasure of placing you safe in France !'

"At the word 'brother,' there was a snicker from some of the wild young divils of cavalry officers; but I soon stopped that nonsense by adding: 'And the man who doesn't treat ye as if ye *were* the sister of O'Brien Dillon, ANSWERS TO ME WITH HIS LIFE!' for the dacent ones among us respected me sentiments, and the others me lunge *en tierce.*

"The girl looked at me with unbelieving, astonished eyes. Finally she muttered: 'Ye heard my offer to that dead ruffian?'

"'Yes!'

"'You will take me safe to France?' she faltered, 'for ten thousand crowns?' turning such grateful eyes on me that their beauty caused me to anticipate myself.

"'Yes,' cried I, 'but not for ten thousand crowns, nor twenty thousand—but only for one smile from your pretty face!' Then I whispered, 'And one little 'yes' from your swate lips, for by the blessing of God and the blessing of the priest, I'll make ye Madame O'Brien Dillon as soon as we cross the frontier!'

"Then oh the blushes of her! Rosebuds were lillies to her cheeks. But the next moment she grew very pale, and commanding herself, she placed a little confiding, though trembling hand in mine, and answered: 'Swear to make good your promise!'

"'I made you two promises!' said I, '*one* to get you safe to the French lines, and *the other* to make you Madame O'Brien Dillon. And by my sword I'll make 'em both good!'

"At this she hung her head.

"So to put away her embarrassment, I playfully remarked: 'Just tell me your present name, sweetheart, so I can address ye convaniently until after the ceremony.'

"But at this time the bugle interfered with my love-making, sounding: 'Boots and saddles!' and I had only time to put her into the coach, to which Lanty had harnessed the four horses.

"But as he was bringing out the maid servant, and took some little time to do it, the rascal, I got two more seconds with my sweetheart. So I suddenly gave her two lover's kisses, whispering, 'I haven't time to talk to ye now, *darling*, so keep these for me, and be sure ye return them at the next stopping place.'

"Then away we went again, I riding alongside of my lady love's coach, like a knight of old. And by the blessing of God, that night we escaped from and out-marched the thirty squadroons of dragoons Prince Eugene had sent after us, for with such a treasure in my possession I was mortally afraid of meeting the enemy then.

"That very march we got into Namur, about two o'clock in the morning. There I had a little talk with her, tired as I was, having hardly closed my eyes for four days.

"Then she told me her name was Hilda Van Holst, and that her father and mother were both dead.

"'God bless 'em!' laughed I. 'I always loved orphans!' for her beauty made me crazy with joy at me luck.

"Next she informed me her uncle was a great banker and money changer, one John Lauriston (hesitating a little over the name), a Scotchman, her mother having come from that country; that her uncle was in Paris, where she was journeying to join him, when to her astonishment, she was captured but a few miles out of Brussels. Then she begged me as I loved my mother, to remember my words to her, and to take her safe to France unharmed and scathless.

"'There's no need of remembering my mother,' says I, 'when I look at ye! By the body of St. Peter, I'd take the future Madame O'Brien Dillon through all the dangers of both armies, safe into France! Now, since ye won't return me the two kisses I gave ye,' for she was very bashful and blushing, which only added to her charm and her beauty, 'I'll add two more to the account!' Which I did, and came from her presence happy as a gineral after he has captured a town.

"In the ante-room of the inn I met Mr. Lanty.

"'What are ye doing here?' says I.

"'Like master, like man!' answers he. 'The future Mrs. O'Brien Dillon has a very pretty maid servant— one Rósalie Lutin.'

"Then he says to me: 'By me soul, Major! never let your lady get away from ye! Rosalie tells me her mistress is a member of the very richest trading family in Europe. They've more money than dukes.'

"But love was in my soul, and I wasn't thinking of lucre.

"Two days afterwards I got my sweetheart safe through the lines, and put her down in the little town of Arles, five leagues to the rear of Donay, in as elegant quarters as any lady of the place, for I had come back a rich man from my spoilation of the Low Countries.

"From there Hilda would have journeyed on direct to Paris, but I didn't propose my darling should get any further from me, so Lanty and I, during the journey, had taken possession of all the future Madame O'Brien Dillon's baggage and wealth, I leading her to suppose they had been lost in a desperate fight with out-posts.

"In fact, I only saved for her, according to my account, two dresses, for the clothes Hilda wore were of such superior quality and richness that I was frightened she might pawn one or two of them, and get money enough to take her on her way. And as I considered myself even at that time not only her protector, but her lord and master as well, I said the future Madame O'Brien Dillon should take no more journeys without me by her side.

"Then she forwarded a letter by post to her uncle in Paris, telling him of her whereabouts, and asking him for money and instructions as to how she should reach him. This was addressed to John Lauriston, care Monsieur Poisson, Rue Dauphin, Paris.

"About this time we cavalrymen were having easy work of it, the infantry being very busy with the siege of Douay, which was getting along very nicely. Day after day and evening after evening, I journeyed from our lines to visit my sweetheart, and press her promise upon her.

"But she put me off, urging that she must have her guardian's consent, but not to doubt her—for the faith of Heaven—not to doubt her. Was I not her savior, her preserver, her dear champion, her beloved knight?

"Every time I saw her she seemed more beautiful than ever, the fatigue of the journey having gone from her face, and the two dresses I had left her being of silk brocade, and furbelows worthy of a princess of the blood. She was only nineteen, with the figure of a sylph, and the beauty of a saint and a siren combined; hand, arms and neck soft and white as swan's down, and a pair of feet and ankles that for smallness and beauty couldn't be matched this side of Seville.

"After a few days my heart getting sick with delaying, I suggested would she postpone the great honor of becoming an O'Brien Dillon, waiting for the word of a gold broker or money changer? 'Don't keep me longing, darling! Let me elevate you to the rank of a major's bride,' whispered I into the delicate mother-of-pearl ear she turned to me.

"Then she astounded me. She answered, proud as a peacock: 'Have I not *rank?* Am I not the niece of one of the richest men in Europe? MY UNCLE IS THE GREATEST BANKER IN THE WORLD!'

"At which I had to fight down a laugh. Bankers and the O'Brien Dillons!

"But Hilda declared to me her uncle was a very great man. That he had been the foremost jeweler and banker in London, until he had killed his man in a duel (which did him more honor than the banking, I think).

As his opponent had been a lord, he had been compelled
to leave England, and was now engaged in financial
operations for his Majesty of France.

"Sometimes I thought by the way she hesitated over
her uncle's name that Lauriston was an assumed cog-
nomen for some purpose or other.

"But, though I argued my case like a Dublin attorney,
again she put me off, and that evening Lanty discovered
from Rosalie (he courting the maid while I courted the
mistress), that Hilda had again sent another post marked
'Very urgent' to her uncle in Paris.

"This time I determined to bring matters to a head,
for her beauty was so great she could not walk the street
without being noticed, and a number of the officers—
dashing Versailles dandies from the headquarters of the
Maréchal, the Duc de Villars—were commencing to put
their eyes upon her, and these glances, I had a horrible
thought, were returned.

"So a few mornings afterwards I said: 'Have ye no
dispatches from your uncle yet?'

"'No!' answered she.

"The next day I asked the same question, with the
same reply. Her uncle's silence seemed to anger her,
at which I chuckled.

"Then I became as impassioned as young Romeo in
the play, and she said to me: 'My uncle cares not for
me, or my future. I place them in your hands!'

"'Done!' cried I, and astounded her by bolting from
the room.

"In five minutes I was back again, and at me heels
a priest, the sight of whom gave her a great start,
and she faltered: 'A day or two longer—a little more
time!'

"'Now!' cried I, for I saw she was a woman to be
won like some fortresses—by quick assault, not by slow
capitulation.

"Me impetuosity overpowered her, and though she
pleaded for just another day, I said: 'The priest doesn't
leave the room alive until ye are Madame O'Brien
Dillon!'

"NEITHER HE DID!

"And oh the joy of it! After she had given herself
to me, and became me wife, I thought I had an angel,

and my two days' honeymoon was the delight of
O'Brien Dillon's heart!"

As he says the last there are tears in the Irish soldier
of fortune's eyes.

CHAPTER IV.

UNCLE JOHNNY.

A MOMENT after he tosses tears and emotion aside by
a hurried dash of his hand across his face and goes
rapidly on with his narrative.

"But the third evening, riding in from my quarters
before Douay, I met Hilda walking with her maid, at the
outskirts of the town.

"Pale and trembling she said: 'I have come here to
intercept you, dear O'Brien, before you see my uncle.'

"'He is here?'

"'Yes.'

"'Well, he's come the day after the Fair,' laughed I,
chucking her under her pretty little chin, after the
pleasant manner of a fond and doting husband.

"'Yes,' murmured she, 'he received neither of
my packets until four days ago, being absent in Italy on
business of his Majesty. Then he came quickly to me.
Don't tell him of our marriage!'

"'Why not?' said I. 'Ye're not *ashamed* of being
Madame O'Brien Dillon?'

"'No! but Uncle John will not like it! From the
words he has even now dropped, he has other views for
me—more ambitious ones!'

"'More ambitious than to make ye one of the House
of O'Brien Dillon?' answered I. 'Faith, where will ye
find a finer family?'

"But she reasoned and plead with me, and begged in
the sweetest voice in the world, 'Not for a day or two!'
and I agreed.

"By this time we had come into the house. Here
she introduced me as her preserver, to a man, the like
of whom I have never seen before, and God help me! I
hope I'll never see again. Not that he wasn't handsome—not that his features didn't have more the

expression of a general than a tradesman. Not that
his manners were not more those of a duke than a bourgeois—for he had as pretty a style as ye'd see in any
court of Europe. In fact, from his communications to
me afterwards, I judged he had seen most of them. But
there was a subtle something about him—something
always behind his grayish eyes, that for the life of me I
could not make out, and I am never partial to the
unknown.

"He had brought quite a retinue with him from
Paris, a couple of postilions and an Italian valet with
whom Lanty took up very rapidly. Besides that he had
his own table service with him; silver and gold more
suited to a prince of the blood than to a tradesman.
He had also selected the best accommodation in the Inn,
and as he was very free and liberal with his money, the
landlord and all the serving people about ran to his beck
and call like drummer boys after the drum-major.

"He appeared to take a liking to me; insinuated I was a
fine fellow, a brave man, and as fine a gintleman in my uniform as he had ever seen at the Courts of St. James or
Versailles, and lots of other things that pleased me very
much. We soon became great cronies, Monsieur
Lauriston remarking that he should remain for a few days
in Arles to rest after the dust of posting over country
roads.

"'My niece,' he says, ' has told me *all* about ye!'
At which I couldn't help chuckling to myself, enjoying
Hilda's roguish blushes.

"So that evening the bottle passed between us
pretty steadily, and we fell to gambling, for he was the
grandest gambler I ever met in me life. We had a
great night of it. He told me more stories of court
life than I had ever heard before. And by my faith he
seemed to know counts, marquises, dukes, princes and
even kings—not as their servant and man of affairs,
but as their intimate friend and dearly beloved. Then
he discussed finance, as if he knew all about it—as I
think he must have, for divil a wrap did he seem to
respect a million than I would a *livre*. Altogether he
was so oily, subtle, and insinuating that he was fit to be
a diplomatist to the Turks, and they are the greatest
liars in Europe. Travelers have told me that the

Chinese and Russians beat 'em, but they are barbarians, and don't count.

"But the next day, as I was dressing to ride over, Lanty, who had brought in me shaving water, had tears in his eyes. 'What are ye crying for, ye great gossoon?' growled I.

"'Rosalie!' muttered he, for the lad was very much in love with Madame O'Brien Dillon's maid servant.

"'What's the matter with her?' I asked.

"'She's going away to Paris!'

"'Not till I and her mistress go!'

"'But Rosalie told me her mistress was going to-day. Shure didn't yer Honor know?'

"'Pooh! Nonsense!' said I. 'It's the uncle that's going—not the niece. Ye've been drinking brandy, Mr. Lanty!'

"Though I kept my lips from trembling, I felt as if I needed brandy myself, and as I poured out my glass, the bottle rattled against it, the hand of O'Brien Dillon shaking for the *first* time in his life;—because a sudden fear had come into me that my Hilda, the wife of my bosom, might be desavin' me.

"But it was 'Boots and Saddles!' with me very quickly, and I galloped to Arles, nearly killing my horse, and got there long before I was expected, for Uncle Lauriston apparently didn't enjoy my coming.

"However, we chatted and gambled a little, and all that day I waited, though once or twice my considerate uncle hinted I might be expected at the camp.

"Though I sat on and on, I never had a chance of a word in private with Madame Dillon, who looked at me a little nervously, I thought.

"Finally like a flash it came out!

"Monsieur Lauriston's valet entered and said hurriedly: 'Your trunks and your niece's are ready! The coach will be at the door in half an hour.'

"'To go where?' said I.

"'To Paris!' remarked the uncle, growing slightly pale, I thought, about the gills.

"'Then I hope ye'll have a pleasant journey!' remarked I with an easy off-hand manner, for perhaps I had been drinking a little brandy between times to keep me

spirits up, 'And I and Madame O'Brien Dillon will wish
you a very pleasant journey!'

"'*Madame* O'Brien Dillon?' said he. 'I did not
know you were married. Is she in town?'

"'Faith!' said I, 'she's by your side, and looking
very red and blushing now. Permit me to have the
honor of introducing her, and asking your blessing.
Make a courtesy to your uncle, Mrs. O'Brien Dillon.'

"Which, plucking up courage, she did.

"Then he laughed, and said: 'Bless ye, my children!'
though there was a kind of a crack in his voice. With
that he went on smiling and affirmed he had known it
ever since he arrived in town. That his niece's maid
had felt it upon her conscience to tell him, and that he
liked me very much, and he blessed us with all his heart!

"Just as he was saying this, in runs Mademoiselle
Rosalie herself, crying hurriedly: 'Your traveling-
dress—' but the look on my bride's face stopped her.
Then something awful got into me.

"Up I rose and remarked: 'Permit me to conduct ye
to your room, Madame O'Brien Dillon!' offering my arm
in my politest manner. 'I would like a few words with ye!'

"Her uncle was about to interpose, but I added:
'Your authority ceased when the church gave me mine!
Make way for me, sir!' and I put me hand on me sword
and me voice was as commanding as when I cry
'Charge!' to a battalion.

"Something in my eye caused Hilda to obey me.
She took my arm and walked with me to her chamber,
though her steps were faltering and I noticed the
little hand on my arm trembled as I closed the door
behind us and turned the key in the lock.

"Then another shock went through me, for laid
out for use was the traveling dress I had first seen
her in. 'One question, Hilda,' said I, 'and answer it
true, or, by me soul! when I go to the front, I'll lock
you up in a convent. I know an abbess who will keep
you safe for me until my return! Were ye going to
desert me?'

"Perhaps what came after was a judgment on me
for my stern words—the first ones I had ever used to
her—but the thought that the wife of my bosom might
be desaving me, made me almost out of my reason.

"On this she uttered a cry: 'Desert you? Leave you? Go to Paris without your consent—without your permission, husband of my heart?' Then she fell on me neck with loving kisses and tender tears and a beauty that could turn a man's head by a glance, till I laughingly said: 'How about the traveling dress?' for I was very easily cajoled by her eyes—which were dark when full of passion; blue when merry.

"'Oh, that?' she laughed. 'That is the one upon which I was showing my uncle the blood of the man who had insulted me—Captain Ducroc—the man against whom you risked your life for me that night. These drops fell from your sword, dear husband, as you first told me that you loved me!'

"Her words made me happier than a field marshal. I ran back, laughing, and clapped old Lauriston on the shoulder.

"Then he laughed back at me, and said: 'I must go on my way now, nephew, but I thank Heaven I'm leaving my niece with a husband that has the spirit to command her. You'll find her a little wayward, me boy!' A moment later he asked: 'Have you considered when you go to the front, and I'm far away, who'll take care of Hilda?'

"'Perhaps, then, I'll send her to Paris to you,' said I, with a grin, 'and let her play the fine lady at court.'

"'Have you money enough for that?' he queried, rather eagerly.

"'Money enough to give Madame O'Brien Dillon a coach and four!' I cried. 'I have sixty thousand crowns on deposit with the Commissary General—me spoil of the Low Countries!'

"On this information we had a glass together, so I told him how I had won not only the booty of Captain Ducroc, but how Lanty and I had pillaged from his niece something like twenty thousand crowns' worth of jewelry and gewgaws to compel the future Madame O'Brien Dillon to keep her bargain with me, and prevent her running away to him in Paris.

"As I told him of all the money I had, a peculiar subtle something came into his face—something that might have warned any one but a fool made confiding by too great happiness.

"A few minutes after, a packet was brought to Monsieur Lauriston from Paris, upon reading which he said that there was no need of haste and he would remain a day or two longer with us, to see what a happy family we made, ordering his coach to be put back in the stable.

"That evening my uncle remarked he should like to take his niece, with my permission, to Valenciennes for a day or two, before returning to Paris.

'To Valenciennes?' said I. 'That is almost in the enemy's country.'

"'Oh, no!' replied he, 'Valenciennes is not in their lines. Besides I have heard the Austrians are gradually being driven back by your brave soldiers!'

"'There's no doubt of that,' returned I, 'but I don't think it's exactly the place to risk Madame O'Brien Dillon!'

"But he overcame my objections, saying he had a very beautiful chateau near the town as well as a little business to transact there. That now he was near gave him the opportunity.

"'You're not afraid of visiting your wife there, eh, Major O'Brien Dillon?' laughed he.

"I said: 'I'm not afraid of visiting my wife in—in Heaven!' I changed the word as I said it; the name of the hotter place was first on me tongue.

"So the next day, after I had obtained leave, we journeyed to Valenciennes, and made a very pleasant day of it there, taking a promenade of the town, where I purchased some of that lace that women wear out their eyes making, to adorn the beautiful figure of my bride, whose looks were swater and more alluring and siren-like than ever before.

"By the blessing of Heaven I had taken with me Lanty, who was as much in love with the maid Rosalie as I with the mistress.

"Late in the afternoon we went to Monsieur Lauriston's chateau, as pretty a little half villa—half castle—as I ever walked into. After a perfect jewel of a dinner, for my uncle played the host to a nicety, Hilda sitting beside me, and making me very happy by her beauty, for never in my life did I see her as lovely as the evening I lost her.

"She was dressed *en princess,* as Madame O'Brien Dillon should be, her white brocaded silk not half as white and shining as her fairy shoulders. Her hair, like the gold dust of Arabia with the sun shining through it, and her eyes roguishly blue and bewitching, though they seemed to droop when mine looked love into hers.

"After desert she laughingly proposed to leave us gintlemen to our tobacco and cards.

"'Pooh! stay and see us play pharo,' remarked her uncle. 'I am going to teach the new game to the Major.'

"'Faith, tobacco needn't drive you from me, Hilda,' laughed I. 'You told me you liked smoked mustachios before marriage; so sit down by your husband's side, my darling, and give me luck.'

"At this Madame O'Brien Dillon said she would help me play, and tossing herself most coquettishly and alluringly by my side, her white hand arranged the stakes for me.

"So we fell to gambling again, Monsieur Lauriston and myself, at the new game that they call pharo, which was invented by the divil to make rich men poor, Uncle John kindly taking the bank, and the stakes grew heavier and heavier, and I lost and lost, Hilda shrieking with laughter at me bad luck.

"'Faith,' said I, 'I don't see why you should enjoy it. The poorer your husband gets, the fewer jewels and gewgaws he'll be able to buy you, my beauty.'

"'Pshaw!' she cried, in roguish tones, 'Isn't it all in the family?'

"And Monsieur Lauriston said: 'Major, resign from the army and I'll make your fortune my personal endeavor in Paris. Pass the bottle. Let's play another case!'

"Just then said I, 'What's that scratching at the window?'

"The card dropped from Uncle Johnny's hand, but his niece cried, 'That must be one of the dogs trying to get in. I'll see about it,' and jumped up to leave the room.

"At the door Hilda paused and looked back at me;

her eyes seemed as if she was about to say something. They wandered from me to her uncle, but as they rested on him she appeared to change her mind, and said with laughing piquancy: 'Adieu, bad luck husband. Save enough to buy us breakfast to-morrow.' Then tossing me a kiss she floated through the door, while her uncle and I went at the cards again.

"Then the divil's own luck came to me. Quarter of an hour more and all me plunder of the Low Countries had left me, and I had given Monsieur Lauriston an order on the Commissary General for everything I had in the world, and was only plain Major O'Brien Dillon, of De Crissey's Regiment of Dragoons, without a *louis d'or* in my pocket.

"But still I thought myself rich—I had my darling wife, she loved me, and I was happy.

"Just then there came more scratching at the window.

"'It's that cursed dog again,' laughed Uncle Johnny. 'I'll go out and see what Hilda has done with the beast.' So he left me, going into the front hallway, following the steps of my wife, putting very carefully in his pocketbook his plunder of the night.

"As he did so, Mr. Lanty came in from the kitchen, bringing with him some whiskey and water, crying jovially, 'Here's yer Honor's night-cap!' Then seeing we were alone, a sudden change came into his voice. He whispered in my ear: 'The Austrians are surrounding the house, but our horses are saddled outside.'

"After an old campaigner's habit I always sat with sword and pistols. I followed Mr. Lanty quietly into the kitchen, and opening the door found myself in the darkness face to face with a couple of Austrian hussars. Not recognizing my uniform in the gloom, one of them, an officer, said: 'This is the house, I believe.'

"The thought of treachery shot like a stream of fire through my soul as I whispered 'Right ye are,' and passed my sword through his body, while Lanty, who was at my side, pistolled the private soldier, and sent him after his master.

"'Quick, to the horses,' Lanty whispered.

"But I said, 'No! Back and defend my wife.'

"'There's no danger to her, but there's death to us,'

he whispered. 'Sure, she knows all about it. Didn't her maid servant confess to me only three minutes ago that the Austrians were sent for last night, Lauriston's Italian valet carrying word to the commander of the German outposts. Quick, they're coming. Follow me to the horses.'

"With my brain in a whirl, I sprang after him, for I saw the Austrians pouring into the grounds and up to the front door. A moment after we were mounted and cleared the fence Irish fox-hunter fashion. Three or four were after us, but they would not risk the jump, and had to go round by the gate.

"Then I heard Hilda's cry. Good God! was it despair?

"I turned to cut my way back through the troopers to save her or die with her, but Lanty seized my bridle and implored, 'She's playing the Banshee on you. She's alluring you to destruction. I saw her talking to the Austrians myself.'

"'I'll not believe ye,' I groaned, and turned my horse again towards the gate. But just at this moment I saw her uncle Lauriston, the Scotchman, in the light coming from the hall door, talking to two or three of the Austrians, and pointing out the way I went.

"Then I knew, traitoress or true, Hilda was safe; and made up my mind to live that I might measure it out to the ·man who had ruined me in purse, and perchance ruined me in heart. So I thundered away, pursued by twenty Austrian dragoons and hussars, but Lanty and I out-ran them, by the blessing of God, and though a few bullets whistled about us, came into camp unscathed about two o'clock in the morning.

"By four I had permission from headquarters, and taking a couple of squadrons, galloped back to the place. If I had put my hand upon my dear Uncle Johnny I would have hanged him without a court martial to one of his own trees. But I found the chateau deserted. They told me in Valenciennes that Mr. Lauriston and a lady had passed through *en route* for Paris very early in the morning.

"It was late in the afternoon when I got back to our camp before Douay, when it suddenly occurred to me I might at least save my money. Up I hurried to the

Commissary General's to stop payment on the order I
had given Lauriston for my riches. But even as I
entered, one of the clerks said to me, 'I presume,
Major Dillon, you've been investing your spoils of war
in Paris.'

"'What makes you think that?' gasped I.

"'Why, Monsieur Lauriston, the great financier,
presented your order quite early in the day, and carried
off your plunder of the Low Countries.'

"'You know him then?' asked I very eager.

"'No; never saw him before to-day.'

"'Then, what makes you think him a great
financier?'

"'Oh! from his conversation. He knows more about
exchange and the values of rare coins than any expert I
ever met.'

"'Oh yes!' I replied, quite easily, 'My Uncle
Johnny is a capitalist. I presume he had my wife
with him!'

"'Then let me congratulate you,' said the young
man. 'I noticed in the coach the most beautiful
woman I ever saw.'

"'That's the description of Madame O'Brien Dillon,'
laughed I; but it was a very yellowish laugh, as I
rushed from the room to headquarters, to try and get
leave so that I could pursue my Uncle Johnny. For I
had made up my mind to overtake him, and to have his
life, if necessary, to bring my wife back with me, where
I would have taken precious safe care of her.

"But, divil any leave could I get, and they sent me
on a scouting expedition to the front, and kept me very
busy till the end of the campaign. Then, the winter
coming on, I said: 'I'll try and find her in Paris,' and
applied for leave again; but there was no leave for me
and I stayed in winter quarters eating my heart out.

"Here an idea struck me—Lanty could get leave
though his master couldn't. I sent him to Paris to make
inquiries as to the health of Madame O'Brien Dillon.

"But he was brought back to me nearly beaten to a
jelly. It seems that he arrived at the capital all right,
and had located Rosalie, the maid servant, and the
Italian valet, Malavello, and was getting along swim-
mingly, when, one night, four bullies fell upon him in

the dark streets of Paris, and cudgelled poor Lanty insensible.

"After that, all he cared for was getting back to me
alive. One of the ruffians, he told me, when he was able
to talk, was the Italian valet, for he heard him chuckle,
while he was beating him to death: 'Take this with
Madame O'Brien Dillon's compliments!'

"Shortly after Lanty's return from his unfortunate
journey I received a note that set my heart beating.
I can tell ye without producing the paper, for its words
are burnt on my heart.

"It read as follows:

"'Do not, for your own safety, attempt to follow me. Above
all, as you value your life, do not visit Paris.   HILDA.'

"That's a dare I won't take. If I live, I will visit
Paris. Oh, Raymond! sometimes thinking the matter
over, I guess Lauriston may not have been my villainous
Uncle Johnny's real name. When I think of his influence—court influence, it must be—keeping me without
leave of absence all winter, and the style in which he
lived, his plate and jewels;—sometimes, by my soul!
I wonder if I may not in my arms have held as
my wife perhaps a princess of the blood. But when I
dream of her I go like mad, so I'll finish my story.

"As I thought of nothing else all winter, I was glad
when the spring opened and we got to soldiering again.
And then the divil's luck seemed to come upon
De Crissey's Regiment of Horse. We lost four hundred
men, as I told you, during the assault on Landau, and
four hundred more in that beastly swamp outside the
place. Then there being no regiment of De Crissey's,
I was transferred to Clancarthy's Irish Foot.

"With that, the same black fortune seemed to come on
them. They got all the hot and deadly places, and
now there's only twenty-five men and myself left alive.

"Somehow I think it is all owing to my cursed
uncle, John Lauriston—that in trying to murder me, he
has murdered my two regiments, and by the blessing of
God I have escaped to avenge them. Sometimes I
think a woman knows all about these infamies, and
that woman my wife! I try to believe her angel, but
divil will come in my mind. But I try to live on and

fight it out, for I know one man's my enemy; that same John Lauriston, gold dealer and money changer to his Majesty, who, after plundering me of the fine fortune I had made in honorable warfare in the Low Countries, would have sold my life to the Austrians, to get me out of his path that night at Valenciennes.

"That's my story, Raymond. That's who I think are my enemies. Now tell me about your wife, and who you think are yours."

But Raymond d'Arnac shakes his curly head and laughs. "I have no wife. I have no enemies."

"Ah, then, ye must be one of the other kind," cries the Major, excitedly.

"What other kind?"

"The *rich* men. The kind that dirty villain Lenoir is using his power as Chief of Staff——" Here O'Brien Dillon suddenly checks himself and whispers hurriedly, coming close to his companion: "But I make no charges. I am simply going to tell ye a few facts from which ye must draw your own inferences."

Then his voice grows sad as he mutters: "You remember poor Raoul, the Marquis de Pasmontain?"

"Yes. As noble a young Frenchman as ever drew sword," rejoins Raymond, astounded at the turn the conversation has taken.

"As noble and as *rich* a Frenchman as ever drew sword," answers the Irishman. "He fell defending the little bridge over the Meuse, his detachment outnumbered four to one; and into his estates, valued at 500,000 *livres* a year rents, in came his cousin, a dirty little Parisian gambler, they tell me. Then ye remember the Chevalier de Lavalle, killed at the assault on a mined tower, with no more chance than a rat."

"Yes, before Douay," answers D'Arnac.

"And rich, also," goes on the Major. "An income of two hundred and fifty thousand *livres* rents, all coming to his step-brother, one of the gambling courtiers at Versailles. So also the Viscomte de Pressieu, you recollect him?"

"He fell a month ago, defending the retreat from Brisac."

"With no cavalry to help him!" cries the Major, "and *richer* than any of them. One hundred and fifty thousand *écus* income. Who benefited by his death? His step-mother, the notorious beauty and spendthrift of the court, Madame de Cambray. Besides, I can mention half a dozen more, all rich, and all with heirs to be benefited greatly by their death, that fell not altogether by the chances of battle, but by being placed in situations where no gallantry could save them from death by the enemy. And each time after his man fell, Lenoir, though he has nothing more than his pay, has had all the money he wants to squander at the gambling table, or to use in his visits to the court, where, they tell me, he lives as extravagantly as if he were a sur-intendant of finance. Now, my boy, put two and two together, and think for yourself. You have no wife. You have a very pretty income, I am told, and some day will have very much more. Who will gain by your death?"

But Raymond's face, at these last few words, grows gloomy and agonized. He cries out: "Mother of Heaven! I don't want to think! You have opened a suggestion to me that makes me shudder. My God! I'm too young to believe the man I love—my own flesh and blood—plotting my taking off. For these are no chances of battle you are talking of, but murders as cruel and cowardly as the poison drops of the Borgias." Then he mutters: "For God's sake, don't let me think more about it—at all events not at present," and suddenly remarks: "But to your business. You are not rich."

"Not since I lost my spoils of the Low Countries!" answers O'Brien Dillon grimly.

"Then why do you think Lenoir is plotting against your life?"

"Because he is Lauriston's instrument."

"You guess that?"

"I *know* it."

"Why?"

"Because on his return from Paris, at the opening of this campaign, Gaston Lenoir, Count du Bourg's Chief of Staff, had upon his table several of the golden goblets and other pieces of plate that I lost to my kind Uncle Johnny that night!" remarks Dillon grimly, "and I know enough about my same uncle, John Lauriston, to

know that he never pays his money without value
received."

"Then I will confront Lenoir with his treachery!"
cries Raymond, the enthusiasm and impetuosity of youth
blazing in his blue eyes.

"Not if you want to live!" answers Dillon very
gravely. "Gaston Lenoir is the deadliest swordsman in
France!"

"As deadly as Ducroc, whom you killed?" returns
Raymond with a confident laugh.

"Worse! Besides you wouldn't have Mr. Lanty to
throw the fire in his face, as I did. Go to the Maréchal.
Tell him the facts in my case, my boy. De Villars has
the true justice of a great soldier. Avoid any complication on my account with Lenoir. Promise me that,
or I won't let ye out of my sight. Because perchance
I'll never see ye again alive, and I can't afford to lose
my only friend now I've just gained him!" whispers the
Irish Major, with so much concern in his voice that D'Arnac knows Lenoir's sword must be very deadly to cause
such warning from a tried soldier, who has faced death
on many a battlefield, in many a cavalry charge, in
many a desperate deed of assault and escalade.

"You have my word!" says the young man shortly, and
wringing the hand of this man, who has received injustice
for saving his life, the young Comte d'Arnac hurriedly
leaves the tent of the Irish Major, and, springing on his
horse, makes his way through the crowded military
streets of the French encampment towards the headquarters of its Maréchal and Commander in Chief, the
pet of fortune and beloved of his Most Christian Majesty,
King Louis XIV., the Duc de Villars.

CHAPTER V.

THE ONE CHANCE OF LIFE.

As HE RIDES, Raymond thinks of Dillon's suggestion that his life is not bearing merely the natural
risks of battle, but also that of some plot instigated by
some one who will gain by his death.

Soon the high spirits natural to strong young manhood overcome these gloomy thoughts; he mutters:

"My cousin Charles—absurd! impossible!" and devotes his mind to contemplating his coming interview with De Villars, and how he may best battle for the Irish Major.

Thinking over this, he finds himself halted by the sentries of the French Garde, who are on duty in front of the Maréchal's quarters. This is the handsome summer residence of a rich German burgher, who has fled before the war, leaving his goods and chattels behind him.

Escorted by the sergeant of the guard, he walks up to the house to find an *aide-de-camp*, who tells him that Monsieur le Duc is at present inspecting the town of Friburg.

" For which we may thank you, Monsieur le Colonel!" adds the officer, who has evidently heard of last night's assault.

Half an hour after, the Duke's carriage drives up, for that officer cannot mount his horse, the effect of a wound received the preceding year.

The next instant the hearty tones of the old campaigner cry: " Show our boy Colonel in!" and D'Arnac finds himself confronting the most successful French commander of that day.

The Maréchal is in the good humor that always attends success. He has thrashed Prince Eugene at Denain, has got his hand on the town of Friburg, and will soon have its mountain covered with forts, and is fighting on that side of the Rhine on which all true French soldiers like to fly their battle-flag—the German side. Naturally of a genial and hearty disposition, he is even more genial now. Instead of the military salute of ceremony, he holds out his hand, saying: " My boy, your grand uncle, the great Turenne, taught me the art of war. Your father rode by my side in the battle at Friedlengen! Now, what can I do for you?"

Raymond, his cheeks flushing under this reception in the presence of a staff brilliant both in names and achievements, says shortly: " Thank you, Monsieur le Maréchal. I only ask a private interview of a minute."

" With pleasure!" answers Hector de Villars, promptly leading the young man into an adjoining apartment. " Now," he says, kindly and reassuringly, throwing off the difference in age and military rank between them, " what can I do for the hero of last night?"

" Reward him!"

" You have been made colonel. Do you want to jump from a captain to a general?" laughs De Villars.

" Reward the true *hero* of last night!"

" I fail to understand you!" remarks the Commander, opening his eyes. " You do not refer to yourself?"

" No; to Major O'Brien Dillon, of Clancarthy's Irish Regiment of Foot."

" Humph!" grunts the Maréchal, his face growing cloudy. Then, stepping to the door, he says suddenly: " The order book of to-day! That of Count du Bourg's division!"

In a moment he has this in his hand; the good nature passes out of his face, and the sternness of military discipline flashes in his eyes, as he says shortly: " Major Dillon is under orders for court martial, for deserting his command in front of the enemy. Did he not desert his command?"

" Yes."

" Ah!"

" By going *ahead* of it. His command joined him in the morning."

" When?"

" When it *overtook* him. He charged the enemy one hundred and fifty yards ahead of his men, and that one hundred and fifty yards was so terrible his grenadiers could not fight their way to him for two hours!"

" *Diable!*" remarks the Maréchal. " This is a new story to me." Then he adds kindly: " Sit down, and tell me all!"

This Raymond does, giving clearly, yet enthusiastically, the account of the Irish Major joining him in the first bastion, and telling them that it was a mine under their feet. That when the men had muttered " *Back!*" O'Brien Dillon had cried " *Forward!*" and led them to attack the second bastion—the one that gave entry to the town—and how they had held it against Baron de Arsch's Austrian Infantry. This is interspersed with one or two of Lanty's remarks, that make the Maréchal chuckle.

Finally the boy concludes, carried away by the impetuosity of youth: " I wish no promotion for the affair of last night, until justice is done to its true hero—the man who saved my life and gave you Friburg—Major O'Brien Dillon!"

"And it shall be!" answers the Maréchal enthusiastically. "Justice to the Major, and justice also to his Irish servant!" For Raymond's words have carried conviction to the heart of his father's old friend.

Then De Villars says more slowly: "Major Dillon committed a military indiscretion that only success in war warrants; had he failed, a court martial might have taken his life. But he won! And egad! I'm too much of a gamester myself to balk any man who risks his life to win glory!" and going to the door, he summons an *aide-de-camp*, saying: "Write instantly to General du Bourg, directing him to cancel order of court martial on Major—no, *Colonel* O'Brien Dillon of Clancarthy's Foot!"

"Colonel ? ' echoes Raymond.

"Of course—you're a colonel—did the Irishman not do as well as you ?" laughs De Villars.

Then, after a moment's consideration, he turns to Raymond and remarks: "From your account there is no regiment of Clancarthy's Foot?"

"Only twenty-five men!" mutters D'Arnac.

"And a colonel should have a regiment!" suggests the Maréchal pleasantly. "The Count de Belleisle has just been relieved from the Regiment of Alsace;" then commands his secretary: "Make an order transferring Colonel O'Brien Dillon from Clancarthy's Foot to the Regiment of Alsace!"

Next turning towards Raymond, he says: "Will that satisfy you, Colonel ?'

"More!" cries the young man. "Now I am really the happiest man in the army!"

"Except Lanty!" remarks De Villars, handing him a slip of paper, upon which he has been hurriedly writing while he is speaking. "This releases Lanty from the guard tent, and makes him a sergeant!"

As Raymond, overwhelming him with thanks, is about to leave, the Duke goes on: "When you left Major Dillon, he thought himself ill-used ?"

"Very!"

"Well! The man who helped you give Friburg to me must not think Hector de Villars ungrateful. Please take my compliments to Colonel Dillon, and ask if he will not, with yourself, do me the honor of dining with me this evening. An Irish soldier of fortune always enjoys a good dinner; foraging is light—and I hope mine will be to his liking."

"I will carry the message to him, Monsieur le Duc, and make his heart as light as mine!" cries D'Arnac, his dark eyes lighted by gratitude and love for his chief.

"Very well!" responds De Villars, "let me see your friend, the Irish Colonel, at seven! Good-bye, as I must make arrangements for the reduction of the forts on the Schlossberg."

"Ah!" answers Raymond, a happy idea striking him, "Monsieur le Maréchal as usual leads the assault in his carriage?" referring to an affair that had made De Villars famous; when being wounded in a previous campaign and unable to take horse, his Excellency had led a charge propped up in his coach.

"No, by my faith!" chuckles the Duke, for even Maréchals of France like flattery when well put. "After that last affair my coachman ran away, and I have too expert a whip to risk my present one. Remember at seven!"

As Raymond takes his leave he is congratulated by several members of the Maréchal's staff, Monsieur de Sartimes, its chief, saying to him: "My young friend, you will soon be as celebrated as your great uncle!' for the pet of the Commander is generally the favorite of his *etat major*.

With a light heart Raymond hurries towards the tent of his Irish friend, but suddenly seeing some ominous movement at the office of the Provost Marshal, turns rapidly to the dispenser of military justice bearing the order for Lanty's release, and finds himself *just in time*.

After the manner of that day, condemnation was prompt for the common soldier, and punishment followed very rapidly thereafter; and he discovers them preparing to make Mr. Lanty uncomfortable, by stringing him up by the thumbs for the night, a mediæval military punishment under the name of *estrapade* then in use in the French army.

On hearing the news, Mr. Lanty, who has been looking on with savage concern, cries to the guard about him: "Take off my irons, and let me jump for joy! God bless his Honor, the Maréchal! Now salute a sergeant, ye murderous villains."

This being done by the grinning privates about him, Lanty accompanies Raymond; but during their journey to Dillon's tent he astounds the young Frenchman by these gloomy words: "By me soul! I was born one hundred years too soon! That's the ruin of me. I know *too much* for the present world."

"What do you mean?" asks D'Arnac. "Hasn't justice been done you?"

"No, and it never will be. Instead of being a common soldier, one hundred years from now, if the world goes on, I would have been honored as a great man; but now my wisdom always gets me into trouble. Look at the lights I made from a revolving wheel, that the priests imprisoned me for. Look at me knowledge of the old forms of gunnery, that rescued us from being blown up in the Escargo Fort, and what has it brought me to—a narrow escape from running the gauntlet, and a whole day lost from foraging. Sure an' the Major will have nothing to eat to-night!"

"Sure an' he will!" laughs Raymond. "*Colonel* Dillon dines with Maréchal de Villars!"

"Dines with the Commander in Chief? Tare-an-ages! And is Sergeant Lanty invited to dine with his staff?"

"No!" answers D'Arnac, "but the canteen furnishes very good meals, and with a *louis d'or*——"

"I can keep fat for a week!" grins Lanty, holding eager hand for the coin the young officer proffers. Then he goes on more solemnly: "But it will be a poor week's living for the Colonel. Sure without the inspiration of an empty stomach, I'll be little good at foraging."

By this time they are at the tent of O'Brien Dillon, who, looking on the faces of D'Arnac and Lanty, cries: "It's good news!"

"The best in the world!" answers Raymond. "Colonel Dillon, Maréchal le Duc de Villars presents his compliments to you, and asks the honor of your company at dinner."

"*Colonel*, did ye say?" cries O'Brien.   Then he goes on gloomily: "But without a regiment! Only twenty-five of me poor fellows left!"

"No, nine hundred!"

"What do you mean?"

"You command the Regiment of Alsace!"

"Faith, then, I'll eat a good dinner with the Duke this evening, and thank him for his command at the same time!" returns Dillon, in a hearty voice; next groans, "God save me! My only uniform was spoilt in last night's fight, and my only wig pulled off my head in the street skirmish."

"We're about the same height, accept one of mine," suggests D'Arnac.

"'Deed and I will! My coat has lost one sleeve, my right epaulette is naught, and I'm never above accepting a favor from a friend like you've proved yourself to me to-day!" cries O'Brien, with outstretched hand, and tears of gratitude in his frank Irish face; then he mutters gloomily, "I've never been able to afford but one uniform since my Uncle Johnny stripped me of my plunder of the Low Countries."

So Raymond leaves him, but he does not forget his promise, and an hour afterwards the two ride up to the headquarters of the Maréchal of France, O'Brien Dillon remarking complacently: "I think my figure does your uniform honor, Colonel d'Arnac!"

A minute later they are shown in, and the Duke, putting them very much at their ease, and treating them with distinguished consideration, they sit down to table with De Villars, some of his staff, the Count du Bourg, his Lieutenant-General, and a gentleman upon whom Raymond would glare with indignation, did not Dillon, who sits next to him, give warning pressure with the foot. This gentleman is Du Bourg's chief of staff, the Chevalier Gaston Lenoir, about whom several pertinent words had passed in the afternoon between the Irish Colonel and the young French officer.

"Don't let him take away your appetite," whispers O'Brien. "He has not succeeded *yet* in taking away your breath. Smile on him, and don't let him think ye suspect him, or he'll do you certain!"

Thus warned, Raymond contrives to keep a pleasant face, and replies to the remarks of Lenoir, who is a handsome man of about thirty; dark, of a Spanish demeanor, punctilious address, and said to be the best swordsman in the army of France.

Monsieur Lenoir is very polite to both the newly promoted ones, and apologizes to Dillon for the mistake in the report furnished him by his Adjutant that had caused the Irishman's arrest.

"But I have rectified your error!" laughs De Villars, from the head of the table, for the wine has been circulating very freely, and they are all very happy.

"Bedad! you can arrest me to-morrow, Monsieur Lenoir," answers O'Brien, "if the Maréchal will make me a general to correct your next error!"

This sets them all to laughing, Lenoir remarking, perhaps with intention: "I hope to give Colonel Dillon a chance to gain another step before the end of the campaign!"

"Then you will have to do it soon," says the Duke, who has got to talking very freely, "for our attack upon the forts on Friburg mountain will probably be the last of it. Eugene can't get any aid from the States, and dare not give me battle with the troops he now has. His Imperial Majesty of Austria will now be very glad to stop fighting His Most Christian Majesty of France, for the Turks are again becoming troublesome, and he fears a second siege of Vienna!"

At this there is a little snarl of rage from the officers about the table: "The infidels besiege Vienna!"

Then man after man cries:

"I'll volunteer for the defense of Christendom!"

For though the French officers did not particularly care for the Emperor of Austria or his fortunes, still all Christendom had been trembling thirty years before at the conquering march of the Turks up the Danube, and had not got over their hatred and terror of them at this time.

"Besides Colonel Dillon, I hope to give another chance to Monsieur d'Arnac," murmurs Lenoir in his soft, purring voice.

"I have done that for him myself!" remarks De Villars.

"How?" asks Raymond, eagerly.

"By appointing him on my staff as extra *aide-de-camp*. His regiment consists of four men, which is hardly enough to do honor to our young Colonel!"

As Raymond falters out his thanks, the Maréchal leaves the table, saying: "Business takes me away, but the wine is still with you, gentlemen, and I hope you will have a pleasant evening."

Cards and dice being brought in, they all go to playing. The stakes are not very high, though the Irish Colonel, backed by D'Arnac, wins one hundred *louis*, and feels himself rich again.

In the conversation over the card table Lenoir mentions his last visit to Paris, rather ostentatiously naming a number of the beauties of the capital, its gayest sights and brilliant life and terrific gaming at the Foire de Saint Germain.

"You know Paris very well, Monsieur Lenoir," remarks O'Brien. Then he says, suddenly: "Talking of the gambling table, have you ever met a gentleman named Lauriston, who is the greatest player of pharo that I know?"

"No," replies Gaston, "the greatest gamester I ever encountered or met is Monsieur Lass. I have seen him risk one hundred thousand *livres* on a card, and win as much as five hundred thousand in an evening at the house of the charming Duclos."

"Faith, then, he played a bigger game than my man. My Uncle Johnny only won sixty thousand crowns from me. But it was all I had!"

And the party soon after breaking up, O'Brien Dillon strolls off arm in arm with D'Arnac, laughing and chinking the coin in his pocket, crying: "That's the best dinner I've had since the one with my Uncle Johnny. A colonel and a hundred *louis* to-night! This morning, a major, and not an *écus* in my purse. Raymond, you've brought me good luck!"

The next day the Regiment d'Alsace is ordered into the town as skirmishers and occupy the houses fronting the works of the Austrians on the Schlossberg immediately opposite the almost impregnable Fort St. Peter.

Meantime, Raymond, as extra *aide-de-camp* of the Duke, has opportunity to go to the town in search of the mother of the waif he rescued in the street fight. To trace her he finds is impossible. Half the inhabitants have fled, the little provisions in the place having been promptly taken, with mediæval military etiquette, by the troops. Inquiries bring no news to him, strolling players are not apt to have permanent friends.

"Jeanne's mother was probably killed in some one of the houses—at all events I cannot find her," the young man reasons to himself, as he makes up his mind to take the little girl, on his return to France, and place her under the direction of the ladies of his own family—if they will receive her. A pertinent question in the year 1713, when grand dames of the ancient *noblesse* looked upon those beneath them as almost of a different race—and the ladies of D'Arnac's family carried in their veins some of the oldest and proudest blood in France.

While making these researches Raymond has little time to cultivate his Irish friend, for the Maréchal keeps his young *aide-de-camp* very busy, sending him on many long rides to his entrenched camp that he has built to defy the attack of the Austrian Prince; and many long rides to the Rhine to hurry up reinforcements, forage and commissary stores.

Yet chancing to see the little girl at the Carthusian Convent the evening before the day the assault is to be made on Fort St. Peter, she, with childlike frankness, gives D'Arnac some curious information.

He comes hurriedly back from his visit to his charge, goes into the headquarters of the Maréchal, and getting an opportunity asks the Chief of Staff if he knows the dispositions made for the assault the next day.

"Yes," replies De Sartimes, "if the Baron de Arsch does not beat the *chamade* by to-morrow morning at eight o'clock De Villars has notified him the assault will take place and no quarter be given!"

"You are sure it takes place to-morrow?"

"Certainly! What can interfere? D'Asfeld reports the facines are ready to throw into the ditches, and the temporary bridges and ladders for escalade are built. Prince Eugene has given up all hope of raising the siege,

and has retired to his lines at Etlingen. It will certainly
be to-morrow at eight."

·" Then," returns Raymond eagerly, " would you
mind giving me the dispositions for the assault ? "

" As *aide-de-camp* you should know them," replies
De Sartimes. " It may assist your duties to-morrow.
The left of our line is the division of the Marquis de
Vivans. At the center is the brigade of De Nangis with
the regiments of Valenciennes and the Guard de
Boulogne. Du Bourg assaults the right. As usual your
Irish friend is in luck again. The Regiment of Alsace
leads the assault supported by De Pescux's Picardy Regi-
ment and Chambard's Bretons."

" That means," mutters Raymond, with compressed
lips, "that Dillon's command storms the bastion of St.
Peter ?"

"Yes."

" The one by the gate of Swabia ? "

" Certainly!—*Morbleu !* but you are in a hurry,
Monsieur d'Arnac!" ejaculates De Sartimes.

For at these words Raymond has suddenly run out of
De Villars' headquarters, mounted his horse, and is
spurring with white lips along the road, up the valley of
St. Peters, straight for the Carthusian convent, for what
the child has prattled to him makes him know his Irish
comrade will have but one chance of life in to-morrow's
battle—AND THAT CHANCE HE MUST GIVE HIM.

CHAPTER VI.

THE MOUSE AND THE LION.

BUT HE arrives to find the convent's portals closed.
His watch, as near as he can discern by sparks from
flint and steel, shows eleven o'clock. He thunders on
the door with his fist.

No answer.

He assaults the heavy oaken barrier with the butt of
his pistol.

No reply.

" Unbar the gate, or I'll blow the lock off! "

No sound.

"Open in the name of the King of France!" he shouts.

Then the shrill voice of the old German lay sister who keeps the gate is heard crying, "God save us! Is the monastery to be sacked?"

"No; but open in the name of the King!"

At this a little wicket is slowly opened, and the pale-faced lay sister whispers tremblingly: "You will not kill us, neither will you defile the convent?"

"No; but I must see the lady superior."

"She cannot be disturbed. The convent is never opened after eight o'clock."

"She must see me—NOW! I come on the King's business."

By this time there is a commotion inside, the lady superior appearing at the head of her frightened nuns, for even convents and the power of the Church did not always prevent riot and outrage of the licentious soldiery of the early eighteenth century.

Fortunately, the Abbess recognizes the young officer, and says imperiously: "This is an unseemly interruption of our hour of prayer, Colonel d'Arnac."

"Life and death hang on it."

"What do you wish?"

"I wish the child I placed with you."

"To take her away at night is against the rules of the convent."

"I *must* have her."

"No man enters these walls after nightfall."

"Within ten minutes she must ride on my saddle into the town of Friburg," answers Raymond, forcing his way past one or two nuns who would bar his passage.

"Enter here and the curse of Rome will be upon you," utters the Abbess with upraised crucifix.

"It's my soul for my friend's life and the lives of three hundred men. I MUST!" moans Raymond. But even as he says this, the young man, filled with the superstition of his time, pauses and crosses himself; for D'Arnac had been brought up very carefully by pious mother and pious priest in the beliefs of the Holy Catholic Church. Then he says beseechingly: "I pray you, lady superior, do not make me commit a mortal sin. Though it is against the rules of the convent,

don't force me to break into your sanctuary and carry
the child off, but her presence in the town of Friburg
to-night means the lives of a whole French regiment.
You have been protected here.   No French soldier has
entered your walls to carry off your provisions, or the
treasures of the Church.   Think!   The lives of *three
hundred* men against *one* of your rules."

The lady superior, looking at him, sees, in spite of
her monastic vows, he is a very handsome youth, and
returns: "You have been well brought up, I am happy
to learn.   You beg—you do not command.   At your
prayer, I relax the rule, but will do penance for it.
Bring the child hither."

A few minutes after, little Jeanne, with a pale face,
stands beside Raymond and his panting horse.   She
says, hurriedly: "Have you found my mother?"

"No! But you remember the story you told me of her?"

"Yes!"

"Come with me!   You are not frightened?"

"Not frightened with *you!*" laughs the child, as he
swings her onto the saddle in front of him, and holding
her in his arms gallops to the town of Friburg.·

Here, giving the word of the night and the countersign,
he is admitted at the gate of the Preaching Friars, the
one he and Dillon had captured, and riding as quickly as
possible through the mediæval streets, crowded by
soldiery, past the old town hall built four centuries
before, to the houses immediately in front of the
bastion of St. Peter, he is halted by a sentry of the
Regiment of Alsace, and demands to be led to its
commander.

"Musha!   How are ye, Colonel?   The Dillon's been
longing for you for weeks," cries the familiar voice of
Lanty.   "I'll take you to him at the sign of The Golden
Calf!"

In this little hostelry, half in ruins from shot and shell,
D'Arnac discovers Dillon, chatting and playing cards
with two or three of the officers of his regiment.

"God bless you, my boy?" cries the Irishman, springing up from the table and seizing Raymond's outstretched hand.   But there is something in Raymond's
face which makes Dillon say hurriedly: "You want to
see me?   Something important?"

"Life and death! And in a devil of a hurry!"

"This way!" and the Colonel leads the young man into a private apartment; the little girl following after them.

"We don't want you here, little Fraulein!" says Dillon, shortly. "Give me a kiss and run away!"

"NEVER!" cries Jeanne, with vicious stamp of little foot.

"Oh, ho! Mademoiselle Vixen!" laughs O'Brien; then he cries suddenly: "*Parbleu!* it's your little captive of the other night!"

"Yes—come here to save your life!"

"Faith! and she looks like a good angel!" remarks the Irish Colonel. As in truth she does, for *la petite Quinault*, dressed in the uniform of the convent, which is sufficiently religious to take from her piquant face its earthly archness and alluring *moue*, some of her fair hair floating out from under her coif, her blue eyes big with excitement, her little hands trembling with nervous tension, appears a saint. The disorder of a house occupied by soldiers that are battling day by day, and drinking night by night, their cries and curses even now coming from the surrounding rooms, in contrast with her slight girlish figure and innocent face, makes her appear more ethereal than she is.

"Now," interjects D'Arnac, hurriedly, "tell him the story!"

"The story of the subterranean passage into Fort St. Peter?" says the girl.

"By Jove!"

"Yes!"

The first comes from O'Brien—the second issues from the lips of D'Arnac.

"Then," says the child, "I have told you, dear Monsieur Raymond, my mother is very beautiful, and a very great actress, and she has had, as is usual with all grand artistes, admirers, for we gave three performances here in the town during the siege. One of these gentlemen is Monsieur le Baron Reinhart, aide to General de Arsch, the Austrian Commander. He had his quarters in Fort St. Peter. Sometimes he could not get leave, and at his request, my mother (taking me with her) would visit his quarters in the fort. At first my mother had objected to this, saying that she would

not pass tne gateway of the bastion in company with
Baron Reinhart; neither would she be willing to pass
the sentries, as it might cause gossip; for my mother is
a very prudent lady.

"Whereupon the Baron said: 'That can all be
avoided. There is a subterranean passage through
which you can pass unquestioned to the Fort St.
Peter!' Twice I went with her through it. It was long
and damp and gloomy, and filled with barrels so close
together we could hardly walk between them. And
Monsieur le Baron being with us, I said to him, 'What
are those?'

"'Those, my dear, are what you must be very careful of!' he replied. 'They hold the gunpowder with
which we will blow up the French, if they ever try
to storm the fort.'

"'But,' said my mother, who is a very wise woman,
'are you not afraid your enemies might make their way
into the fort, through this very entrance?'

"'No! If we are compelled to evacuate Friburg, we will close up the town entrance to this
passage, which is known only to me, a few of the
officers, and the Sergeant who is accompanying us now,
and who will escort you back on your return.' Then
he went on very sternly, 'If you or your daughter ever
utter a word of this I will have you shot to death.'"

"Faith, an' ye're not afraid of the Baron," mutters
Dillon, looking meditative.

"Of course not, with my guardian, Monsieur Raymond, *here!*" says the little maiden, confidently, giving
D'Arnac a roguish glance and courtesy with the words.

"Do you know the house you entered the subterranean passage from?" asks Dillon, springing up.

"Yes; the third from the Inn of the Golden Calf."

.."'The Golden Calf!' That's where we are now!"
cries Raymond.

"We entered from the cellar of the house."

"Quick! show us!"

And the three run down the stairs into the streets,
and forcing their way between some loitering soldiers,
march straight for the house which the little girl
indicates. It is unoccupied, its inhabitants having fled
with most other civilians, from the storms of war.

A moment after, Dillon, going back to the Inn, returns with a flambeau, and they enter the house. Pulling up a trap door, they find a little stairway, which has apparently been made in a hurry, and which is unusual, as a ladder was commonly used in those days.

"Now," says O'Brien, looking around the walls, "where?"

"There!" cries the little girl, and points to a heap of rubbish on the side of the apartment nearest Fort St. Peter.

"I'll bring three sappers and miners at once!" cries Dillon.

"A dozen! The assault takes place to-morrow morning at eight!" whispers D'Arnac.

"Only seven hours—that is little time! God bless the child all the same! How innocently she told her story, and never guessed she was letting us know her mother was a very naughty girl. Faith I'll bring two dozen—this must be a quick job!"

As the two have been whispering, they have sprung up the stairway, carrying Jeanne with them, and Raymond going to the Inn, gives instruction to the host and his wife—who are risking German bullets for hope of profit—to take very good care of the child for the night.

Then he and Dillon and relays of men, lighted by the sickly flicker of flambeaux, attack the *débris* and the stones and boulders and portions of the ruined masonry that have been thrown in by the Austrians to close up and conceal any trace of the passage into the Fort St. Peter.

"It doesn't even sound hollow!" mutters Lanty, who has come down to help them. They have worked for two or three hours, and O'Brien mutters: "Do you think little Jeanne has been fooling you, as the lady I captured fooled me?"

"No," answers D'Arnac, "I believe her so well that I think our lives depend upon our finding this passage before the signal for assault is given!"

"*Our* lives!"

"Yes! I go by your side!"

"Absurd!"

"I have already volunteered!"

"You foolish boy!" whispers Dillon, leading D'Arnac to a corner of the cellar, where their voices are drowned by the blows of the sappers and miners that are working incessantly. "Don't you see that you are giving our friend, Lenoir, two birds to kill with one stone? Don't you know that the Regiment of Alsace are now getting the posts of danger and certain death? Didn't I have nine hundred brave men with me when we manned these houses, and after fusilade, assault, and counter-sortie, haven't I only three hundred of them left! Faith! I shouldn't wonder if Du Bourg's Chief of Staff knew of this very mine that is to blow us all up!"

"Then, we must work the harder to disappoint him!" answers Raymond.

They urge on the men, relays are brought, and all work like demons — for Dillon has told them their lives depend on finding this passageway, before the assault is ordered. That when the bugles sound "The Charge!" this passageway, filled with gunpowder, is what they'll have to run over before they reach the glacis of the Fort St. Peter.

Stones are dragged away, and the men work stronger than slaves under the lash—stronger than money could make them—stronger than anything but the fear of death.

So they toil on, and it is now six o'clock, and Lanty, sounding, says: "Faix! I think I hear a hollow ring through the stone work and the rubbish now."

Encouraged by this, a new relay is brought in, and fresh men attack the stone work, and then they come to some impenetrable obstacle, and D'Arnac cries: "Good heavens! they have made a solid wall of masonry from the inside!"

"Murder! One we dare not blow down on account of the powder beyond us! The mortar's been setting for the last two weeks, and is now as hard as flint!" groans Lanty.

But they attack this with drills and crowbars and struggle on, while overhead the firing of musketry and boom of musketoons tell of coming daylight and beginning battle.

It is now seven o'clock!

Lanty gives a howl of joy.   His drill pierces the wall and finds open space beyond.

Working like men whose only chance is speed, the miners chisel and pry out the solid masonry.   "Faix! This gate of St. Peter's is as difficult to get through as if it was the *real* gate of Heaven!" mutters Lanty.

Half-past seven !

The bugles and drums are sounding the assembly.

"Malediction! We'll not have time!" mutters Dillon.

"I'll fly down to Du Bourg and ask him for half an hour's delay!" cries D'Arnac, and hurries away.

But in the narrow mediæval streets now crowded with soldiers marching to the ramparts, he cannot find his General of Division.

Good Lord! he is too late! for even now De Vivan's drums,from the left are sounding the charge.

Then Raymond suddenly gasps: "The child! The explosion will kill her!" and flies back into the inn to find the "Golden Calf" is deserted.   All have now fled from it, save a few soldiers, who are now acting as sharpshooters from its roof.

D'Arnac speeds back to die with his Irish friend if he cannot save him.

Springing into the cellar he finds the miners still working like beavers, but a girl's voice horrifies him.

Little Jeanne is standing by the Irish Colonel and eagerly saying: "I could show you the way, if you could crawl through like me.   Why are you so big and broad-shouldered?"

"Quick! Jeanne! Away!" commands Raymond, hoarsely.

"I— I— only came here to see if you had found the passage.   Don't be angry, dear Monsieur Raymond!" pleads the little girl.

"Yes, take her away!" mutters Dillon.   "For God's sake leave us! The long roll is beating and I must charge with my men!"

Just here there is a cry from Lanty: "Faix! I have got another beastly stone out!"

"If you could get through, I could show you where the trench is dug!" persists the child.   "It is marked with small flags."

"What trench?"

"The one the Sergeant said would light the gun-powder!" explains Jeanne. Then she suddenly cries: "Oh, goodness gracious! you *have* done it!"

For at this moment D'Arnac, with the agility of twenty, has forced his way through the hole, which is just large enough to permit his lithe, scarce fully developed body to squeeze through. In fact he leaves half his uniform behind him.

"Holy St. Patrick! The fool's goin' to fight the Austrians alone!" screams Lanty, for none of the men can follow the young officer, though some have tried.

"Give me a hatchet!" answers D'Arnac.

"Powers of Heaven! what are ye goin' to do?" whispers Dillon, seizing Raymond's arm that is now thrust back in the cellar, groping for some sharp weapon.

"I am going to cut the port-fire so they can't explode the mine. Let go my hand!" returns D'Arnac.

"Not without me?"

"You can't get through! Colonel Dillon, your place is at the head of your men. Hold them back as long as you can with *honor*—then CHARGE! If I cut the port-fire, you're saved from the mine! If not, we go *together!*"

"Together!" whispers Dillon, wringing his friend's hand.

"*Together!*"

To this the Irishman cries: "Go in God's name!" and places a sharp tomahawk in Raymond's groping fingers.

Then D'Arnac disappears in the gloom of the passageway.

"Come, child, quick, run back into the town!" shouts O'Brien, hurrying from the cellar, for his orderly has just cried to him his regiment is mustered and waiting. But on getting to his place in front of his command, Dillon sees no child has left the house.

Then the drums roll out the *pas de charge!*

Forward he must go, over the place of death—he and his three hundred!

But oh! what is going on below among the gunpow-der?

In intense gloom, Raymond crawls along.

He dare not walk. A stumble that would disable him would destroy him.

It is pitch dark.

He holds out groping hands. They encounter wooden staves and iron hoops—*the kegs of gunpowder!*

He is among them—they surround him. Have they been moved? Is all passage through them barred to the port fire that may even now be burning to destroy him? Must he stay here till the awful roar and— NOTHINGNESS!

As he stumbles about he feels a clutch upon his arm.

"God bless you, Lanty!" he whispers, for he knows the Irish dare-devil has a gaunt frame and may have squeezed through.

"No, it's I!" whispers a girlish voice.

"Jeanne? Back for the Virgin's sake!" groans D'Arnac.

"No! I can show you how to get forward. You've turned wrong. Follow me!"

No time to argue—only to act! He gropes after her.

"Quick! take my dress in your hand. This way! I can show you how to go when in the Austrian fort!"

In the Austrian fort? Will they get there, or will the gigantic roar and death reach them first?

They are groping on! His grasp meets only barrels and barrels—gunpowder everywhere! How slow they move, creeping on hands and knees. *At this pace* they are lost!

"Quicker!" he gasps. "Jeanne, *quicker!*"

"I can't! The barrels stop me!"

"*Mordieu!* you've lost the path!"

"No! I've found the turn!"

"Thank Heaven!"

"Now we can walk—the walls are higher—we can run!"

"Thank God!" whispers D'Arnac, and speeds after her; slime under foot, a faint glimmer in front, and sudden death all about them.

Will these barrels never, never end?

At last a vaulted way, subdued light and THE LAST BARREL!

"Quick! the trench of the port-fire!" he gasps.

"There! See the little flags!"

"My God! the smell of burning fuse!" he groans. "Fiends of Hell! The slow match is lighted and burning towards the powder!"

He runs back to the last barrel and feels in semi-darkness for the port-fire!

He has it—where it enters the bung hole! Then his axe flashes and he cuts the fuse just in time!—ONE INCH AND ONE SECOND AHEAD OF THE SPARK OF DEATH!

Then a great, strong breath of relief! He pulls the disconnected fuse away, and tossing it on one side, stands dazed, trembling, almost unnerved—death has looked him so straight in the face.

A second after a little hand is laid upon his arm, and a voice that has grown dear to him whispers: "The coming steps."

The Austrians! Come back to see why the mine has failed! They'll overpower him, and his risk has been for naught.

"Quiet!" he whispers to the little girl as he peers out of the darkness.

Two men are coming—a sergeant and a corporal. Brave men they must be, to volunteer to enter a mine already fired.

They are looking for danger, but not such as meets them.

He is the unexpected!

As they bend down over the severed fuse, with his tomahawk he brains them both! Without a cry, almost without a shudder, they fall and die.

"Assassin!" shrieks little Jeanne, and, wringing her hands, she flies from D'Arnac.

Raymond must overtake her. If she alarms the fort before it is gained by his friends, he is lost. He follows her and catches her just as she enters the main vaults of the bastion. But the soldiers are all on the ramparts, away from the expected explosion. D'Arnac hears distant cheering though there is no firing.

"Don't be frightened, little one," he says, holding her hands.

"Let me go, murderer!" mutters the girl, shuddering from him.

"It was not murder."

"Not murder?" The blue eyes open wide at him.

"It was war!"

"War? Then never let me see more of it!" And the child would shrink from him again, but he retains her, speaks soothingly to her, telling her that she holds his life in her hands. If the Austrians discover him he will be killed. That he had to do it to save the lives of all those brave men she saw working all the night. That he has always been kind to her.

And she murmurs: "Always kind to *me!* But, oh! how cruel to *others!*"

Even as D'Arnac whispers, he knows danger has passed from him. The Austrian drums are beating the *chamade* on the ramparts above him—a token of surrender, for their mine has failed them.

Another second, and he hears the wild cheer of Dillon's regiment climbing over the ramparts.

Then he rushes up the stairs from the vaults to the battery, and before his eyes are reconciled to the bright light of the sun, he is in the arms of his Irish comrade, who is embracing him, and crying over him: "Thank God! You got through in time! You stopped those beggars blowing us up to Heaven or Hell!"

And Lanty, forgetting discipline, is thumping him on the back and yelling: "Musha! 'twas hard work walking over the gunpowder! What must it have been to crawl through it? God bless ye for saving our lives!"

But D'Arnac simply says: "It was not I who stopped the Austrians firing the mine!"

"Faith was it bad powder?" asks O'Brien.

"No! only the little girl! She saved us all!"

So D'Arnac telling them the story, the soldiers crowd round the little maiden, and thank her, and O'Brien Dillon walking up, says: "My little lady, you've preserved the lives of three hundred brave men to-day! As Colonel of the Regiment of Alsace, I shall ask permission from the Maréchal to carry your name on our banner!" With this he makes her the profound bow of ceremony, but does not offer to kiss 'Miss Distant,' as he did the night before.

Perhaps there is something in her eye that still says: "NEVER!"

A moment after, he incidentally remarks to Raymond: "By the powers! It was the old story of the mouse and the lion, over again!"

This the little girl, who chances to be near them, overhearing, she laughs in the Irish Colonel's good-humored face: "But you were not my lion! Pooh! Do you suppose I risked my life to save yours?"

"Faith I seldom compliment myself when ladies are concerned!" replies O'Brien. "Whom did you do it for?"

"It was to save *his* life!"

"His! Whose?"

"The hero of the play, of course, Colonel Raymond d'Arnac, my guardian!" And she walks to this young gentleman, who is conversing with some of the Austrian officers (for both sides in this war of enmity between two kings generally treated each other very much as comrades, when truce or parley permitted), and courtesying humbly to the astonished Raymond, she kisses his hand and makes obeisance to him, saying: "*Mon Seigneur!*"

CHAPTER VII.

LOOK FOR ALL THINGS IN PARIS.

As THIS happens, Dillon and D'Arnac receive orders to make their reports in person to De Villars.

At the very gate of the bastion they are halted by an orderly, and asked to step into a house that is occupied as the temporary headquarters of the Maréchal of France. Here they find De Villars and De Arsch, the Austrian commander, who are settling the terms of surrender.

"What new adventure is this, I hear?" cries the Maréchal. "Have you both gained another step? I see you've got the bastion."

"You needn't thank me for this one, Monsieur le Duc!" answers Dillon. "Thank your own countryman —the Frenchman."

But D'Arnac laughs: "If there is any promotion give it to this young lady!" And introducing Jeanne to his chief, Raymond says: "Tell him your story, *petite!*"

At which the little girl becomes a *comedienne* and tells her tale to De Villars and his staff, and to the Austrian Commander, who looks very gloomily on, as he learns how his fort was lost—through the *amours* of one of his officers.

This little Jeanne does, with all the airs of her profession, imitating Dillon, until he blows his nose to conceal his confusion, and taking off the brogue of Mr. Lanty, in a wild kind of Irish-French, that makes the tears roll down the bronzed and wrinkled cheeks of the old Maréchal of France.

As she concludes, he takes her in his arms and kisses her, though she cries "NEVER!" But a maréchal of France is not put off so easily as an Irish colonel, and he says: "*Petite!* were I King of France, I would make you a countess—but as I am only a gruff old soldier, all I can say is, call on Le Duc de Villars when you want a friend!"

Then he turns to De Arsch, the Austrian Commander, saying: "The terms of the surrender, as I understand it, agreed upon by us, Baron, are, that you march the garrison out with the honors of war, and join Prince Eugene at Etlingen, leaving all stores, ammunitions, and the batteries uninjured, to be occupied by the army under my command. Is that the understanding!"

"Yes, Maréchal," replies De Arsch, who has been chewing a grizzled moustache very savagely as he has listened to the little girl's recital, "with one condition."

"Humph! no condition!"

"One! Listen to me. I demand ten minutes before I surrender!"

"Why?"

"Five minutes to assemble a drum-head court martial and try Reinhart for neglect of duty! Five minutes more to shoot him to death with a file of musketeers."

"And if not granted?" says De Villars.

"Then I will fight you until I have time to execute the traitor."

"Under these circumstances, the ten minutes are allowed!" remarks the French Maréchal, and De Arsch eagerly pushes his way through the crowd, muttering

between his clinched teeth: "Though he is my cousin,
I'll teach him to betray the secrets of my fortifications
to aid his assignations with an actress!"

Ten minutes after there is a sound of plontoon firing
on the glacis of Fort St. Peter. Then the flag of Austria
is lowered. A moment after the German bugles
sound and the fifes play the quick march, as the infantry of the House of Hapsburg march out with drums
beating and colors flying with the honors of war, and
defile through the streets of Friburg, to take route for
the camp of Eugene of Savoy.

The next day the Maréchal sends for the two comrades. "Three months ago," he remarks to them,
"the exploit of yesterday would have given you both a
step; you would have become generals. As it is, I
fear now the war is closed, promotion will be slow, and
the army will be cut down You probably will not
receive your rank immediately, though I shall send my
recommendation to the King to that effect. As it is,
all I can offer you as certainty is an empty honor—
that of attending me, as members of my suite, to
Rastadt, where I am going to meet Prince Eugene, to
arrange the terms of peace between his Most Christian
Majesty of France and his Most Imperial Majesty of
Austria."

A mark of such favor from the Maréchal in Chief is
equivalent to command and is immediately accepted by
the two young men, for Dillon himself is only twenty-
eight as he stands a Colonel of France before De Villars.

The day after, relays being furnished by the French
Government, De Villars, attended by a magnificent staff,
journeys up the Rhine past Strassburg, and in three days
finds himself at Rastadt, little Jeanne accompanying
the cavalcade in a coach furnished her by subscription
of the officers of the Regiment of Alsace, who are
inclined to make her their goddess, for the child's
piquant beauty and theatric airs have won the hearts of
those she has saved from death in the assault.

Several times, De Villars himself, at the towns they
stop at over night, has her at his dinner table, gives her
bon bons, and makes much of her, in his courtly, yet grave
way, and one evening says: "We must find a husband
for you, my little princess!"

In truth, that is what she looks, for Jeanne is dressed now after the *grande monde*, Raymond having squandered almost his last *louis d'or*, as her guardian, to give her a proper outfit of linen, silks, satins and laces, and a maid to attend on her, for he is very proud of his protégé—his ward as he calls her—and very grateful to her, for he knows he owes his life to her.

To this speech the little lady bows with graceful ceremony, and surprises the Maréchal by replying gravely: "On that you must ask my guardian, my *Seigneur*, Colonel le Comte d'Arnac—I have made oath of fealty to him, and he has the disposal of his vassal."

"Mon Dieu!" answers the Duke, "You talk as if it were two hundred years ago, in the Feudal ages."

"Yes; I got that speech out of a masque played before Louis the Ninth," returns Mademoiselle, courtesying again.

At which De Villars bursts into a laugh; but Jeanne having gone away, he suddenly orders: "Send Colonel d'Arnac here at once!"

Then the two being alone together the Maréchal looks sternly at his colonel and says: "D'Arnac, what are you going to do with this pretty captive of your bow and spear?"

"You mean little Jeanne?"

"Yes!—Answer me as man to man."

"Then, as man to man, I am going to take Mademoiselle Quinault to the ladies of my family in France. If they will accept her care she shall stay with them. If not, she shall be educated in a good convent."

"And afterwards?"

"Afterwards! I shall provide for her future as if she were a daughter of the House d'Arnac." Then, seeing the cloud on his chief's face, Raymond bursts out: "My God! What do you think of me that you ask such questions? Don't I know she saved my life as well as that of Dillon and all his regiment?"

"I think of you," answers De Villars, his face growing genial and his voice hearty, "as a very young and very honorable gentleman. I am delighted, Raymond, the camp has not destroyed your good heart as it does so many of my officers. This little lady has given herself into your keeping; see that you use wisdom as

well as honor in her direction; for, by my troth! a few
years from now she'll be more difficult to manage than
an army.   But if trouble comes to you call on De Villars.
He has beaten Eugene of Savoy, and 'll help you manage
this young woman, and also assist you as to her 'dot.'
There will be many suitors for her bright eyes.   Some
day she will think of marriage.   Now good-night, my
dear boy.   I'm very much pleased with you."   And the
Maréchal of France gives his young colonel a mighty
squeeze.

Coming out from this interview, Raymond thinks:
"No wonder he wins his battles!   Who wouldn't die for
De Villars?"

The next morning they journey on, and one fine winter
day toward the last of the year 1713, with sounding
salute of cannon, De Villars and his party ride in and
take quarters in the palace of Rastadt.

Here he is shortly joined by his old but honored
adversary, the Prince Eugene of Savoy, who comes,
attended by a brilliant suite, from his lines at Etlingen.
And for sixty odd days these two semi-mediæval
warriors alternately entertain each other at dinner each
night, and talk politics and terms of armistice and
surrender of fortresses, and replacement of national
lines during the daytime, though even in sixty days
they do not agree as to conditions, and the terms they
have partially drawn up are referred to their respective
courts.

But within two weeks afterwards, on the 6th day of
March, 1714, are ratified by the Treaty of Rastadt.

During this time Raymond, finding safe convoy for
Mademoiselle Quinault, dispatches that young lady with
a long letter of introduction to the care of his aunt,
the Countess de Crevecœur, in Paris.   He feels
relieved to get rid of the immediate charge of her,
especially as the beauty of his protégé has caused
remarks that are, some of them, not altogether equiv-
ocal as to his generosity in regard to the little lady's
clothes and equipage.

So la petite bids him good-bye, though her blue eyes
are very teary as she says, playfully, but pathetically:
"Adieu, Monsieur Hero of the play, till the hammer
raps for the second act."

As she is driven away, D'Arnac reasons that little Jeanne is much better off in the care of the ladies of his family than in this town of Rastadt, with its crowds of gay officers dicing and gaming; for many of both the Austrian and French armies have congregated there, and *fêtes* and dinner parties are taking place by day and by night.

At one of the last of these, given by the Austrian General in Chief in celebration of the signing of the articles of peace, that have this day been ratified by both governments, it chances that both he and O Brien Dillon are present. Prince Eugene, having heard of their very distinguished conduct at Friburg, both by general report and the very flattering words of Maréchal de Villars, spoken to him privately, is inclined to make much of them, and these young gentlemen find themselves much higher up the board than officers of their rank or their age might expect.

This dinner, drawing towards its close, and the wine being passed very freely (as it always did among the military of those days, when they could get any), they are all in a laughing and happy humor, and the formal toasts to the rulers of both countries being drunk, and the conversation growing informal, De Villars, who sits at the right of his host, in post of honor, and has been chatting and laughing with him, for these two old antagonists have always respected each other's fighting qualities, and their sixty days' diplomatic intercourse has made them great friends, says laughingly: "I presume your next campaign, your Highness, will be on the banks of the Danube, and not against Christians, but against the Infidel. May it be as fortunate as that of your last defense of Christendom!"

Then rising, he calls out in his hearty voice: "Gentlemen, fill your glasses! I drink to the hero of Zenta!" — referring to that battle in which Prince Eugene had given the Ottomans their most terrible thrashing since the siege of Vienna.

At this there is great cry and wild applause for the hero of Zenta.

Returning thanks for this compliment, Prince Eugene of Savoy, warming to his subject, depicts the awful horrors of Mohammedan invasion, when the ladies of Austria and Hungary were carried off to the harems of Constantinople, the captives of higher rank held for exorbitant ransom, the captives of lower rank sold for slaves, and the country made a waste of destroyed castles, violated homes and burning villages. Then he goes on: "But with such armies as that of yours, Monsieur le Duc de Villars, and that of my own, Christendom no longer fears the Ottoman. For I know both of them would use bayonet and sword and musket against the legions of Allah, even more stoutly than they did against each other!"

This being received with great clinking of glasses and shouts of applause, his Highness of Savoy, who is an excellent recruiting officer, cries out: "What Frenchman will volunteer to go with me and fight the Turk?"

At this, O'Brien Dillon, filled with wine and enthusiasm, springs on the table and, drawing his blade and waving it on high, cries: "Here's an Irish sword for you as well as a French one!"

In a second, Count d'Estrades and half the French officers in the room are on the tables beside him, flashing their sabres and crying: "Death to the Ottoman!"

"*Morbleu!*" laughs De Villars himself, carried away by the enthusiasm, "we'll all go with you, Prince, if we can get the permission of our master, his Most Christian Majesty of France."

"On that subject I would talk to you," says Eugene, and, after a little, the two leave the dinner party together, which shortly after breaks up, with no more result than that a number of French officers, obtaining permission from the French Government, do in the course of the next few months, volunteer to assist the Emperor of Austria against the enemy of the Church of Christ.

In O Brien Dillon's case it takes more immediate and pointed result.

The next afternoon D'Arnac sees Mr. Lanty hurriedly packing up his master's impedimenta, for O'Brien and he occupy the same quarters.

"You're in a hurry to go to Paris to find Madame O'Brien Dillon, eh?" laughs D'Arnac, noting the excitement of the Irishman.

"To go to Paris? Musha! we're bound for Constantinople!" cries Lanty. "They say the plunder is something beautiful in that country."

"You don't mean it?" ejaculates Raymond, excitedly.

"Shure as I'm a Catholic!" answers Lanty.

This information is confirmed by O'Brien, who comes hurriedly in, saying: "Faith, my boy, good-bye is the word! I'm going to Vienna!"

"Impossible! You're an officer in the French service."

"Yesterday I was. To-day I'm an officer in the Austrian!" Then the Irishman continues, hurriedly: "This morning Maréchal De Villars, God bless him! sent for me, and spoke the kindest words I have ever heard in my life. It was something to this effect: That his Highness, the Prince Eugene of Savoy, had asked for me especially, upon hearing the Duke's report of my conduct at Friburg, and had offered me a colonelcy in the Austrian army—a crack regiment of dragoons at that! At first I hesitated, said I hoped to go to Paris, as I had a little affair to settle with me Uncle Johnny.

"'Never mind your uncle,' said he. 'Let me tell you *entre nous*. You won't have any money to go to Paris. Don't you know the army is in arrears for over twelve months?'

"'Faith, my pocket knows that too well!' said I.

"'Do you think there will be any money now to pay the army? Don't you know the country is entirely bankrupted by this war?' said De Villars to me confidentially. 'Besides that, the number of our regiments will certainly be cut down. Even with my interest, I doubt whether I can retain you in the service. There will be too many of high family and courtly influence running around after my master, the King, for even De Villars, his old servant, to be able to save all the officers he wants. Now, if you leave the French service with my permission, I can get you immediately your arrears of pay. I will take that upon myself! You, as I understand it, depend entirely on active service for your success in life. Think of the spoils of an Ottoman camp.'

"His talk of 'spoils' made me remember my plunder of the Low Countries and I became as anxious as a terrier dog smelling rats.

"'Do you think there will be much plunder, Monsieur le Maréchal?' said I.

"'Faith!' laughed he, 'you'll never know what plunder is until you get there.'

"With that I give him my word, and my papers are even now being made out.

"Then he went on, crying: 'Colonel, if there was any employment for you in the army of France, do you suppose I'd give you up to any other general on earth?' And complimented me and made me feel a hero; and then said: 'Good-bye! God bless you! And don't come back unless you're a general!'

"'Faith! you might as well make it a field marshal!' I remarked.

"'Faith! and you may!' he replied, laughing, 'and with a handle to your name besides. Look at Count Browne. The Austrians are very partial to your countrymen, and the Emperor throws his titles at the feet of good generals. Besides, the Vienna ladies are very rich and very beautiful!'

"At which I came away very thoughtful, for the Maréchal's little joke had put Madame O'Brien Dillon in me head, and by me soul! if I had enough crowns in my pocket to take me to her in Paris, and to give her the establishment of a gentlewoman, as my rank and her beauty entitles her to, all the Turks in the world would not drag me from seeing Paris. As it is, Raymond, I want you to do me a favor when you get there."

"Anything!" replies D'Arnac.

"Well, this is simple. Find Madame O'Brien Dillon. She's somewhere in high society, you can be sure of that. Find her and give her this letter that I have written. Will ye do it?"

"As I am your friend!"

"Then it is settled," answers the Colonel delivering the epistle. "Now, please don't talk to me of her again, because when I think of her, I grow desperate!" and O'Brien goes off with tears in his eyes to see that his horses will be ready for him within the hour.

After he has gone, D'Arnac, meditating upon his errand, concludes the finding of his friend's wife will be a difficult matter, as she doubtless does not bear O'Brien Dillon's name. For further information consequently he applies to Lanty, who is busy about his master's baggage in the next room, and is easy of access.

"You heard," Raymond says, "my promise to deliver a letter to Madame O'Brien Dillon?"

"Faix and I did! I was wondering to myself how you'd find her!" laughs Lanty.

"That's why I ask your assistance. Give a description of her!"

"Musha! I can do better than that," says Lanty with a grin. "I'll give you her likeness."

"Her what?" gasps Raymond, astonished.

"Her miniature! It's with diamonds all 'round it on ivory! When the Colonel and I stole her baggage that night, we were conveying Miss Hilda Van Holst from Namur. For my portion of the plunder I secured *this!*" and Lanty, producing from his haversack a little tin case covered with velvet, opens it, and placing it in the astonished D'Arnac's hand, says proudly: "What do you think of Madam O'Brien Dillon?"

"A-a-ah!" This is a gasp of astonished wonder and delight from the young Frenchman. He had thought Dillon's rhapsody on his captive bride the raving of a wild Irishman's romance, but the face before him defies description, for the first moment he looks at it, all it means to Raymond is beauty bewildering, alluring.

No blue eyes so dark before, but still so blue, so passionate, so appealing; no hair so Titian red though every lock has golden gleams; no mouth so alluringly romantic as her coral lips laugh "Love me for I love you—*and another ;*" no cheeks so rounded yet delicate and blushing.

Beneath this face, a neck of ivory satin, and arms, shoulders, and bosom of Greek's fairest statue, with gleaming snow tints; for this miniature is the work of some Flemish master. And after the custom of the time and the school of Sir Peter Lely, the girl has been painted in a *déshabillé* of light lawn and fairy lace, that scarcely conceals the marvelous beauties of her form and graces of her figure.

"By the divil's tail! Do you think Saint Antony could have turned a cold shoulder to that!" mutters Lanty, glancing at the picture. "Don't I myself, when the master ain't about, sneak a look at it on the sly, it's so beautiful!"

"But this is not her *real* likeness?" asks D'Arnac. "It exaggerates her loveliness!"

"Oh wirra! It don't do her justice," laments Lanty. "Add to that the fascinations of the Queen of Sheba, who ruined Solomon, and the divilish arts of Cleopatra, who put Antony in her pocket, and ye've only half the charms of Madame O'Brien Dillon. Bad cess to her!'

"And her husband never spoke to me of this!" returns D'Arnac, his eyes still devouring the beauty of the portrait.

"Faix, and he doesn't know anything about it. The diamonds around it are worth one hundred *louis*. I was keeping it for a very rainy day, and, by me soul! if he'd seen her features he'd never let me sell it, or pawn it, or make any decent use of her treacherous face. In fact, I've been afraid to let him put eyes on it, because when he thinks of her, he goes into such spasms of jealous rage against her and her Uncle Johnny, it makes him sick for a week. Besides, the less he thinks of that divil the better it is for him."

"You don't seem to like her!" remarks D'Arnac. "You think she betrayed him?"

"She did worse!"

"Worse?"

"She betrayed *me!* Faix, I could forgive her betraying the Colonel—he's her husband—that's natural. But she betrayed me also! Didn't I see her speaking to the Austrians while they were surrounding the house, when she pretended she'd gone out to look for her dog. Musha, was it a dog that was scratching at the window? Don't I know it was an Austrian officer? Didn't that Italian valet, Malavello, say to me, when he, with four other wretches, tried to beat me to death in Paris: 'This is with Madame O'Brien Dillon's compliments!' By the snakes of St. Patrick! look out for her! beware of her! She'll be your death if she knows you're looking for her! She's got some influence in high quarters that gives her a hold on the very King of France, I belave! Musha, once or twice I've thought she might be Madame de Maintenon herself!"

"Madame de Maintenon! that old hag!" shrieks D'Arnac. Then he bursts into a fit of laughter, but a moment after goes to the door and looks out nervously and returning says: "Lanty, never speak of the power behind the throne — even walls have ears."

For though Louis XIV. had but a few more months to live, the power of his mistress was so great in France that even the princesses of the blood cringed to her, and doffed their hats to her, and the ladies of the court were more obsequious to her than if she had been Queen of France.

"Now," says D'Arnac, his eyes still lingering on the beautiful picture, "you kept this for a rainy day, Mr. Lanty. Your master's purse is not over well-filled to support the position of a colonel in the Imperial army. Permit me to give you, for the Colonel's use, the hundred *louis* you think this is worth."

"Not when it's for me master's business you're takin' it!" answers Lanty.

"And it's for your master's good that I give you this!" replies D'Arnac, who has hastily written an order on the Commissary General. "Do not fail to remember one thing—that your master and I are *comrades*. I know he is too proud to even hint of money to me——"

"Wirra! we've been nearly beggars since we came here, and divil a word has he ever said to anybody?"

"But remember this," goes on Raymond, "that my purse is O'Brien Dillon's purse, as his sword is my sword and my sword is his. Notify me if your master wants funds to pay his debts, or friendship to help him spend his money."

"God bless you for that first!" cries Lanty. "Faix, I'm very glad now I saved ye from bein' blown up that night!"

Then he gives Raymond a leer and whispers: "I hope your honor will have better luck with your captive than my master did with his."

Here their conversation is interrupted by the return of O'Brien Dillon.

A few moments after D'Arnac and he, followed by Lanty, go off to his horses that are already saddled; for Prince Eugene is about leaving Rastadt, and the Irish Colonel travels in his suite.

Just before Dillon mounts, these two, whose sixty days of peace has cemented a friendship caused by two nights of battle, bid each other adieu as men who love each other.

There are tears in O'Brien's eyes as he wrings Raymond's hand, and mutters: "You remember the word, my boy—*together*. Wherever you hear it, 'TOGETHER' will make you think of O'Brien Dillon. Now, good-bye, my dear boy, till I come back to you a general, from the Turks, with Ottoman plunder enough to support Madame O'Brien Dillon like a lady of the land. Don't forget you've an enemy in Paris who wants your blood, as well as I have. But get all there is out of life, even, if necessary, a gallant death."

And so, with a last grip of friendship, the two part, Dillon riding away with the Prince Eugene to fight the unspeakable Turk on the banks of the Danube, and the next day D'Arnac, in the suite of his chief, the Duc de Villars, turning back to the pleasant country of France, which is just throwing off the snows of Winter and putting on its Springtime hues.

BOOK II.

THE SPECULATION IN BEAUTY.

CHAPTER VIII.

COUSIN CHARLIE.

So it comes to pass, about a week after this, Raymond d'Arnac follows his chief along the Rue de Charenton to the barracks of the the *Musquetaires Noirs*, just outside the gates of Paris.

Here they are met by a number of the great officers of state and many of the nobility, and congratulated with great show of enthusiasm upon the success of the French arms in the last campaign.

Curiously enough, though there is a large crowd of voluble Parisians who have come outside the walls to see the return of France's victorious Maréchal, there is but little enthusiasm among them. Even the volatile French find it hard to cheer and *viva* when their purses are very empty, and in some cases their stomachs also.

In the enthusiasm of youth and the joy of return covered with the laurels of the battlefield, D'Arnac's mind does not rest upon this.

After he has been dismissed by his chief, with a hearty pat on the shoulder, and "run away to your sweetheart, my boy!" he rides into the town of Paris, through that great arch Louis XIV. has just erected to the victories of his reign, at the place called the Port St. Antoine, and coming through the crowded commercial part of the city's streets (now getting too narrow for its business), he crosses the river by the bridge Notre Dame, and by the time he has reached the Rue St. Andre in the Faubourg St. Germain, and stands in front of the Hotel de Crevecœur, one of the handsomest residences in that quarter, occupied by the nobility of France, he has forgotten all about it.

The streets have seemed as busy, the rush of people as great, as he had ever before seen in the capital of France. His mind, however, is occupied not with the state of the people, but with the state of his family, for a courier two days before had reached him, bearing the news of his uncle's illness, to hasten his return to Paris.

The bowing flunkeys have scarcely ushered him into the main salon before his aunt, Clothilde the Comtesse de Crevecœur, has her arms around his neck, whispering: "You come to a house of mourning!"

"Dead!—my uncle!" gasps Raymond, for D'Arnac's father had passed away some ten years before this, and had left his little son Raymond and his only daughter Mimi to the care of their uncle, and Henri de Crevecœur had been very kind to the two orphans.

"Of course not dead!" says his aunt sharply, "but very sick."

As the Comte de Crevecœur has been very sick, according to his wife's statement, for the last four or five years, Raymond recovers from the shock and says rather snappishly: "Pish! why do you always make a tragedy, my dear aunt? I suppose the dying one is at breakfast!"

"Yes, he's eating a little."

At which Raymond bursts into a laugh, and his aunt says: "I am ashamed of you—in the house of mourning, too!"

"*Diable!* he's not dead!"

"But he is always threatening to die!" answers his aunt. "However, I suppose we must not put on black until he is no more." Then she becomes voluble and babbles: "Raymond, how handsome you look—and a colonel—you will be a general at an earlier age than your poor father was! And how becoming! I always liked uniforms, even before I left the convent." With this a pair of plump arms go around Raymond again, in an embrace that is almost maternal, for young D'Arnac has a taking way with all women—even those of his own family—and the Comtesse de Crevecœur's heart has not been withered by age. She is scarcely forty, and has the plump *embonpoint* of a lady who has lived very comfortably and contentedly, though she has often remarked during the last few years, that hers is a house of mourning.

"I think I'll go in and see him!" says Raymond.

"Yes, he has been inquiring for you. Every day—every hour—he has asked for you. Between every meal he has said: 'Will Raymond come *in time?*'"

"In time for what—dinner?" cries the youth, irreverently, and laughing lightly steps into the dining room and slaps a hearty old invalid on the back.

The invalid is breakfasting upon two chops, an omelet *aux fines herbes*, a pint of Rhine wine, and some sweetmeats. He also has a cup of the coffee of Mocha in front of him, an essence introduced some forty years before this by Soleman Aga, the distinguished Minister from the Sublime Porte to the French capital, where it has now become the rage, little restaurants for its sale bearing the signs of *cafés* being common in most of the fashionable streets.

"You are doing very well for a dying man in Lent," says Raymond.

"Ah! Ha!" grins the invalid, "I always grow very sick in Lent. Then I need not abstain from meat."

"Neither shall I, as a traveler," replies Raymond, "and with your permission I will join you—my uncle."

"Not in these chops!" cries the invalid. "Order more for yourself, and tell me of your glory."

And the two have a very pleasant meal, towards the close of which, however, Raymond says, after recounting his adventures in the army: "A courier came to me to hasten my return. What did you want to see me about?"

"Oh, nothing! I imagined, perhaps, you would not mind returning to Paris a little sooner. Then I thought we might discuss my will. De Moncrief was here and drew it up for me. You know I am poor now," mutters the Comte de Crevecœur.

"Poor!"

"Yes, my investments in the *billets d'etat* have turned out very badly. They pay no interest. The country is ruined—bankrupt!"

"What makes you think that!" asks Raymond.

"Have you had your pay for the last twelve months?"

"No!"

"When are you going to get it?"

"I don't know."

"Neither do I know when I'm going to get my interest. That is what makes me anxious for your future."

"I have my own estates."

"Yes, but they are too small; for you will be the head of the house when I die, my boy. De Moncrief, you know, as cousin, comes after you."

"Oh, don't think about dying," laughs Raymond, looking at his uncle, who is perhaps sixty, and remarking sententiously: "You've a good twenty—perhaps thirty—years before you. I shall, doubtless, be killed in some engagement long before that. In fact, twice—three times—yes, four times—in the last campaign I was nearer death than you have ever been."

"*Diable!*" shrieks his uncle. "Do you think gunpowder as dangerous as doctors?"

This gunpowder idea sets D'Arnac's mind on the little Jeanne. After a few minutes, he excuses himself to the Count and getting converse of his aunt, he says: "Where is she?" for he thinks it is curious that the child does not come to welcome him.

"Julie! You know she is at Melun."

"No, I was not referring to her!" mutters Raymond, biting the end of an adolescent moustache, for the little Comtesse de Beaumont is a child of twelve, and the rich heiress the family have set their hearts upon his marrying when he has sown his wild oats and she has left her convent.

"Who?"

"Little Mademoiselle Quinault."

"Oh, that brat!"

"Brat?"

"Worse! I could not have her in the house. She objected to eating with my maid. She—the daughter of a strolling player woman!"

"But she saved my life!"

"Well, I have done my duty by her!"

"In what way?"

"I have placed her at the convent *Les Filles de la Croix!*"

"*Morbleu!*" gasps D'Arnac, "that is a school for the daughters of valets and cooks."

"Precisely! You would not have had me send her to '*L'Assumption* or *Saint Cyr*."

"That is just where I would have her!"

"What? Doing her lessons with the daughters of marquises and dukes and counts? Why she'd have a bowing acquaintance with some of the royal family soon. She's brazen enough for it!" remarks Madame de Crevecœur. "She told me"— here the lady's voice almost falters with emotion—"she told me there was the aristocracy of art as well as the aristocracy of birth. But the mother superior of *Les Filles de la Croix* has pertinent instructions about her!" mutters Clothilde significantly.

"In that case," returns Raymond, "please give me an order on the convent for the child." Then, seeing his aunt hesitate, he goes on commandingly: "Just sit down and write it at once!"

"What are you going to do with her?"

"I am about to put her in a school where she need not associate with the daughters of valets and cooks!"

"*Mon Dieu!* Would you treat her as a countess?" shudders Clothilde; but is wary enough to make no direct opposition to her nephew's wishes.

Seizing the note the Countess hands him, D'Arnac says: "You meant for the best, but you hardly understand little Jeanne's spirit." Then he continues in tones that send shudders through Clothilde's plump members, "Le Duc de Villars and I are going to do great things for this little lady. The Maréchal himself has promised to help me with her *dot.*"

"*Mon Dieu!* You are not going to marry her? Raymond, remember your family—the blood of the Turennes!" screams the Countess wildly.

"Not to myself!" laughs the young man so heartily that he partly relieves Clothilde's fears, as he makes his *adieux.*

Coming out from the great hotel he is soon at the Rue Dauphin.

Here he encounters a *voiture* driving along with great cracking of whip, for the jehus of old Paris were just as vociferous as those of to-day, and even more brutal and savage in their use of the *fouet* upon their unfortunate animals.

The vehicle is empty. Springing into this he commands: "Hotel de Chateaubrien!"

"All right! I know it—Rue St. Honoré, Colonel!" returns the *cocher* noticing Raymond's epaulettes and uniform.

"Very well! Drive as if the archers were after you!" replies D'Arnac, and with much cracking of whip, the wretched beast flies across the Pont Neuf, jostling its crowd of hucksters, and shortly after turns into the Rue St. Honoré, where Madame de Chateaubrien occupies the great hotel of that name in the new Faubourg that is just being built up by the nobles around the palace of the Tuileries.

The young man finds his sister at home. "I have been expecting you, Raymond," she cries, "ever since the courier, three days ago, brought news of the signing of the treaty of peace."

Then she pats him on the shoulder, and calls him her brother, Monsieur le Colonel, and gives him some kisses in a piquant yet sisterly way, her bright eyes shining with joy over the return of her brother.

Mimi de Chateaubrien is one of the most dashing young matrons in France. Scarcely over twenty-one, she has made a very great match, her brother assisting her even to the depletion of his own fortune for the *dot* necessary for so grand an alliance as she has made, Le Marquis de Chateaubrien being one of the very great nobles of the court.

After a moment Raymond asks: "Your husband?"

"Oh, Raoul is at present in Southern France. The winters of Paris are too severe for him."

"I came up hurriedly from Beaupere (mentioning her beautiful little estate on the banks of the Rhone) a few weeks ahead of my husband. Madame d'Orleans honored me by requesting my presence. You know," here Mimi glances about the apartment and lowers her voice, " it is expected after the demise of the King, the Duke will be Regent, and the Duchess has been kind enough to suggest to me I may be one of her ladies of honor."

" That's no news in the army," answers D'Arnac, " even now they're betting at the Hague that his Majesty will not live out the month."

" Hush, not so loud! " mutters Mimi, " Cousin Charlie is in the next room! "

" No, Cousin Charlie is in this one! " says a voice so suddenly that it makes them start, as rising from a large *fauteuil* upon which he has been sitting, the back of which has concealed him, Charles de Moncrief, a little grin rippling his somewhat senile but intellectual countenance, rises and continues: " Raymond, *mon garçon*, welcome to Paris! "

Then he laughs again " Mimi, don't look so pale! Though I am the Procureur du Roy I shall not mention to his Majesty that the world knows of his bad health —*entre nous*, I think the King knows it also, better than any one."

With this he gives a welcoming hand to Raymond, and pats Mimi's cheeks till they blush, for he is very much older than his two cousins, having full sixty years to his credit on the book of time, of which Cousin Charlie would like to wipe out about thirty-five years.

In fact, though a little shaky even now, De Moncrief lives the life of a young man, as far as his strength and health permits, and there is no gayer nor wickeder courtier at Versailles, and no greater roysterer at the Foire de Saint Germain than this man, who had been once an abbé in the French church, appointed under De Fleury, but whose methods of life had brought such scandal on his religion that it had been suggested to him by the Cardinal that he should forego all hope of preferment in the Church, and take to that of the law, " a profession you are much better fitted for, my dear De Moncrief," had whispered his Holiness.

" And if I prefer to remain in the Church and become a cardinal ?" the young abbé had sneered.

" In that case your diocese will be the Bastile! " Monsigneur de Fleury had replied, with a grin, which

settled Cousin Charlie's occupation in life, and he is
now the Procureur du Roy.

Notwithstanding his rank, which gives him *entré*
to the court and association with the great nobles, he
is one of the most astute lawyers in the kingdom,
believing that the "end always justifies the means," a
maxim of Cardinal Richelieu that he has stored carefully
away in his mind.

For he revered and admired the memory of that great
statesman, though he did not love it, for Charles de
Moncrief never in his life loved anything but himself, save his *porte-monnaie*, for which he would even
sacrifice his own personal wishes and pleasures.

But over all that cynicism which generally comes to a
man of his temperament in later years, he has thrown
the *bonhomie* of youth, its vices and its associations.
He is more apt to be found with the young officers of
the Garde, or the young nobles of Versailles, than
with the great officers of state.   Consequently he
affects the society of young women, loving them as well
as if he were a young man, and expecting them to love
him likewise.

This very lightness and effervescence of character
has made him a favorite with young D'Arnac, of whom
he playfully says: "We have been boys together!"
and also would make him a favorite of Mimi de Chateaubrien did she not somewhat distrust him, for one or
two anecdotes have come to her ears through ladies'
lips.

Altogether she thinks Cousin Charlie very nice, if
he were not such a wicked old gentleman, and did not
wish to appear such a young one.   Besides, the same
blood flows in their veins, and the Crevecœurs,
D'Arnacs, De Turrennes and De Moncriefs have always
hung together as a family, backing each other up,
and fighting right manfully to give each other titles,
place and wealth, and consequently have succeeded
better than a good many other families who have
fought among and destroyed themselves.

"Now, Raymond, you are in Paris again, we'll have
some gay evenings together," continues De Moncrief.
"I know half a dozen of the leading actresses of *Le
Français* and *Des Ita iennes*, as well as one or two of

the ladies of the opera, who will be delighted to meet such a dashing young colonel."

Whereon Mimi bites her lips, but a moment after she smiles and says, rather too pointedly to please this youthful old gentleman: "Brava! Introduce him, Cousin Charlie. The ladies of the opera and theatre of *your* day must have forgotten how to be very dangerous!"

At this Raymond, stifling a laugh, remarks: "*Apropos* of ladies of the theatre, I have a very young one under my charge."

"A *young* one! Introduce me, my boy!" cries De Moncrief, enthusiastically.

"I will!" says Raymond, and astonishes both his sister and Cousin Charlie by telling them the story of *la petite* Quinault and asking Mimi to accompany him to *Les filles de la Croix.*

"I'll go this instant!" answers Mimi. "She saved your life!" and, summoning a lackey, orders her carriage.

"The sisters will probably imagine Madame la Marquise visits them to obtain a new maid-servant," sneers De Moncrief. "Supposing you and I, D'Arnac, go together and rescue the little beauty. Then we will bring her here and see what we will do with her! You say Jeanne is pretty and fourteen. Egad, Raymond, my boy, I feel like her guardian myself!" laughs Cousin Charlie.

So the two depart upon their errand, arriving at the convent in the Rue Saint Antoine to receive a surprise.

The mother superior reads the note of the Countess de Crevecœur; then says, devoutly crossing herself: "Thank God for His blessings! You've come to take her away!"

"Certainly! Please bring her here," replies D'Arnac, who has got to thinking of the last time he took Jeanne from a convent, the night before Friburg.

This the mother superior is pleased to do quickly, remarking, "Present my humble salutations to Madame la Comtesse, your aunt."

Little Jeanne, being brought down, gives a cry of joy, and astonishes Raymond by shouting, merrily: "Hurrah! the curtain's rising! Act Second at last!"

Then, coming to him, she kisses his hand and courtesies, saying: "*Mon Seigneur* has come to take me away?"

"Of course," mutters D'Arnac, and, presenting her formally to Monsieur de Moncrief, he puts her in the coach, where the girl says, complacently: "Now I feel comfortable once more! I am in my own rank!"

"What makes you so pale, Jeanne?" asks Raymond, who has been looking at the child's face and has seen some new emotion in it.

"Discipline and bread and water!" she answers, savagely; then continues: "They said I had a proud stomach. I would not sit down to eat with offspring of the rabble of Paris—I whom Le Duc de Villars called the little Princess."

Then warming to her wrongs during the ride across Paris, she sends the Procureur du Roy into spasms of laughter by describing her efforts to assert her dignity among the daughters of the fishmongers, butchers and cooks of Paris.

But while he laughs at the little girl, Cousin Charlie is deeply disappointed in her beauty. And shortly after, arriving at the Hotel de Chateaubrien, he excuses himself to its mistress and goes down the steps of the grand house, bitterly thinking to himself, "*If* she had been beautiful, it would have been another chance! He has escaped Monsieur Lenoir and German bullets— when will I get another opportunity?"

De Moncrief's idea as to Jeanne's beauty seems to be coincided in by Mimi, as gaining opportunity, she whispers to her brother: "Why, I thought you said she was pretty!"

"So I did!" returns Raymond; then looks at the child, astonished, for somehow Jeanne seems to have grown awkward since he saw her two months ago, being at that age when girls do not know what to do with their hands and feet. This is emphasized by the short, prim and coarse uniform of a poor convent which displays uncompromisingly every angularity of incipient womanhood.

However, half an hour afterwards, little Jeanne is a different being. She has thrown off convent garb, and is once more dressed in the fine clothes that her guardian had furnished her, before she left Rastadt. She has eaten a dainty dinner, and her eyes are sparkling with happiness as they follow Raymond, her little lips whispering to herself: "*Mon Seigneur!*"

"Yes, she is rather a better figure now to present to the Chanoinesse," remarks Mimi, taking in the picture before her. Then she asks Raymond, seriously: "You still wish to place her at *L'Assumption!*"

"If that is the best school in Paris, yes."

"It will be difficult, but we'll try."

A step along the Rue St. Honoré, and they, together with little Jeanne, are introduced into this very fashionable convent and received by the head of this aristocratic *maison des filles*, the Chanoinesse de Chevreuse.

This lady, a daughter of one of the proudest families in France, of course has heard of Madame de Chateaubrien. On little Jeanne being presented to her care, she looks astonished, and then says hesitatingly: "She is not your—your daughter, Madame la Marquise?"

"*Mon Dieu!*" shudders Mimi. "Do I look so old?"

But this speech is mistaken by the little Jeanne, whose sojourn at "*Les filles de la Croix*" has made her both sensitive and haughty. She interjects savagely: "No, I am not Madame's daughter! My mother was an actress. I was born in Strassburg in 1699. My father was the grandest acrobat of his age. He was the only man who could turn a triple somersault—and broke his neck doing it. He was called the Chevalier of the Spring-board! Now there are no more like him!"

This pedigree settles the affair. The Chanoinesse, struggling to keep the laughter out of her eyes, remarks: "It is impossible to receive any one but the daughter of a noble here, no matter if you are her guardian, Monsieur d'Arnac," for Raymond has hurriedly told her his story; "no matter if she has saved your life. Our rules are imperative. I think, as you seem to wish to do very well by the little girl, you had better take her to '*Des Capucines*,' Place Louis le Grand."

And as they go out, Beatrice de Chevreuse mutters to herself: "He is a good youth, a handsome youth. To-night I'll pray for his good guidance, for some day this

child will be a beautiful woman. He has the same
face as Claude," and there are tears in this white-
haired woman's eyes, for she is thinking of a youth who
had left her side to march under Turenne to the Rhine,
and who had never come back to her.

Taking Madame de Chevreuse's advice, they find *Des
Capucines* a very comfortable school, where the
daughters of attorneys, notaries, silversmiths, and the
better class of *bourgeois* send their daughters. The
mother superior, bowing to the ground to Madame la
Marquise, tells her that she is a protégé of the Chateau-
briens, that they had furnished her convent dower. Here
they leave her, D'Arnac especially stipulating there is
to be no discipline and bread and water for Jeanne, no
matter how naughty she is.

"I think it is the best thing you could have done for
her," remarks Mimi, as they leave the convent.

The immediate care of little Jeanne being off his
hands, Raymond suddenly turns his mind to the mission
of O'Brien Dillon.

His sister being a very competent authority on the
beauties of Paris, he goes to questioning her upon the
latest sensations in the line of professional beauties at
the French court. Finally growing enthusiastic, he
describes the miniature so vividly that Mimi returns
laughingly: "There is no one like the beauty you speak
of in this world!"

"Then," she jeers, "Raymond, you are in love! You
have seen this wonder, this paragon, these eyes of
'pathetic violet,' this hair of gilded Titian red!"

"No," says D'Arnac, chewing his moustache, for
most young men do not care to be laughed at, "I
have never seen her, but I have seen her picture."

"Her picture? Tell me!"

And this compels him to disclose the story of O'Brien
Dillon.

"Very well," replies Mimi, "bring me the miniature.
Then I can tell you if I have ever seen her. I will look
at it through my own eyes, not through yours."

"I will!" answers D'Arnac, and being full of his
subject, he goes hurriedly to the Hotel de Crevecœur,
and shortly returns, bearing in his hand the tin case
which contains the miniature he has been describing.

Then, opening it, he places it in front of his sister, and says: "Tell me, did I rave about *this* ?"

"No," ejaculates Mimi. "She is more beautiful than even you said. But it is not a real picture. No woman was ever as lovely as this. It is an ideal!" then laughs. "You will have to go to Heaven to find the prototype of this, for it is not in Paris. Madame de Parabère, the prettiest woman of the court—the last lady whom Monsieur le Duc d'Orleans has honored with his far-reaching attentions, is ugly compared to it."

An instant after she says: "Have you investigated the whole of this miniature?"

"What do you mean?"

"I mean what there is behind the picture, perhaps. This box is too large to be occupied entirely with this little ivory." And her facile fingers search hurriedly for some concealed spring in the case.

An instant after they find and press it, the miniature flies up—there is an open space behind.

"Pish! It is empty!" ejaculates D'Arnac, disappointment in his tone.

"Save this little piece of paper," returns Mimi, "which may give you a better clue than diamonds," as she reads hastily from it,

Address Monsieur Poisson,
Rue Dauphin,
Paris.

"Poisson! I've heard that name before," mutters Raymond. A pause of thought and he ejaculates, "The address of the letter to her uncle. The one Dillon spoke of in his story. Mimi, have you ever heard of such a man ?"

"Yes; in the playbills of Le Français," answers his sister. "He's the man who does the old pompous comedy rôles. He makes every one shriek with laughter as 'Crispin.'"

"'Crispin!' I know the fellow! I fell out of my chair laughing at him six months ago, before I joined my regiment," replies D'Arnac.

"But he may not be the one. There may be a hundred Poissons in Paris," suggests Mimi.

"I'll discover where he lives. If it's Rue Dauphin that will probably settle it."

"Well, if you want to learn about actors, I know
some one who can give you the history of every one of
them, and actresses also."

"Who?" asks Raymond, eagerly,

"Cousin Charlie," answers Madame la Marquise,
with a mocking laugh.

"Then, to-night at dinner I'll nail Cousin Charlie,"
cries D'Arnac, enthusiasm in his voice and confidence
in his manner, "for he doesn't know he is beginning a
task to which the siege of Friburg and the assault on
the German infantry of stout De Arsch were almost as
the play of infants."

CHAPTER IX.

POISSON THE LIAR.

RAYMOND strolls to dinner that evening in a very easy
frame of mind. The brilliant sights of the city are
pleasing to him after his campaign. He looks at the
principal thoroughfares, lighted with oil lamps, and
thinking "What a grand civilization!" jostles his way
quite cheerily along the Rue Dauphin with its crowds of
beseeching mendicants, for in the year 1714 there are
plenty of starving people, both in the great City of Paris
and the Provinces of France, some of which had been
devastated by war, and all of them devoured by the
Farmiers Generals who collected taxes from them.

Soon the quick steps of youth bring him into the Rue
de Fosses Saint Germain, and a few minutes after he has
passed through the Rues de Condé and Des Maries and is
at Pascal's Armenian Café in the Foire de Saint Germain.
Here, mid the light of flickering candles, he finds a
section of gay Paris. Cousin Charlie is seated at a little
table where preparations for a feast for the gods are
going on rapidly, for Monsieur le Procureur, loving
himself, loves his stomach.

De Soubise of the Garde and De Rohan of the
Musquetaires Noirs, two dashing young officers, are with
him. Abbés, generals, nobles, and a smattering of
hangers-on of the court, make the rest of the company
at the surrounding tables.

"I have the pleasure of knowing Monsieur d'Arnac's sister!" remarks Soubise on introduction.

"And I have the honor of greeting the hero of Friburg!" adds De Rohan, who has seen service in Flanders and on the Rhine. "How is our old Chief?"

"The Duc de Villars was very well this morning when I left him," replies Raymond, as they sit down to dinner.

A moment after they are taking their soup. Soubise remarks: "We heard as much in Paris about D'Arnac's lucky escapes at Friburg as you did on the Rhine, De Rohan. De Moncrief told the whole town the details of his cousin's taking two bastions."

"Yes, I had a few letters from the front, speaking in very high terms of your conduct, my boy—so I made them public;—they won't hurt you with the young ladies of honor at Versailles!" laughs Cousin Charlie.

"Letters from whom?" asks Raymond, carelessly.

"From the man who knew the most about your gallantry—the Chief of Staff of your Division—Monsieur Lenoir!"

As the name leaves the lips of De Moncrief, his eyes turn on Raymond, and he notes that a drop of soup falls from the boy's uplifted spoon.

"Yes, no one should know it better than he!" returns D'Arnac. Then breaking into a forced laugh, he says: "*Pardieu!* I sometimes thought Lenoir, by the places he put me in, meant I should not live through the campaign."

"Perhaps that was owing to me, my dear boy!" utters De Moncrief proudly.

"You!" gasps Raymond, astonished at the confession.

"Yes, as I know Lenoir quite well I said to him as Chief of Staff: 'Please give my cousin a chance to win his spurs—I want him to be a general before his father was.' *Parbleu!* I'm glad Lenoir did not forget it. Instead of colonel you would now be a captain."

"Yes, I've done very well," returns Raymond, looking at his epaulettes and forgetting in the pride of military glory Dillon's remarks about the young officers who did not come back.

Shortly after the conversation changes to the doings of Paris and Versailles, De Soubise expatiating on the

beauty of Madame de Parabere, the last favorite of the
Duc d'Orleans, and De Rohan remarking upon the
reigning star at the opera—the dancer, la belle Françoise
Prevost. This brings them easily enough to the Theatre
Français.

"By-the-bye, would you like me to show you some of
the heroes of the boards?." remarks De Moncrief, who
is rather proud of his knowledge of the stage, an
unknown land always interesting to the uninitiated.

"*Morbleu!* I prefer the *heroines* of the stage,"
laughs De Soubise.

"I expect we can find some of the heroes at Pro-
cope's!" suggests Cousin Charlie. "Shall we step over
there?"

"Agreed!" cries Raymond, thinking of Poisson.
"Instanter!" rejoins De Soubise, for the dinner is finished and he is anxious by means of the heroes of the
stage to get introduction to one of its heroines, the
beautiful Mademoiselle Seine, who is at this time making the hearts of Parisian gallants beat very fast, as they
gaze on her charms across the candles of the Theatre
Français.

De Rohan, however, excuses himself, remarking that
he has an appointment this evening.

"Ah," chuckles De Moncrief, "we are about to worship
Thalia, while you seek Venus, I presume, my young
gallant!"

"No, only a lady of the opera!" laughs De Rohan,
and departs upon his way, as the three others stroll
toward the Rue de Fosses Saint Germain and Café
Procopé.

As they step along Monsieur Le Procureur oracularly
remarks: "I hope to introduce to you my old friend,
Michael Baron! You boys never saw such an actor.
He has left the stage now these twenty years, but I
remember him in the days of Molière. We will probably
find him and two or three others of his cronies playing
dominoes this evening."

"Will we see the man who makes all Paris laugh
with his 'Crispin?'" queries D'Arnac, leading up to his
subject.

"What? old Paul Poisson, the idol of the pit. You'll
find him wherever there are cards and dice."

"Ah! great at cards and dicing!"

"Yes. And a hint to you, you can gamble with him *now*. Since Lass, the great pharo player, was here my friend Poisson's purse has been full enough to pay his losses."

This information causes Raymond to think he is warm on the scent. His friend Dillon's "Uncle Johnny" is a great gambler, and arriving at the Café Procopé he is delighted to find the elder Poisson is one of the company.

This place, one of the most popular in Paris, stands immediately opposite the *Comedie Française*, that had been turned out of its more commodious theatre in the Palais Royal by Cardinal Mazarin to first accommodate the Italian comedians whose patron he was, and afterwards to make room for the Royal Academy of Music, now called the "Opera."

For Richelieu had founded the *Comedie Française*, and Mazarin had brought the Italians to Paris, and he gave the French actors a kick with his ecclesiastical foot whenever he could bring it to bear on Monsieur Molière and his companions of the footlights.

But Mazarin having passed away, and the King having exported the Italian troupe for playing "The False Prude," a comedy that Madame de Maintenon maintained, quite wisely reflected upon her, the *Comedie Française* had become again the fashion, and still sustained its prestige, though another troupe of Italians, lured by Gaelic gold, had by this time come to Paris to play against it.

The popularity of the Theatre Français made the popularity of the Café Procopé, which, being opposite to it, was convenient both for its actors and its audiences.

To the glow of tallow dips, François, its proprietor, had added the dazzle of oil lamps, and the place was considered the most brilliantly illuminated of its day. Its sawdust the cleanest, its wines of the finest vintages, its coffee the most genuine of Mochas—chicory was yet to come.

It is by no means crowded as Cousin Charlie and his party enter ; but in a retired corner. several guests are gathered together, some sitting at a table, the others lounging near them.

"*Parbleu!* we're in luck," whispers De Moncrief. "There's Baron, and beside him is the man you asked about, Raymond, old Paul Poisson himself."

"Which is Baron?"

"Baron is the tall, well-built fellow, sixty years of age if he is a minute, but doesn't believe he is any older than I am."

This produces a snicker from De Soubise, who is following immediately after them, as the actor designated has the appearance of a Hercules and the apparent activity of a Mercury, compared to the somewhat emaciated five feet two and rather trembling movements of Cousin Charlie.

As they approach the group at the table, Michel Baron rises and says heartily and easily: "Welcome, Monsieur de Moncrief!" then cries: "Quasimodo, quick! Chairs for the gentlemen of the court and the gentlemen of the army!"

While these are being brought by a hump-backed *garçon*, who has the enormous shoulders of an acrobat and the light flying legs of a rope dancer, a wonderful leer in his sharp twinkling eyes, and an agile flourish in his strong, powerful arms, introductions have been going on, and Raymond finds himself acquainted suddenly with some of the great lights of literature and the stage.

Old Prosper Crebillon, whose romances and plays have given Paris many nights of naughty enjoyment, says he is pleased to meet the hero of Friburg.

Little Jacques Campistron, who has just been button-holing Baron for his influence to get a hearing for a play of his at the Français, is delighted to return the bow of De Soubise and D'Arnac, thinking a stroll in the Gardens of the Tuileries with these two dashing officers will add to his literary reputation.

A second after Baron, who has just been introduced to Raymond, begs to have the honor of presenting his friend, Paul Poisson, of the Français, to the gentleman who has been so much talked about in Paris during the last campaign.

"*Pardi!* you'll make him think he's De Villars himself, in a minute!" laughs Cousin Charlie, as they all sit down, for Quasimodo has piled seven chairs on each other, and brought them with one quick skip to the group.

"Isn't he a miracle?" chuckles Baron, delighted. That imp of Hercules can carry ten chairs in each hand, and a table in his mouth.

"We've christened him Quasimodo, Junior, after the old bell-ringer of Notre Dame," remarks Poisson. "*Sapristi!* when I look at him, I shudder to think what a success he would have made in comedy rôles!"

Then the conversation drifts towards the stage, for the actors of that day were even more cut off from the general run of men than those of the present time; though they associated with the gentlemen of the court, the court looked upon them as its servants, and the Church anathematized them as the servants of the devil. They get to speaking of the rival company.

"Those Italians," remarks Baron, oracularly, "disgust God!"

"While we only disgust Saints!" laughs Poisson so infectiously that all the company burst into a shriek at his humorous countenance.

"Yes, your jokes go because you laugh at them yourself, Poisson!" returns Baron. "*Diable!* who can help laughing at your grimaces?"

"Do you mean to insinuate," says Poisson, indignantly, "that my grimaces are the only funny things about me?"

At which there is another shriek of laughter, because Poisson's rage is funnier than his humor. Just here Quasimodo makes his appearance with several flasks of Italian wine, ordered by De Moncrief, and the opening of the bottles closes the actors' mouths.

"*Ma foi!*" remarks Cousin Charlie, "you think Italian wine better than Italian comedy."

"*Pardieu!* I can stomach their wine though I can't their Venice farces!" says Baron, putting his glass down with a smack.

Then Moncrief and Soubise getting into some discussion on Italian vintages, and a crowd of people coming in from across the street, for it is now an *entr'acte* in the performance going on at the theatre, Raymond draws his chair alongside of Paul Philippe Poisson, and gradually leads the conversation from the stage to the

gambling table, which will put him in position to ask
questions about John Lauriston, and his niece, Madame
O'Brien Dillon.

While doing this he incidentally receives some other
curious information, as he begins his conversation rather
deftly for a blunt young soldier in complimenting
Poisson on his performance of "Crispin."

"*Parbleu!* I am pleased to have obtained Le
Comte d'Arnac's approbation in the rôle!" remarks
Paul, solemnly; then says with a sigh: "It may be
my last great success, as I do not appear very regularly
now."

"*Mon Dieu!* that is unkind to Paris!" returns
Raymond, who has shrewdly discerned that old Poisson
is a mass of vanity, like many other actors.

"Then Paris must suffer. At present I am instruct-
ing some of the younger members of my family in the
arts of the stage, one of whom, Arnoul, they say will
excel his father, because, hang their impudence, they
say he is *uglier!*" answers the comedian with a chuckle
so hideous that it would send Raymond into a spasm,
did not at this moment the old actor add: "You
must visit me at my school Rue Dauphin, No. 17."

Rue Dauphin is the address that O'Brien Dillon
mentioned. Raymond is on the *qui vive* at once.

"I shall be most happy," he replies. Then a gleam of
cunning flying to his mind, he suggests: "I presume you
have some beautiful pupils, as well as intelligent ones."

"You mean girls?" cries Paul. "No girls! I
would not be bothered with the minxes. Let Duclos
take care of them."

Then a new idea suddenly coming into his vivacious
brain, he continues: "There is only one woman to whom
I would like to teach my art, and she is beyond me! She
has such *beauté de diable!*—such grasp of emotion—such
intelligence and finesse—such a concentrated infernal
topsy turvy erratic nature, that she would make the
greatest actress in France! Duclos would be a *comedienne*
to her in tragedy, and poor Desmares would be a *tragedienne* to her in comedy if I could get her on the stage
—but that is impossible! At present she is a *relegieuse!*
She walks the boards of a convent. They mean her for
greater things."

"**Greater things** ! what can be grander than the triumphs of the stage ?"

"The triumphs of the court ! She is destined for great things, when certain little things happen!" answers Poisson, whose tongue is beginning to babble under the influence of the wine of Italy.

By this time the two are quite alone, as most of the patrons of the café have gone back to the theatre, in their company Baron, Cousin Charlie and De Suboise, who want to have a glance at beautiful Mademoiselle Seine, especially Suboise, whom Baron has promised to present to her.

"Let's have **another flask of** Chianti!" suggests Raymond.

And Quasimodo bringing it, the two continue their conversation, D'Arnac leading up to his subject by giving a little account of the desperate dicing and card playing that took place in Rastadt between the officers of the French and the German armies.

"Twenty thousand *livres* on a card! Did Monsieur **de Sartimes** think that a **big** bet ?" jeers the comedian.

"It is among gentlemen of the sword, but perhaps it is not among *fermiers généraux !*" returns Raymond.

"*Fermiers généraux a la diable!*" cries Poisson. "I have seen my friend Jean Lass risk one hundred thousand on the turn of a card, or the throw of a die, and think no more of it than you do of spiting a German!"

"There is another friend of yours, I believe, who is a great gambler—a John Lauriston," queries Raymond, trying to hit the nail on the head.

"John Lauriston!" says the old comedian. "John Lauriston!" Then his eyes suddenly have a perturbed, perhaps frightened look, and he mutters: "I do not think I have heard the name, though my memory is sometimes treacherous."

"He had his letters addressed to you in Paris, a year ago! You remember him—tall—well-formed—gray eyes!"

"Had his letters in my care ?"

"Yes, Rue Dauphin!"

"I—I have a great many pupils at my school. He may have been the father of—of one of them!" stammers the old gentleman. "I—I will look over my books. Perhaps the name is on them."

"Very well! I will call on you to-morrow!" says D'Arnac, who is determined to see No. 17 Rue Dauphin, and find out what he can discover with his own eyes, for somehow the sudden change in the bearing of the gentleman he is addressing produces a suspicion that Monsieur Poisson's memory is not as bad as he would have Raymond believe it.

A moment after the comedian rises. Apparently anxious, for some reason, to end the conversation, he says: "You will excuse me now, Monsieur le Comte! I have to go on the stage. One of my sons appears this evening, and it is necessary for me to speak to him!"

"What! Arnoul, the ugly one?" laughs Raymond.

"No, I shall not let him appear until I have taken my leave of the stage. I still wish to be considered the ugliest actor in France!" chuckles Poisson.

"Very well," replies D'Arnac, "to-morrow morning —Rue Dauphin!"

"Yes, if you wish it; though perhaps you had better call a—a few days later. It may take me some time to look over my books."

"I will take my chances of that, and I hope to have the pleasure of calling on you often," returns Raymond, diplomatically, as the old gentleman, with a profound bow and somewhat disturbed countenance, takes his leave.

The next morning one o'clock in the day finds D'Arnac at the house of the comedian, who laughingly remarks: "You come too late to see my pupils. They have finished and gone away."

"Then I hope you have had time to examine your books, and see if you have discovered the name of John Lauriston. He did not have a niece he wished to put on the stage?" suggests Raymond, making a wild shot.

It is a shot which apparently tells in some hidden way, for Paul Poisson's eyes roll about in a wild and disturbed manner as he receives it.

A second after his mobile features become calm, as he says: "Yes, I have discovered the name, and I believe the gentleman did have a niece. He spoke to me about her. That is the way I knew him. He had a desire to put his niece upon the stage, but it came to nothing."

"Why?"

"Well, as I recall the facts now, Lauriston received an order from Monsieur d'Argenson——"

"What, the Lieutenant of Police?"

"Yes—to leave France."

"You astound me! Why?"

"Because, I have been informed, Monsieur Lauriston was too great a gambler!"

"As great a one as Monsieur Lass?"

"About the same," returns Poisson, struggling to fight down a hideous grin.

"So he is not in Paris?"

"No; I believe he went to Venice or Bologna—somewhere in Italy."

"And took his niece with him?"

"I imagine so. I do not think she would have made a success on the stage. She was a poor, skinny, washed-out kind of a girl!" adds Poisson easily and affably.

Either this description or O'Brien Dillon's miniature is a lie, but Raymond, turning the matter suddenly in his brain, thinks it is best to say no more. At all events, if Dillon's "Uncle Johnny' has been ordered out of France, that would indicate no great political influence, and no high rank in life.

So departing on his way, he hunts up several of his old friends in Paris, and making cautious inquiries, discovers that no one has ever seen John Lauriston in Paris. That no gentleman of that name has ever been heard of at the great gambling salon in the Foire de Saint Germain. Consequently this must be another fib *de theatre* of Monsieur Poisson.

Filled with this information, Raymond turns to the Rue St. Honoré to seek counsel with his sister, and telling his story, interests her to such an extent that she says: "There is something that we cannot understand here!"

"Would you like to help me solve the enigma?"

"With all a woman's inquisitive soul!" cries Madame la Marquise.

"Very well! What does your bright brain suggest?"

"Make sure if Lauriston has been ordered out of Paris."

"How?"

"Monsieur d'Argenson is under obligations to my
husband. Though he is the head of all the police of
Paris, and people tremble at his name, and his spies are
everywhere, still I think he will do me a slight favor.
A letter of introduction to him from me, and he will
probably answer your question as to whether he ever
ordered a Monsieur Lauriston out of France!"

Ten minutes afterwards D'Arnac drives hurriedly to
the Ile de la Cité, and going to the Bureau de Sûreté, is
affably received by D'Argenson, who, as chief of the police
of Louis the XIV., holds in his hands the city of Paris.

On Raymond asking his questions, Monsieur le Lieutenant replies: "There never has been a Lauriston
in Paris, as far as I know, consequently I have never
ordered him out of it."

Then summoning one of his assistants, he says:
"Have you ever heard the name?"

"Yes, Monsieur d'Argenson."

"Where?"

"It was on several letters addressed to the care of
Monsieur Poisson, Rue Dauphin; but I have never seen
the man."

"You see?" D'Argenson remarks as his assistant
goes out.

Then turning to Raymond, he says: "I would like
to do you any favor in my power, Monsieur le Comte,
both for your sister's sake and for the sake of your
dead father, who some fifteen years ago, long before I
obtained my present rank, was kind to me. This man,
Lauriston, has not been ordered out of Paris. The
only great gambler to whom I ever sent a polite request
to depart from France was Monsieur Jean Lass. He
was also a friend of the comedian, Poisson; but that is
not curious, as Poisson is intimate with all great gamblers. Lass' greatest friend among the profession, however, was Madame Duclos, the celebrated tragedienne.
But I did not give his *congé* to Monsieur Lass on
account of his gambling, but on account of other things,
in which I would not advise you to interest yourself,
my young friend."

So Raymond, coming out from this interview, concludes that Dillon's Uncle Johnny and his niece are
beyond his finding.

Returning with this news to the Rue St. Honoré, he receives a tremendous shock.

He is met almost at the door of the salon by Mimi. Her dark eyes are flashing with excitement, and very wide open with astonishment; but her brother's become even more excited and more wide open, as she says to him: "I have found her!"

"Who?"

"Madame O'Brien Dillon!"

"*Sapristi!* Where?"

"At the convent *Des Capucines* where I went to visit little Jeanne. I thought the child might be lonely. The lady you seek is there as one of the pupils!"

"And beautiful?"

"As beautiful—more beautiful than the miniature!"

"You have made some inquiries about her?"

"Yes, she was placed there as the ward of Poisson, the comedian!"

"Poisson, the comedian—Poisson, the LIAR!" shrieks D'Arnac. Then he chuckles to himself: "We must outwit this farceur of the *Comedie Française*. Will you help me, Mimi?"

"With all my heart," returns La Marquise with excited face and beaming eyes.

CHAPTER X.

THE LIEUTENANT OF POLICE.

"You made these inquiries—you learned this from Madame O'Brien Dillon personally?" asks Raymond, eagerly.

"Partly! Of course I had *entré* to the convent when you were not with me. I was shown into the private parlor. There Jeanne came to me and was delighted to see me. We're going to be very great friends. She has wonderful *esprit*. She said she would like the place very much—for a year or two, because a great *artiste* should have a grand education."

"But the other one?" questions D'Arnac, biting his moustache with impatience.

"Oh, I'm coming to her! In her remarks about the school, Mademoiselle Jeanne expatiated upon the beauty of one of the scholars.

"'In your class?' I asked, carelessly.

"'Oh, no! she's by herself! She is much older than I—almost nineteen or twenty' But she has the beauty of an angel and a fascination *au diable.* Sometimes more of the first, sometimes more of the second,' remarked the little Quinault, whose theatrical experience," continues Madame la Marquise, with a slight laugh, "has given her a most precocious understanding of human nature. Well, Jeanne went on, with almost childish pertinacity, about the wonderful loveliness of the girl, and as she described her, somehow the miniature of yesterday came into my mind. La Quinault's description recalled it.

"'Nonsense!' said I, 'you're extravagant,' for her persistency wearied me.

"'Extravagant! Look at her, and say I exaggerate! Out in the garden. She's there now!' cried Jeanne, and pulled me towards the window, and under the budding trees I saw Madame O'Brien Dillon!

"'Ah! who's extravagant now!' said little Jeanne, for I had given a gasp of surprise at the discovery and a gasp of astonishment at the beauty of the girl herself, which is greater than her miniature. Even her uniform, for she was in full convent school girl's dress, could not modify it; in fact, ' continues Mimi, with a laughing blush, "it rather added to it, for very short skirts revealed feet and ankles adorable."

"You spoke to her," asks Raymond, eagerly.

"Yes, a few words, but very guardedly. To do this I amused myself with Jeanne and then proposed a walk in the garden. Here I met the young lady herself, and Jeanne cried out in her impulsive way: 'Come here and make your courtesy to Madame la Marquise de Chateaubrien. I told her you were the beauty of the school. Come here and live up to your reputation.'

"At this, Madame O'Brien Dillon, giving me a rather haughty salutation, said: 'I come to you, Madame la Marquise, to show you little Mademoiselle Jeanne sometimes tells fibs.'

"'Not this time, Hilda!' answered La Quinault."

" Hilda is the name! " cries D'Arnac.

" Yes, but her other one is not ' Van Holst ? ' "

" Ah! it is ' Dillon! ' "

" Not now! She calls herself ' Poisson! ' "

" Poisson ? "

" She was left there by the comedian as his niece and ward nearly two weeks ago," answers La Marquise.

"The niece of Lauriston, the niece of Poisson, and still Madame O'Brien Dillon. There's more mystery here than ever."

" Lots more," cries Mimi, " I've some now on my lips if you don't interrupt me.

" On coming away, as I was bidding *adieu* to the mother superior, I incidentally mentioned the wondrous beauty of her charge.

" ' Yes, too beautiful! ' she replied. Then the good woman whispered quite tremblingly to me: ' She has been here but two weeks, and already an attempt has been made to carry her off. If it had succeeded, what a scandal on *Des Capucines!* '

" ' Ah, she does not wish to remain with you— Mademoiselle is naughty and would run away,' sneered I, to draw her on.

" ' No, I don't think she knows of the attempt at all,' replied the mother superior. Then, after a moment's hesitation, she continued: ' Madame la Marquise, you are a woman of the world. Your husband is my patron. May I ask your advice upon this matter ? '

" ' Certainly,' said I, trying to restrain my eagerness.

" ' It only happened yesterday afternoon. You remember, just as you left, a carriage drove up to our door.'

" ' Oh, yes ; the one with the arms and liveries of the Prince de Conti,' I remarked.

" ' Ah! that is what nearly deceived me,' cried *la Superieure.* ' A gentleman coming in that carriage presented me with a note, apparently written by Monsieur Poisson of the Français, who is the girl's uncle and guardian. It directed me to deliver the young lady to him, as Monsieur Poisson had determined to place her in another convent. This seemed to me quite natural, as her guardian had said she would not

probably remain long at *Des Capucines.* I was about
to deliver her up, when suddenly, to my astonishment,
in walked Monsieur Poisson himself. He had come
accidentally to see his charge. As he entered, the
gentleman (for his bearing was that of a courtier)
muttered some excuse about going to arrange the coach
for the young lady, pulled his hat over his eyes and
went hurriedly out.

"'You have come to get your ward in person?'
said I.

"'No; only to speak to her, and to leave her a basket
of bonbons and fruits, with your permission,' replied
the actor.

"'Then, what means this note?' I gasped hurriedly,
handing it to him.

"'He glanced at it, shrieked "Forgery!" and was so
overcome that he sank on a chair trembling, muttering:
'If he had succeeded, what would I have said to the
Prince?'

"'I stepped hurriedly to the window to recall the
man who had delivered the letter, but he was driving
away like the wind, in the carriage that bore the Conti
arms.

"'So you think the Prince de Conti tried to abduct
your charge?' suggested I.

"'Certainly not!' said the mother superior, excitedly. 'It was the Prince de Conti's recommendation
that made me take the young lady into our convent.
Monsieur Poisson said he used the Conti arms on his
carriage as part of his plot. Oh! I fear there is some
extraordinary intrigue—something perhaps political;
something that may bring trouble upon *Des Capucines.*
If I had known I would never have accepted her care
—not even if all the princes in France asked it.'"

"So the Prince de Conti requested them to take
charge of her!" says Raymond, as his sister stops.
"Then O'Brien may be right; she may be a princess
of the blood."

"Nonsense, it is her beauty, not her rank, that
makes Madame O'Brien Dillon important," rejoins
Mimi. A moment after she cries: "How I would
like to guess the mystery—who is trying to abduct
her?"

"That you shall do very shortly, with my assistance," remarks D'Arnac, in the superb confidence of youthful manhood.

"How?"

"Arrange an interview for me with Madame O'Brien Dillon. You can see her again to-day?"

"Yes, I left some unfinished directions to *la petite* Quinault to give me an excuse to return to *Des Capucines*," answers La Marquise. Then she says suddenly: "What can she tell you? The beauty inside the convent doesn't seem to know of these men's plots outside it."

"That information I shall get from another quarter," laughs Raymond, very wise and deep about the eyes.

"Ah! How?"

"From *Monsieur le Procureur!*"

"Brava!"

"I'll go to Cousin Charlie. Who can tell me better about a court intrigue? Who knows more about the gossip of Paris? Who is deeper in the law? Who can better advise me how to protect my friend, O'Brien Dillon's wife, than Cousin Charlie?"

"Bright boy!" exclaims Mimi. "While you go to Cousin Charlie, I'll do Madame Dillon."

Leaving his sister, Raymond hurriedly crosses the Pont Neuf to the Ile de la Cité, and in a few minutes is on the Quai de l'Horloge. Entering the Palais de Justice he soon finds himself at the offices of the Procureur du Roy, and shortly after is shown into the private apartment of De Moncrief.

"A visit to my office? Raymond, my boy, that must mean business!" says Cousin Charlie, motioning D'Arnac to a seat.

"Yes. Important business!"

"Your own?"

"That of a friend—a brother in arms—Colonel O'Brien Dillon, who saved my life at Friburg! Whose business I will make my own."

"Oh, the wild Irishman! He's off fighting the Turks, isn't he?"

"Yes, but he has a wife here."

"*Diable!* a pretty one?"

"Very beautiful! though I have never seen her!"

"But want to.   Where is she ? "

"She is a school-girl in the convent *Des Capucines,*
Rue Louis le Grand! "

"A school-girl—the wife of Colonel O'Brien Dillon ?
and most beautiful!   This sounds interesting! "
chuckles the Procureur, and would give the young man
a sly nudge, did not Raymond's severe manner check
such youthful indiscretions on the part of the aged
lawyer.

"Well, what do you want to do for him, or—his
wife ? "

Thus requested, Raymond commences to hint and
beat about the bush, telling of his interview with Poisson, the comedian.   But in the midst of this the lawyer
stops him by saying: "Enough! I won't take your
case! I won't give you my advice! "

"Why not ? "

"Because you are not telling me *all!*   Now, if you
wish my counsel as your cousin, tell me what you
please.   If you wish my counsel both as your cousin
and as your lawyer, tell me EVERYTHING! Which do you
want ? "

"Both."

"Then the entire story."

Thus compelled, Raymond gives a complete history
of Colonel O'Brien Dillon, from the time he had met
him up to the present moment.

As it goes on the look of pleasant interrogation on
the lawyer's face changes gradually into that of most
intense and personal interest.   As his cousin reaches
the description of Madame O'Brien Dillon and the
attempt to abduct her by an individual in the liveries
of the Prince de Conti, De Moncrief's concern becomes
so dominant that he hardly breathes.   And as Raymond
concludes, a sigh of rapturous delight floats from his
thin lips as he murmurs: "Is that all ? "

"Everything.   Now what do you advise? "

After a moment's contemplation, Cousin Charlie
promptly gives council that he knows will *not* be
accepted.   He says: "If I gave you the advice of a
lawyer I should say, 'Do nothing about it. You may
burn your fingers pulling your friend's chestnuts out of
the fire.'"

"But that is not what O'Brien would do for me!"
cries D'Arnac, impetuously.

"No? I suppose he is hot-blooded like yourself,
and would protect the Countess d'Arnac (if you were
foolish enough to have one) with his life, his sword, and
his honor!"

"And I will do the same by him!"

"Then you want my advice as your friend?" says
Cousin Charlie, looking very curiously at Raymond
over his eye-glasses.

"Yes, as my cousin and one of my family, and—as
a man of honor!"

"Very well. Here it is: I would protect Madame
O'Brien Dillon by every means in my power   Then I
would, if possible forward her to Vienna.   My purse is
at your service for that purpose."

"I do not need that, but your counsel will be very
valuable to me."

"Very well. The first thing you must do is to
protect this beauty from any further attempts at abduction by force or artifice.   Monsieur d'Argenson, the
Chief of Police, will attend to that for you."

"You would go to him?"

"At once! and tell him your story in full.   It is but a
step to the Bureau de Sûreté.   After your interview with
D'Argenson, return to me, and tell me what he says!"

"Immediately!" replies D'Arnac, and bolts from
the office, as the Procureur du Roy, emitting a hoarse
chuckle, sits hurriedly at his desk and writes a little
note.   Then calling in an attendant, he says: "Take
this in person to Monsieur d'Argenson."

"And leave it?" asks the clerk.

"No! In all probability my cousin,• the Comte
d'Arnac, is at present with him.   You saw him; the
young officer who just left me?"

"Yes, sir."

"Go to the Office of Police and wait until you see
Monsieur d'Arnac ushered into the private apartment
of the Lieutenant.   Wait then five—no—ten minutes—
and then say you must see Monsieur d'Argenson at
once!.   No matter what they say to you, insist, and
interrupt the interview!   Give D'Argenson this letter in
person, and then return to me!   Remember that the

time of the delivery of the letter, ten minutes after my cousin has been closeted with him, is of vital importance!"

"Yes, sir; ten minutes after the Comte d'Arnac goes into the Lieutenant of Police's private office!" and the assistant, who understands Monsieur le Procureur's methods of business very well, departs upon his errand.

Meantime Raymond has bolted to the Bureau de Sûreté, and astonished Monsieur d'Argenson by being announced a second time.

Curiosity obtains him an immediate interview, for the Lieutenant mutters "*Parbleu!* Twice in one day! There must be some new developments!" and bids his attendant show Monsieur d'Arnac in at once.

Here Raymond hurriedly tells of what he has discovered in regard to the niece of Lauriston, and the attempt that had been made to abduct her but yesterday, and astonishes Monsieur d'Argenson.

Then the Lieutenant of Police makes reply, and astonishes his visitor still more.

He says, shortly: "You are not speaking of the niece of John Lauriston, but of Monsieur Jean Lass, called in his own country, Law!"

"You astound me! Is it possible?"

"It is certainty! Monsieur Law—called here in Paris, Lass—sometimes travels, on his gambling expeditions through Europe, under assumed names. What more natural than that he should take the name of his estate, Lauriston, in Scotland? Besides, I have known of this affair you speak of for some time. Not that the lady was married to your friend, the Irish officer, and that her real name is Madame O'Brien Dillon—but *other* things about her. I am delighted to have the opportunity of stopping this intrigue now. I will give you my assistance. The whole power of the police of Paris is yours to take this lady who has kept me awake at nights, from the convent, and send her to her husband in Vienna, where I wish him joy of her."

Astonished and delighted, D'Arnac is about to thank the policeman. But D'Argenson goes hurriedly on: "You're under no obligation to me in this matter. It's what I've wanted to do ever since I gave his *congé* to Monsieur Lass."

"Then I can rely on your stopping all attempts at abducting her?"

"More! I know who is the instigator of them, and if necessary I will report his conduct to the King. Then we will see if Philippe Duc—" checking himself—"we will see if the party in question dare raise a hand, high though he is, against the command of his sovereign!"

As the Chief of Police says these last words, there is a hurried rap on the door.

"I must not be interrupted now!" he calls out.

"It's a letter," answers one of his clerks, "one of imperative importance, I am told, from the Procureur du Roy!"

"Give it to me—I'll glance at it!" says D'Argenson suddenly. "Excuse me a moment, then I will arrange the details of my assistance with you, Monsieur d'Arnac."

With these words the Lieutenant of Police breaks open the letter of Monsieur de Moncrief, and as his eyes run over it, says: "Pish! it's but official routine!"

But towards the close of the letter his features become contracted, as if in deep thought, his face grows pale, and crumpling the missive in his hand, he shoves it angrily into his pocket.

Then his manner suddenly changes. He turns to D'Arnac and astounds him with these words: "On further consideration I deem it best to leave this matter of Madame O'Brien Dillon entirely alone, and let it take its natural course!"

"You will not aid me?"

The Lieutenant hesitates a moment, then says sharply: "It's impossible! I cannot!"

"You cannot?"

"To be very frank with you," returns the Lieutenant, noting the distress in the young man's face, "I dare not!"

"Something in my cousin's letter has deterred you?"

"Not at all. His note was simply routine business. But I have made up my mind." Then D'Argenson goes on more cordially: "My young friend, take my advice! Let the matter severely—entirely alone! You do not know what you may encounter in protecting the wife of your friend."

"But I shall attempt it, even if Monsieur le Lieutenant de Police does not dare it!" replies D'Arnac with a ceremonious yet haughty bow, and leaves the office of the Chief of Police, while that official looks after him, muttering to himself: "*Pardieu!* I wish him joy of his bargain!"

A second later a little official shiver runs through him as he thinks, "How near I came to putting my foot in it!"

But Raymond does not entirely believe the statement of Monsieur d'Argenson, that the letter of his cousin had not altered his determination, and he bursts quite indignantly into Cousin Charlie's private office, crying: "I would have had his assistance had it not been for your infernal note."

"Oh, the one I sent to the Lieutenant of Police during your interview?"

"Yes."

"Did it prevent his making a move in the matter?"

"It did!"

"But it also showed me that you should make no move in the matter, because now I know who is trying to abduct Madame O Brien Dillon!"

"*Sapristi!* Who?"

"Monsieur le Duc d Orleans, who will very shortly, unless the stars fall, become Regent of France!" This last is whispered into D'Arnac's astonished ear.

"How do you know that?"

"I discovered it from your interview with Monsieur d'Argenson!" remarks Cousin Charlie, smiling, and happy as a child that has solved the secret of a new riddle.

"How?"

"You told Monsieur d'Argenson your story?"

"Yes!"

"He agreed to aid you?"

"Most cordially! He said he would go, if necessary, to the King."

"Then my note came, and he suddenly said he would have nothing to do with the matter?" returns De Moncrief, with a chuckle.

"Yes."

"Well, what did my note contain? Simply this: a statement of various official data that it is necessary for

me as Procureur du Roy to render to D'Argenson as
Lieutenant de Police. But at the close I added two
lines: 'By-the-bye, have you heard that His Majesty
had yesterday another attack of his stomach trouble,
and is at present very low at Versailles?' Then
Monsïeur d'Argenson said he would not aid you! Why?
Because he feared there would soon be a Regent in
France, during the minority of the young King, and
that Regent Philippe d'Orleans, who has seen Madame
O'Brien Dillon and fallen so deeply in love with her that
he would even risk the King's displeasure to gain her for
himself. You know Monsieur loves every pretty woman.
Think how he must love one as beautiful as the minia-
ture you showed me when you told me the story of
Madame O'Brien Dillon!"

"Well, what do you advise under these circumstances?" asks Raymond.

"There is but one chance for your friend! That is
to get his wife out of France immediately. Certainly
before the Duke becomes the Regent, and all powerful!"

"That I shall attempt at once?" replies Raymond.
"Thank you for your advice!"

"But be wise, my boy! You're running against
another bastion, mined like that of Friburg."

"Yes; but O'Brien Dillon did not hesitate to enter it
to save my life—shall I hesitate now to save his honor?"
cries Raymond, the enthusiasm of twenty blazing in
his eyes, and giving intensity to his voice.

"Then God be with you!" remarks Cousin Charlie,
as D'Arnac, wringing his hand, leaves the office.

His eyes watch the retreating figure of the young
man, and as Raymond disappears, De Moncrief, clos-
ing the door of his office, bursts into such chuckles of
joy and merriment that old Satan, down below, snickers
to his imps: "Has our old friend the Procureur up
stairs got a new ballet girl or a new villainy?"

CHAPTER XI.

THE PIE OF THE PRINCE DE CONTI.

A FEW MOMENTS devoted to joy and De Moncrief
comes to business. He thinks: "Now I can get my

finger in this great pie that is to be cooked on the death of his Majesty. Now the estates of Count de Crevecœur will surely be mine, because my cousin, who would inherit them before me, will certainly pass away !''

But a second after he mutters: ''I must be moving! Strike while the iron is very hot, and this one is 'in the forge *now !*''

And leaving his office takes carriage, for he fears his shrivelled legs will not carry him fast enough, to the Hotel de Conti, the palace of that Cadet branch of the house of Condé Bourbon—the youngest, yet the haughtiest of the family of France.

Arriving there, he begs the gentleman in waiting will take his name to Monsieur le Prince and tell him Charles de Moncrief, his humble servant, must see him on a matter of most immediate and urgent business.

A few minutes after he is shown in to the private apartments of the head of the younger family of the house of Bourbon. These are situated in a pavilion that occupies a portion of the court yard of the great house and are arranged in the Italian style as the Prince likes that country and spends a great portion of his winters in Venice, Florence and Rome. They are filled with furniture bought at great price from the Palazzos of Italian noblemen and have been frescoed and adorned by artists imported from that country. Every fitting of these rooms indicates a lavish prodigality in money matters—so great that the house of Conti was regarded as very bad pay by the usurers of Paris.

As the Procureur enters, Louis de Conti, rising from a chair, says in the easy way of the most affable, yet the most villainous, most unprincipled, most scalawaggy Prince of those most scalawaggy times: ''Take a chair with me, Moncrief. I have shoved the Burgundy your way, and will you join me in a pipe ?'' For tobacco was at that moment the newest fad in Paris.

''No! Perhaps you would prefer snuff ?'' And this affable yet haughty prince passes his snuff-box embossed with jewels that form his crest, towards Cousin Charlie, who pounces upon it and enjoys it.

''Now between sneezes,'' laughs Louis de Conti, ''tell me why you must see me at once!''

"Why?" says the lawyer, "because if *we* don't act on the instant, the great scheme of your life—the one you've been working on for the last year—the one you think of at night—the one you dream of by day—will be smashed into ten thousand pieces, and we will not be able to pick up one of them!"

"WE? What dream of my life? What scheme that I have been working on for a year? Do you mean my new device to pay my debts with nothing?" laughs De Conti, though his eyes are serious, almost menacing.

"Yes, for your great scheme includes that lesser one."

"What do you mean?"

"I mean," says Cousin Charlie, though his legs tremble under him at his audacity, "the scheme you have with Monsieur Jean Lass, financier and gambler, on the death of one to whom we doff our hats and bow our knee, when the Duc d'Orleans becomes Regent, to obtain from him, first the charter of your National Bank, next the revenue of the French Colonies—ultimately the control of the finances of France!"

"You must be mad!" gasps De Conti. Then he grins hideously and says: "Charles de Moncrief, the words you have used are petty treason!"

"But you will not report them?" whispers Cousin Charlie, agitated but determined.

"Why not?"

"Because I will show you that it is to your interest to make me a member of your combination—that it is fatal to you not to do so!"

"*Morbleu!* you are out of your senses! The lunatic asylum, not the prison, will be the proper place for you!" blusters De Conti.

"Yes, but these will be my ravings": cries de Moncrief. "De Conti being for a Prince of France most infernally hard up, and Jean Lass, the greatest gambler on earth being most ambitious, the two have thought to get a great concession from Monsieur le Duc d'Orleans, when he becomes the Regent. That is, the concession of a bank, next of a great commercial company, and perhaps ultimately control of the collection of taxes for France itself. These concessions they expect to win, first by the great friendship of the Duke for the Prince de

Conti, and his belief in the financial abilities of Jean
Lass; next, and most potent, by Philippe d'Orleans' love
for the mistress of Jean Lass, whom the Regent has
seen twice, and whose beauty has ensnared him as no
other woman's has ever done, because it is beyond com-
pare. That when they saw D'Orleans' passion for her
had become such that they knew he would grant them
all privileges to obtain her, that they had removed her
secretly, and by aid of the comedian Poisson, entered
her as his ward in the convent *Des Capucines.* Just as
this took place, D'Argenson, Chief of Police, suddenly
ordered Jean Lass out of France, on the pretext of
gambling, but really to stop their scheme. Therefore,
they expect to hold this paragon of beauty, who is
herself willing, having tremendous ambitions, to wait a
few months until the proper time comes, to become perchance a second Madame de Maintenon. Thus holding
the meat, as it were, beyond the reach of the dog to
make him lick his royal chops the more.

"Now bring in your keepers and I'll begin to rave!"
concludes the Procureur, smiling at De Conti, who during the last part of this oration has been going about
eagerly from doors to windows to see that none of his
maids or flunkeys have been listening, and who now
regards De Moncrief with a hang-dog, half frightened,
half surly air.

A moment later the Prince, attempting a laugh, says:
"Have you any more ravings, my wise lunatic?"

"This one, that this fine plan has suddenly been
stopped by the Duke discovering the whereabouts of
the woman he adores, and his attempt to abduct her
yesterday, from the convent *Des Capucines,* Rue Louis
le Grand!" whispers De Moncrief.

"Discovered her! Abducted her!" shrieks De Conti.
"By Heaven, that cursed comedian shall answer to me
with his miserable soul!"

"Oh ho! the lunatic's ravings were right!" chuckles
Cousin Charlie. "But I said 'had discovered her' not
'had abducted' her. Furthermore, I can tell you how
he shall never abduct her!"

"What do you want for this assistance and this
advice?" cautiously remarks De Conti, who knows
De Moncrief is a wary bird.

"Just my chance to put my own hands into the pie, when it is cooked—nothing *down* and NOTHING ELSE!" remarks De Moncrief.

"Very well! Then assist in this pie's baking!"

"Won't I?" cries Cousin Charlie. With this he sits down and tells the Prince the whole story of D'Arnac and of the Irish Colonel, who is fighting the Turks, and who is married to the beautiful object of their speculation, and concluding, says: "My cousin will attempt to remove our prize from the convent. We must do so first, and send her to Italy to Monsieur Lass, before D'Orleans makes another attempt, or becomes Regent."

"But if your cousin should interfere? I've heard D'Arnac's a dashing fellow and has a ready sword!"

"Then my cousin must take his chances as any other ENEMY!"

"Ah, you do not object to treating him as if he were an outsider?"

"No, I sacrifice my cousin up to your plans, very willingly," laughs De Moncrief.

"Oh, yes, he has estates, I presume."

"Yes, and will have more handsome ones if he lives. I make this confession," remarks Charlie, "to show you I am bound to you as well as you to me."

"Very well, my old fox!" replies De Conti. "But how did you discover all this you have told me?"

"By mathematics?"

"Mathematics? *Morbleu!*"

"By putting two and two together, and seeing it makes four. By the babbling of a drunken comedian to me over his wine, a little each night, but, adding them together, they made a revelation; by the conduct of Monsieur d'Argenson, the Chief of Police to-day——"

"So this Poisson is the babbler?" growls De Conti, interrupting.

"Yes! We must take the girl out of his hands. He plays the buffoon off the stage as well as on it!"

"She goes to Italy to-night!" answers the Prince determinedly. "That shall be my personal charge."

"It is our only safe move from both D'Orleans and my impetuous cousin!"

"You are sure D'Arnac acts on behalf of the Irish officer? She is beautiful enough to send a boy of his age crazy, both with love and despair!" queries De Conti.

"Certain! Raymond has not even seen the beauty, besides he is devotion itself to the man who saved his life!"

"*Sapristi!* I thought we had got rid of this wild Irishman!" mutters the Prince. "Lenoir tried to put him out of our way by means of military duty, but he escaped the most deadly positions in battle and assault; then we brought influence to bear on Prince Eugene to offer him a regiment in the Imperial Army, and when he accepted and went off to Vienna, we thought it was an end of him; but here he is in the person of your cursed cousin springing up again!"

"Yes, Monsieur Raymond intends to take Madame O'Brien Dillon off to her husband in Vienna if we don't move to-night!" laughs De Moncrief.

"Take *her* to Vienna? Destroy the scheme of my life!" screams De Conti, bubbling over with rage. Then he mutters: "This settles Comte d'Arnac!" and the tone of his voice means death.

"By the way, would you please give me an order to *Des Capucines*, to see our charge? I know Poisson is her guardian, but she was placed there through your influence, and a note from you and my name and official rank will be sufficient," suggests Cousin Charlie.

"You want to see her?" asks De Conti, a trace of suspicion in his voice.

"Certainly! Because she is so beautiful!" returns the Procureur. "Second, she may be unwilling to go to Italy. I wish to ascertain that, and whether it will be better for you to use diplomacy or force to induce her to go there."

"Yes, you're just the inquisitor to get at the innermost thoughts of our fair charge!" laughs Monsieur de Conti, who sits down and writes the order.

As he finishes De Moncrief suggests to him: "Now a line to the young lady just to say she can trust me."

"As you wish," answers the Prince, "but after this no more notes; it's too much work to write them!" and scribbles off two sentences to the girl herself.

As he receives the missive, Cousin Charlie kisses the hand of his ally and takes his leave, saying: "I'll return in an hour and tell your Highness what I discover."

"Adieu, old disciple of Richelieu!" chuckles De Conti after him; then turning the affair over in his mind, he concludes: "It is best to have De Moncrief, the old Renard, in our affair! We need legal minds, and by all the gods there is enough plunder for everybody!"

For this scheme was of such financial grandeur that there was enough in it to bribe Parliament, the Regent, the Court—aye! even the people of France, and afterwards every banker, broker, money changer and speculator in Europe—which meant, at that day, the civilized world.

A second or two of glum consideration and De Conti swears a great Italian oath, and mutters: "*Per Bacco!* this spring-gald of the camp, young D'Arnac, shall not destroy the greatest project of the age!"

With this he calls to his counsel, the gentleman who heads his bullies and bravos who do the abducting, assassinating, and such like duties, for this most Christian prince of the blood.

Departing on this errand, De Moncrief soon finds himself at Des Capucines. Presenting his letter from the Prince, he is very affably received by the mother superior.

"As the Procureur du Roy," he remarks, blandly, "I have heard of the attempted abduction of your charge. I wish to ask the young lady—Mademoiselle Poisson—a few details that may be necessary to the Department of Justice in taking cognizance of the affair. I would like a private interview with *mademoiselle.*"

"It is against the rules of our convent!"

"It is imperative for the affairs of justice!"

"Very well, then," replies the mother superior. "The letter of the Prince de Conti and Monsieur's high position as the Procureur du Roy and his extreme age, induce me to grant his request. Please step this way."

So De Moncrief follows her, wincing and snapping his jaws together in rage at the thought that he is considered by this holy woman too old to be very dangerous.

And perhaps it is well that he is no young gallant of the court, though, oh, how he wishes it!—for the beautiful sight he sees as Hilda comes into the room would

twist the heart and turn the head of any man.   At all
events it does his.

She is in the dress of a schoolgirl, but has the
coquetry of a woman and a loveliness that is hardly of
the earth, and, over all, that wondrous art, indescribable as electricity, ethereal as the breath about us, but
potent as the powers of the air—fascination!—fascination in every gesture, fascination in every pose,
fascination in every glance of the eye, in every tone
of the voice!

To this vision Monsieur le Procureur bows down at
once and worships as other men have done before and
other men will do again.

For a second she stands hesitating, as if half in
doubt as to her bearing, courtesying after the manner of
the school to the old and dignified gentleman who is
gazing at her with all his eyes.

A moment after, remembering him as one of the very
few gentlemen she had seen at Poisson's, for Uncle
Johnny had kept very close watch on his trump card
since she arrived in Paris, Hilda gives a little piquant
pout and half laughs, half sighs: "How do you like
my masquerade?   I am here because I'm naughty.
Monsieur Lass would not trust me in Italy and so
placed me under Monsieur Poisson, who has put me *en
retraite.*"

"*Pardi!* that is a little fairy tale for those who do not
know *all!*" laughs the Procureur.

"ALL!" ejaculates the girl; then says hesitatingly,
but inquiringly: "You come—?"

"From the Prince de Conti, the ally of Monsieur
Lass in *our* little affair.   This note will prove to you
that I am one of your adherents and promoters of your
interest."   This last he adds hastily, for at his first
sentence Hilda's eyes have opened with astonishment
and flashed with sudden fright.

In a second she pounces on and devours the missive.
Then reads it over carefully again, aloud:

"You may trust him.   He is one of us!
                                        "DE CONTI."

"You know the Prince's signature!" says Cousin
Charlie, for she is gazing at him very searchingly.

"Perfectly! But I don't agree with the Prince's convictions?" sneers the girl. "Your face is *not* to be trusted!"

"Not if my interests pull the same way?"

"Ah, that is different! Explain how *your* interests are *my* interests!"

"With pleasure!" says Cousin Charlie. "In ten minutes I'll make you believe in me!"

And in five minutes he does so, proving to her as her blue eyes glow like diamonds as they try to read his soul that her elevation will make his success.

"Yes, I see—I understand!" she replies, after a moment's consideration. Then she whispers: "Tell me what Monsieur le Prince wants me to do!"

"Certainly!" and De Moncrief does so lucidly, candidly, and *in full*, placing the whole affair before her, for he has been studying the lovely face he is looking upon, and sees in it great ambition and great passions—and at present ambition dominates. Then he concludes: "If you throw yourself into D'Orleans' arms *now*, you only gain what he can give you NOW— nothing! If you wait—not long—till he is Regent— then he can give you France!"

"And how I will play with France!" whispers the young lady, for the conversation is still in an undertone.

"Then I hope you will not forget old friends!" murmurs Le Procureur, kissing the pretty hand that has been gesticulating so gracefully before him.

"Oh, I shall never forget *you*. You shall always have the privilege of—of *kissing my hand!*" says Mademoiselle Hilda, with fairy archness.

"That will make me *always* happy!" mutters the Procureur, but his wicked old eyes say more than his lips.

A moment after he goes on, for all this time though she bewitches him, he is trying to test her strength for the grand rôle of high priestess in this great political and financial scheme: "By-the-bye, how about your adventure with the wild Irish officer?"

"Who?" The blue eyes open wide and innocently.

"Colonel O'Brien Dillon! Why did you marry him?"

"Who told you that?" gasps the girl, with a start.

"Oh, I know all about your adventures!" laughs De Moncrief; and gives her the story as he heard it from D'Arnac; then repeats: "Why did you marry him to complicate this affair?"

"Why?" cries Hilda, her blue eyes becoming like wood violets with excitement, perhaps passion. "Why? Because he is such a fighter!"

"A fighter!" gasps De Moncrief, astonished.

"The grandest fighter I ever saw! Ah! you should have seen that glorious duel by the camp fire!' and she is up before the Procureur telling the story not only with her voice, but with eyes and graceful gestures, quick as the actions she is describing, as she goes on: "My Irishman, his cavalry jacket thrown off, one white sinewy arm bared to the shoulder! The dark-browed, swarthy scoundrel, who would have made me his slave, stripped likewise for the combat, and fighting almost as well as my blue-eyed knight! The glistening blades gleaming now and then in the flickering firelight! Then only darkness and the clink of steel, as *riposte* follow, parry, and lunge follows counter! Then the fi blazes up again! A wild yell from Irish Lanty, one p: more, and my Irish hero has him through the heart, an the man who would have made me his slave falls dc at my feet, where I can trample him into the dust."

At this last her eyes are blazing with triumph, inc nation, scorn, and one fairy foot is uplifted as if crush the corpse that lies before her.

A second later her volatile mood changes, and laughs: "Would you not have loved, too, old blood, for—FOR A LITTLE WHILE?"

But De Moncrief does not answer this, for in tr the school girl of *Des Capucines* has frightened hi He has now discovered that though she has ambiti great enough to take in France, she has also passi enough to devour the world, and he is thinking to himse rather grimly: "It is fortunate Monsieur d'Orleans i not of a jealous disposition." A moment later he suggests uneasily: "You love this Irish hero still?"

"*Mon Dieu!* How can I tell?" she cries, laughing. "I have not seen him for a year!"

And this reply soothes any concern he may have as regards O'Brien Dillon.

"All the same," he remarks, "my fly-about young lady, your marriage has placed a new and serious complication for your friends to encounter. Will you help them to meet this obstacle to your future greatness?"

Her reply astounds him more. Her face grows vindictive. She mutters: "What? Does he dare to come here when I have written him if he comes, he dies?" Then, her eyes grow tender, she says: "Of course, my Irishman dares anything to see my face!" next mutters savagely: "If he troubles me, let him take care!"

"Not in person," replies De Moncrief, "but Dillon has sent a representative!"

"A *what*?"

"A representative; his young friend, the Comte d'Arnac."

"Ah! that is the reason his sister, Madame la Marquise de Chateaubrien, took so much interest in me!"

"She has been here to see you?"

"Yes, under pretence of visiting a little charge of hers—*la petite* Quinault, who has a wild kind of schoolgirl affection for this young D'Arnac, whom it seems rescued her in some romantic manner, for she is never tired of telling of his exploits at the siege of Friburg."

"You have spoken to Madame la Marquise?"

"Once! and that merely accidentally. The second time she *tried* to see me, but I did not think it wise to meet her, as there is no telling where a court intrigue extends!" replies the young lady with an acumen so beyond her years that De Moncrief gazes at her in amazement.

Then he tells her the story of Raymond's efforts on behalf of his comrade, and his intention, if possible, to remove her to Vienna, to the care of her husband.

"To Vienna?" mutters the girl, her face growing white; "to Vienna? *Never!*" and stamps both fairy feet.

"Why do you fear Vienna more than other places?"

"Because that is where I was born—because that was where they spat upon and degraded my mother in the Market Place because she dared to wed a count of the Empire."

"Your mother was a Jewess," whispers De Moncrief.

"No, a Magyar; she was the daughter of Tekeli by a morganatic wife."

"The last King of Hungary!" gasps De Moncrief.

"Yes, the one even now in hiding with the Turks," cries the girl. Then she whispers: "Wait till I have France in my hands, and Austria shall pay for my mother's tears."

A moment after she laughs—"A truce to history—ambition can wait. Tell me what I must do *now.*"

"*Now!* In order," says De Moncrief, " to stop the attempts of Comte d'Arnac at once and forever, will you do as I tell you?"

"*Diable!* with pleasure. Tell me," remarks *Mademoiselle*, nestling up to Cousin Charlie as he gives to her a little plan that has originated in his fertile and ingenious brain, which sends the young lady into shrieks of laughter, and she cries out: "Brava! With pleasure! This is a comedy!"

"That will be perhaps a tragedy," replies De Moncrief.

"Yes, everything in its turn," laughs Madame Hilda; next says significantly: "This evening I am at Monsieur's orders."

"Then remember—AT TWELVE O'CLOCK!" remarks Le Procureur impressively as he rises to go.

"At twelve o'clock! I see we shall be great friends," she says, taking his hand, "you and I!"

"More, I hope!" replies De Moncrief suggestively. "Then adieu for the present," says Hilda.

But as he is leaving she gives him such alluring glances, such little cries of "Brava conspirator!" "Thanks for to-night's comedy!" such a merry step or two of the dashing *sarabande* that her abandon, *elan,* and general infernal fascination makes this sinner's old eyesroll as he mutters to himself: "I never envied a prince of the blood before—but now I would give my soul to be Monsieur le Duc d'Orleans!"

For the archness, the fascination, the vivacity—aye, even the very passion of the girl, was contagious. And during their interview she had shown such loveliness, such *esprit*, that Monsieur le Procureur was, for the time being, out of his head.

However, Cousin Charlie does not let his semi-insanity interfere with present business, and he drives back to the great hotel of the Prince de Conti, and there, seeing this gentleman, explains his little plan to him, remarking: "If we carry her away ourselves, D'Orleans will never forgive us for having kept his mouth watering so long—even though we restore her to him afterwards!"

"*Sapristi!* how will the Duke know?" growls De Conti.

"He knows already, or why did he use your liveries and crest in his attempted abduction yesterday? Now, by my plan, the blame of the young lady's elopement will fall all upon my cousin, the Comte d'Arnac!"

"*Parbleu!* I believe you are right!" mutters the Prince.

"Then give the orders as I request."

"With pleasure!" cries the Prince of the blood, and calls in again the gentleman who directs his bullies and his bravos, changing certain orders that he has given him; then he chuckles savagely to himself: "This will teach young D'Arnac to put his finger into De Conti's pie!"

CHAPTER XII.

THE ELOPEMENT FROM DES CAPUCINES.

THE OBJECT of these sinister designs on leaving the office of Cousin Charlie has hurried back with his news to his sister, and told his story to her.

Then she has disconcerted him, for she has thrown cold water on his romantic plans with regard to the rescue of his friend's wife.

"You have seen Madame O'Brien Dillon again," Raymond says, "as you promised?"

"No; I tried to, incidentally, but for some reason or other, could not obtain an interview without forcing one, which I thought was unwise. What you have discovered proves the wisdom of my course. Cousin Charlie's advice, as your lawyer, is what you should follow. There is some court intrigue—something that most unscrupulous and wretched reprobate—the Prince

de Conti—is engaged in—in regard to her.   Yes, I will
call him a worthless reprobate, though he is a prince of
the blood," cries Mimi, with feminine vindictiveness,
to her brother's deprecating hand.   "Something that
may be fatal to your career and success in life to
encounter!   You may make great enemies—powerful
at the court—potent in the army.   Promise me, my
brother, you will let this affair drop.   If your friend
O'Brien Dillon wants his wife let him come and get
her.   You only promised him to deliver a note to
her.   Give it to me and I will see that she gets it."

"What good will that do him when there is a plot
now against his honor—when they have already
attempted to abduct her?"

"But she may have been cognizant of it," replies
Mimi, "and willing the abduction should take place."

"What nonsense!   You yourself said the mother
superior told you O'Brien Dillon's wife knew nothing
of it.   There is only one safe place for her—under the
protection of her husband.   And that is where I'm
going to place her," replies D'Arnac, growing sulky
under Mimi's objections.

"That you must not do," urges Madame de Chateaubrien.   Then she says contemplatively: "The beauty
of this woman—I won't call her child, though she is in
a convent school—is of the kind that would not make
her a good wife.   I can tell from her manner she has
ambitions beyond being the spouse of a poor Irish
colonel.   That she means her beauty to be her stepping
stone in life to some high rank or position; that
her loveliness is to be for one of the princes of the
earth."

"Her beauty shall be for her husband, to whom it
belongs," cries D'Arnac.   "But since you will not aid
me——"

He rises to go, but Mimi's arms are round him
entreating him—begging him.   She knows the reckless
disregard of all rights of God or of any man, that he
does not fear of the Prince de Conti.   It frightens her.

To her entreaties and almost tears, Raymond
unwillingly promises to turn the matter over in his
mind for a day or two.

"Then it is a promise," reiterates the sister.

"Of course!" answers the brother.

"Very well!" she replies. "Don't forget it—as you love me, don't forget it."

"Now go and have a pleasant evening with some of your friends of the Garde, and think no more about this," suggests Mimi, whose two years greater age has given her a motherly as well as sisterly regard for her dashing and handsome young brother.

So with this promise on his lips, Raymond d'Arnac sallies from the Hotel de Chateaubrien, and pushes his way through the crowd on the Pont Neuf going toward the Hotel de Crevecœur on the Rue St. André, where he has taken his quarters with his aunt.

In this concourse of hucksters, beggars, hackdrivers and peddlers, mixed with the carriages of the nobility, and some old ladies' sedan chairs, that have not as yet entirely gone out of fashion, Raymond jostles his way with that careless ease peculiar to *le jeune militaire*, and chancing to push past a couple of Italian retainers of the Prince de Conti, one of them whispers to the other: "That's the man! Don't forget his face for to-night!"

"I have him! I remember him!" is the reply.

But this is in Italian, a language D'Arnac does not understand, and he proceeds on his way with all the unconcern of a young man who has thrown, for the time being, a weighty matter off his mind, thinking he will hunt up De Soubise and De Rohan, and one or two other young blades, and make an evening of it.

But at the very entrance of the Hotel de Crevecœur he is stopped by Cousin Charlie coming out.

"I've been here to see you," replies De Moncrief to Raymond's greeting. "I came in person to tell you I have just made a wonderful discovery with regard to that villain, the Prince de Conti!"

"In reference to Madame O'Brien Dillon?" says Raymond, hurriedly.

"Yes. Do you know that unscrupulous Prince is about to remove her from the convent this evening?"

"Why?"

"Why? Because he fears the Duc d'Orleans will get hold of her. He doesn't propose to have Monseigneur Philippe interfering with his prize. He has obtained an order from that old fool, Poisson, to that effect. This

will be your only chance to conduct Madame O'Brien
Dillon to her husband in Vienna!"

"Why my only chance?"

"Because how could you get her from the convent
Des Capucines without scaling its walls, and carrying
her off by force—even if she remain there?   But if you
have a carriage and postilions and horses immediately
behind that of the Prince de Conti, at the door of the
convent at twelve o'clock to-night, when they bring her
out to deliver her to him, you have a quick wit and
ready sword.   Why not pluck her right out of his arms,
into your coach, and presto! away for Vienna!   That
would be an exploit worthy of your friend, O'Brien
Dillon—what he would do for you!"

"And if I do not move to-night?"

"You will never have a chance to move in the matter
again!   I do not advise your doing it, that
must be your own decision; but I could not refrain from
telling you what I have discovered!"

"And how did you learn it?"

"From two ruffians of the Prince de Conti that I
bribed.   I understand Italian.   I accidentally overheard a few words from them in the street, and one
hundred crowns increased their frankness.   These fellows
will sell themselves for anything."

"Very well! here's your hundred crowns!" remarks
Raymond, and astonishes De Moncrief by placing the
money in his hand.

"What have you determined to do?"

"*Nothing!*"

"*Nothing?*"

"NOTHING!   I shall simply think it over, but I'm very
much obliged to you.   Now I must dress for
the evening.   I hope to have De Soubise and De
Rohan to dinner with me.   Won't you make one of
the party?"

"No, I have an engagement!" mutters the Procureur
with a little sigh, and goes away with disappointment
in his heart to take his solitary dinner and commune
with himself on the misadventure that he thinks has
come upon his plans.

But at the close of his meal he hurriedly jumps from
the table, for in his occult mind has suddenly sprung

up this idea: "Raymond is twenty! Youth changes its views quickly! He said he would consider my suggestion. I'll see if he's at dinner with De Soubise!"

And he walks off hurriedly to the Armenian Café in the Foire Saint Germain to discover that De Rohan and De Soubise are both at dinner there, and have not seen young D'Arnac.

"Egad! he's changed his mind—I'll have him yet!" chuckles De Moncrief, and directs his way to the Hotel de Crevecœur.

Here, being shown in, he is shortly received by Clothilde, who says to him hurriedly: "We have such bad news! Raymond is going away this evening!"

"Raymond going—aha!" a sigh of rapture.

"Yes, he follows his sister to Melun. She has received, by courier, news that her husband on his way from the Rhone, has fallen seriously ill there. She has already gone—Raymond follows after. Why, your face is white! I did not know Monsieur de Chateaubrien was so dear to you!"

For De Moncrief's visage has grown pale with disappointment, as he thinks D'Arnac will take post to Melun to be by his sister's side, and that is an end of his scheme against him for the present.

A moment after he makes his *adieu* to Clothilde who overwhelms him with condolences at his sorrow at the unfortunate affair.

But as he passes out of the Hotel de Crevecœur, he is jostled by Raymond's servant.

"Pardon, Monsieur de Moncrief," says the servitor, "but I am going in advance of Monsieur d'Arnac to order post horses along the road."

"Ah, yes, to Melun!" mutters Le Procureur surlily.

"No."

"Where?"

"To Claye, Mieux, Changis. We're to travel quick."

"Well, be careful and order good horses, and wish your master a pleasant journey for me!" says De Moncrief, with such a sudden change in his voice that the lackey departs on his errand astonished.

For joy has come to the Procureur du Roy! "Claye, Mieux, Changis? that, the road to Melun? That's the road to Strassburg, the Rhine and Austria!" chuckles

the old gentleman to himself, for he now knows that
his cousin has changed his mind, and is going to
attempt the restoration of Madame O'Brien Dillon to
her husband in Vienna.

So he goes off carefully repeating the route to himself,
and getting to the great hotel of De Conti, tells that
prince just where he can waylay his cousin on his
journey to Strassburg.

In this he guesses right.   Raymond, turning the
matter over, had flown to Mimi, not only to ask her
advice, but to be relieved of his promise. At the
Hotel de Chateaubrien, however, he had found that
Madame la Marquise having suddenly received word by
courier that her husband was desperately sick at Melun,
on his return journey from Southern France, had ordered
post horses at once, and was now on her way to the
side of Monsieur de Chateaubrien.

"If I do not act to-night," cogitates this reckless
young gentleman, "perchance my comrade's wife is lost
to him. How can I look him in the face, if I could
have saved her, and would not?"

Filled with this generous idea, Raymond had returned
to the Hotel de Crevecœur, told the news to his aunt of
Monsieur de Chateaubrien's sickness, and said he was
going away for some time, she naturally mistaking his
destination for the side of his sister's sick husband.

So it comes to pass that ten minutes before the
clock of distant Notre Dame strikes twelve, Raymond
d'Arnac drives from the Rue St. Honoré into the Place
Louis le Grand, now shrouded in darkness, for its few
oil lamps have been extinguished, and keeping the big
statue of Louis XIV. between his carriage and the
convent, drives straight across the open square towards
the portals of *Des Capucines*, which stands opposite,
where he sees another coach already waiting, and
knows the information the Procureur has given him is
correct.

He whispers to his coachman and the two lackeys
who are with him: "Don't move till you see the door
open and the lady brought out!"

"Ah, trust us, Mr. Wild Blood," answers the driver.
Then one of the other men mutters: "The desecra-
tion of a convent!" and crosses himself.

A moment after, the coachman gasps: "Good God! what will D'Argenson do with us?" For the police had a very nasty way, at that time, of punishing valets and underlings for the crimes of their noble masters and mistresses.

"They can't catch you till you have squandered the two hundred crowns I have promised you! You can hear me clink them in this bag!" whispers Raymond, anxiously.

This sound of silver vanquishes fear of the Church and terror of the police. The lackeys prepare to do his bidding, though in rather a half-hearted manner.

"You saw some one go into the convent? The door opened as we passed the corner?" asks D'Arnac.

"Yes!" replies the coachman.

"Then when the door opens again, it's for them to come out! Move quick when I speak!"

So they wait there for nearly ten minutes, shrouded in the shadow of the great equestrian statue of Louis XIV. that holds the middle of the place.

Then the portals of *Des Capucines* open, a faint light shows upon the street, and a lady, assisted by a gentleman, comes down the steps.

"Now!" whispers Raymond.

The coachman drives rapidly up, running into the coach standing in front of the convent, into which the gentleman has just assisted the lady.

As he passes her in at one door of the carriage, Raymond opens the other, pulls her, with his strong arms, out of the De Conti coach, and swings her into his own.

Then as the gentleman, with an oath of astonishment, attempts to follow, D'Arnac's sword is at his breast, and he whispers: "Back, meddler, or you die!"

A second after he has sprung into his carriage, which is driving rapidly away, while a faint but lovely voice is saying: "Help!—mercy!—spare me!" though could he see it the lady has stuffed her kerchief into her mouth to keep from giggling.

But Raymond reassures her by saying in his noblest tones: "Madame, have no fear! I, the comrade of

your husband, O'Brien Dillon, am taking you to
Vienna, to place you in his arms!"

Then the lady astonishes him by sobbing: "Thank
God! At last I shall see my gallant Irish husband!—
Noble D'Arnac, you are my only trust!" and a pair of
the softest, roundest, loveliest arms in the world clasp
themselves about his neck and a delicate head with hair
of softest perfumed locks seeks protection on his bosom
and makes his twenty-year heart beat wild and furious.

CHAPTER XIII.

THE SIREN'S SONG.

So HE goes to soothing her fears and tremblings;
doing so in the wild way of youth, patting her pretty
hands, stroking her soft hair, and telling her that he
will protect her as faithfully as if her husband himself
were by her side, for up to that time Raymond had only
seen her wondrous beauty as in the miniature—to it had
not been added the marvelous fascinations of her eyes
nor the fairy graces of her person.

But he has not much time for his tender attentions,
as the people in the other carriage are now making
a great show of hot pursuit.

His coachman calls for advice, and he directs him
still to keep to the north, and go out of Paris in
that way. They can make better time through the half
rural lanes they are now coming into than in the narrow
streets of the city proper.

Urging the horses to their full speed, they fly round
the corner into the Rue Louis le Grand, then into the
Neuve St. Angus and the Rue Faideu, next a quick turn
into the Rue Montmartre, and at last, distancing their
pursuers, they see and hear the carriage behind them no
more.

A moment after they are in Le Cours with its great
avenues of trees.

Here Raymond directs his coachman to turn towards
the east, and they journey along this new great drive-
way practically going over the ground on which to-day
stand the grand boulevards of modern Paris. So jour-

neying around the northern portion of the city of that day they come out into the country by the Porte du Temple, and still keeping to the north, past La Courtille, after a little they turn into a cross lane and at last reach the main road leading to Claye, a little town some twelve miles distant to the east.

Driving still with whip and spur, at last its houses come in sight, and they draw up at the post-house. But their enforced detour has delayed them, and it is now three o'clock in the morning.

During this journey, occupied by precautions to prevent pursuit, and in giving directions to his coachman and lackeys, Raymond has been unable to pay anything but desultory attention to his fair companion.

Part of the time he has been on the seat beside the driver, with both pistols ready, as the road has passed through the forest of Bondy, at that time notorious for its foot-pads, highwaymen and bandits.

Fortunately Raymond has been relieved of any great amount of trouble on Madame O'Brien Dillon's account, for after the first quarter of an hour the young lady had settled herself very comfortably in a corner of the carriage, and made warm by the robes her companion put about her, had gone very contentedly to sleep.

As the carriage stops, she wakes up suddenly, gives a little start of surprise, and cries: "We are halted! Are we pursued and overtaken?" clutching the arm of her protector in a feminine timidity enchanting in its appealing helplessness.

"No, only the first post-house! Now to give you some refreshment while we change horses!" And lifting her lightly out of the coach, Raymond assists her into the *auberge*, which in the darkness seems a comfortable though unpretentious hostelry.

Here they are received by the mistress, who is standing at the door, saying: "We expected you! Your courier has given directions. The horses will be ready soon!"

A bright-looking young maid servant who gazes with wide open eyes at the officer and his graceful companion is behind her.

A moment later they are in the main apartment of the place, which apparently does duty as a sitting and eating room combined. A few tallow dips are lighted,

and logs burning brightly in the large open fire-place
add to the illumination.

Then for the first time Raymond d'Arnac truly sees
the loveliness of the lady who has ridden beside him
for the last three hours. He expected beauty—wondrous
—immense. He gets it—but also arch glances from
enchanting eyes—piquant gestures from graceful arms,
tender words from lips carved out of coral, and the
fascination of seeing a loveliness but before imagined;
embodied, living, breathing, moving under his very eyes.

Her very beauty embarrasses him; he stammers, as
she seats herself in alluring pose: "You—you are not
afraid?"

"Afraid?—no!" The blue eyes open wide in innocent astonishment, as she returns, adding subtle flattery
to her other fascinations: "Are you not the hero of
Friburg?"

Then Raymond calls to the post-mistress who has
been looking on, and orders: "Refreshments, quick!"

"What does Monsieur wish?"

"Everything in the house that can make this lady
comfortable!"

And the woman going off on her errand, he turns to
Hilda, standing very much as a young knight might
have done in the days of chivalry, and bowing with the
punctilio of the old school, says: "Madame O'Brien
Dillon, for this journey I am, in duty to my comrade,
your husband—your protector! It shall be made with
every care of your personal comfort that is consistent
with safety. As your escort, I shall ride beside your
carriage to Mieux, where by the blessing of God, I
hope we may be early this morning. There my courier,
who is traveling in advance, will have provided for you
a suitable attendant and maid. You shall journey to
Vienna like a princess!"

"Then, like a princess, I give you my hand to make
salutation!" laughs the young lady.

Kissing her pretty fingers after the ceremonious
manner of that time, Raymond d'Arnac feels something
that is more than chivalry in his veins, for his glance
for the first time meets hers—eye to eye.

A moment after, as if brushing away some insect that
had stung him, he passes his hand hurriedly over his

forehead, then mutters: "I—must see to the horses.
The mistress of the inn will bring you refreshments in
a moment."

"Won't you stay and share them?"

"No, I—I am not hungry. Besides, these lazy post-
boys need looking after!" Then, after a second's hesitation, perchance even a pang, he mutters: "This
letter I promised to deliver into your hands," and
produces the missive with which O'Brien Dillon had
charged him.

"From my husband?"

"Yes!"

And thrusting the letter into her hand, he strides
out, leaving her gazing into the firelight, in which
she sees a handsome figure, short curly hair, dark,
expressive, noble eyes, and drooping moustache *a la
militaire*, and these together make the dashing Colonel,
the Comte d'Arnac.

She mutters to herself: "He is very handsome! I
wonder if he is as great a fighter as they say!"
A second after she laughs: "Perhaps this morning will
show me!"—the letter of O'Brien Dillon still lying
unopened near her hand.

Then, the hostess coming in, Madame Hilda refreshes
her dainty self with the best there is in the house.

As she finishes her repast, her eye catching the letter,
she opens it, reads it very carefully, and her red lips
murmur: "Wheugh! This wild Irishman loves me—TOO
MUCH!" Next mutters: "'He would be jealous of his
honor!' He must cross my path no more.'" then laughs:
"*Adieu, cher* O'Brien!"

So, having bid her husband mentally eternal good-bye,
Madame Hilda sighs discontentedly for another adorer,
murmuring: "That handsome boy is very long away
from me."

As in truth Raymond is, for the stablemen seem
unusually sleepy and stupid, the horses have not been
harnessed in advance, and were it not that the young
officer himself, assisted by his lackeys, handled strap
and buckle, it would be morning before they are ready
to proceed.

As this is finished and D'Arnac turns to enter the
inn, he is met at the door by the maid servant with

the bright eyes. She puts a warning finger to her lips,
and whispers: "Hush! I have something for your ear,
my gallant. I always like to assist elopements. Six
men passed here after your servant had left. They
took the horses already harnessed for you. They went
on towards Mieux."

"*Ma foi!* They could not have been pursuing me!"
laughs Raymond.

"No? Still I think they meant you evil!" whispers
the girl.

"Why?"

"Because I heard them mention your name. You
are Monsieur le Comte d'Arnac—the hero of Friburg,
of whom everybody has spoken so much."

"*Sapristi!* Thanks, my little bright eyes," says
Raymond, pressing a *louis d'or* into her hand.

Then the young man's brow becomes troubled. He
cannot understand how anybody hostile to his journey
can be ahead of him. His sudden assault seemed
such a surprise to the men in the De Conti carriage!
"But for all that," he thinks, "I'll take my precautions.
To do this I'll ride ahead of my charge."

A moment later and he has brought Hilda out of the
inn, and has put her in the coach. His horse, already
saddled, is being held by one of his servants for him
to mount.

Hilda suddenly cries: "You are going to ride?"

"Yes, beside your carriage!"

"But it will fatigue you too much!"

"On the contrary, a little horse exercise will refresh
me!"

"Very well! But before we get to Mieux, promise
me your company for half an hour. I have a few
important things to say to you."

"As you wish!" mutters the young man.

"Then in the morning," says the girl, "we ride
together."

The "together" thrills him, for it is the word of
O'Brien Dillon. The word he had spoken as he bid
him *adieu*—the word he had muttered when their hands
clasped, before Raymond had crawled through the
mine at the Bastion of St. Peter to save the regiment
of Dillon.

The young man thinks of all this as he gallops beside the coach, and curiously enough it frightens him, for he also thinks of the wondrous loveliness that is here in his keeping—that must be in his keeping until she reaches Vienna, and sighs: " I would the journey were shorter! "

But present action drives out introspection. They have come to a little lane that leads towards the south off the main road to Mieux. He hurriedly tells his postilions to take this route, reasoning that if there is danger ahead of him he will avoid it in the by-lanes of the country, and by making a slight detour, reach Mieux without molestation, even if there are people in advance, looking out to waylay him.

So they ride on through country by-ways from which the snow has just departed, bordered by trees which are now taking on the leaves of spring.

Birds are beginning to sing their morning songs, and the sun's first rays are just tinging the horizon, when a white hand is waved to him from the coach, and the limpid voice of Madame O'Brien Dillon cries in coaxing tones: "Come! your promise. Dismount your horse and sit in the coach by my side. I have a few questions to ask you, and some little information to give."

Raymond cannot resist the bright eyes and entreating voice. He gazes hastily about. It will soon be full daylight, Mieux is even now in sight, the sun gilding its distant steeples; there is small chance of danger.

Springing lightly from his horse, he gives its bridle to one of the postilions to lead by the side of the equipage, and jumping into the coach, takes seat by his charge, to listen to the voice of the siren singing the song of innocence. For never was there such piquant candor and such enchanting artlessness brought together to make a young man's eyes grow brighter and his heart beat faster.

As he takes seat beside Hilda the sun falls upon her face fresh, even after this night's travel, as a morning daisy, and illuminates the outlines of a figure girlish as that of Hebe, though rounded contours tell him it is also that of Venus.

No longer in the convent costume, some light traveling dress falls about her and makes her ethereal from

the point of her tiny boot to the glossy golden tresses
of her head, patrician in its delicate beauty and graceful
pose on the white gleaming column that is her neck.

"Behold me," she says coquettishly. Then, having
caught his eye, she whispers: "Do I look guilty?"

"Guilty?" stammers Raymond. "You!" Then he
cries: "Not if eyes show souls!"

"And yet," she goes on pathetically, "my husband's
letter hints as much. As his friend, tell me what
dear O'Brien thinks about me? He must have said
something to you about my enforced flight from him
that awful night at Valenciennes."

This Raymond does not answer. He will not tell
this lovely being that her husband in his wild pangs of
jealousy had ever cried out against her faith to him.

"Ah, he has doubted or you would speak!" she says
indignantly. "Now, I must tell you the truth." Then
she sighs: "Though O'Brien may still suspect me,
you shall believe me innocent. I could not bear to be
doubted by *you!*" blending subtle caress of accent
with appealing hands that seem so white and gleaming in
their graceful movements.

With this she goes on, speaking rapidly; bright eyes
and vivid gestures acting the story her limpid voice
relates:

"That night—it had been such a happy day we had
passed together in the old town—it had been such a
lovely evening—as we dined together in Monsieur Law's
little chateau! And then to be torn from him—my
husband! Is he not handsome—and what a fighter!
You have seen him fight as I have!"

"I have had the honor of fighting by his side,"
replies Raymond proudly.

"Ah, yes, and gained equal glory with him. What a
Paladin you must be also!"

Her blue eyes have in them admiration that is very
pleasant to this young gentleman.

"But Dillon's servant says he was betrayed to the
Austrians!" answers D'Arnac, though his tones say he
thinks her innocent.

"Yes, but not by me!" cries the girl. "That was
Law's plan, the man who calls himself my uncle, but
who is really my guardian. The man who was under

the assumed name of Lauriston, but whose real name is Law, though the French here call him Lass. But I did not know it! As God is above me, when I went out that evening, I thought the scratching on the window was that of my pet dog. As I opened the door I found myself in the very hands of the Austrians. They whispered if I cried a warning, they would shoot him—my husband—as he sat at the table. And so I stayed with them, imploring them—begging them—praying to them to spare his life—and that delayed them long enough for him to escape!"

"So the scratching on the window was a signal!" says Raymond.

"Yes, for my uncle—my guardian. He had, unguessed by me, arranged the surprise with the Austrian officers. He wished, God forgive him! to put my husband out of the way!"

"Why?"

"Because Dillon was my husband. Law had higher views for me than that I should wed a soldier of fortune!"

"Higher views for you?"

"Yes! why not?" she cries. Then she goes on imperiously: "Is that curious for the granddaughter of Count Tekeli, called by his countrymen 'the last King of Hungary!'"

"You, the descendant of Tekeli!" D'Arnac's eyes open very wide, for that unfortunate prince's adventures had been the talk of court and camp in Europe for many a day.

"Yes, when my grandfather fled before the Imperialists, compelled to take refuge with the Ottomans, Monsieur Law, who was employed by him in some plan to raise funds for the Hungarians, received me as his charge, and also a sum of money for my education and maintenance." Then her eyes glow with beautiful fire and she cries: "Do I look so unlike the daughter of a line of kings?"

"Like the daughter of the angels!" replies the young man impulsively, for Hilda's plausible account of her action in O'Brien Dillon's surprise has made Raymond think her not only a marvel of beauty indignant, but a marvel of innocence accused. And to this has been added the thought that in her veins flows the blood of nobles and princes, making her one of the elect of this earth, for at that time there was a wall high as that of China between the *azur sang* of the *gentelhomme* and the noble, and the baser clay of the peasant and the *bourgeoisie*.

"Ah," she says, "you believe me—thank Heaven ! It would have been hard to have been doubted by *you !*" Her emphasis makes the "you" an implied caress.

D'Arnac's eyes return it, for struggle how he may she draws passion from him with every whisper of her lips, every glance of her eye. "I always guessed Lanty was an idiot," he mutters, thinking of the fellow's inventions that now seem to him ridiculous.

"Oh, yes ! Lanty, the scatter-brained valet of my husband ! He said words against me also," she laughs. "But you believe——"

"And love !" the young man thinks in his soul of souls.

But she runs on, "that is enough — youth and faith are by my side ! What a joyous journey to Vienna this will be—eh, Monsieur Raymond !"—FOR SHE HAS FOR ONE MOMENT FORGOTTEN THE PLOT THAT IS TO TAKE HER FROM HIS SIDE.

To this he answers nothing. He is dashing his curly black hair back from his brow that is fevered by passion and tortured by conscience, and his brain is pulsing with this thought: "I did not know she was so fascinating—so adorable! God help me keep O'Brien's honor and my own !'

They are looking at each other. Heaven knows what their eyes are saying, but it is something that makes the dark ones blaze and the blue ones droop like dewy violets —when—

Bang ! *Bang !!* BANG !!!

Pistol shots are flying around ! The postilions are leaping from their horses and scurrying for their lives, for horsemen are riding up before and behind, with Italian oaths and hoarse shouts: "Surrender the girl— or your life !"

But as all this goes on about her, Hilda suddenly gives a stifled shriek of astonishment. Raymond has sprung from the carriage, and is on the back of his horse.

Then she gives another, perhaps louder scream, for she is suddenly dragged out of the carriage, and with one strong swing drawn up on the saddle in front of him, and he is speeding along a little country lane that leaves the larger road.

For D'Arnac's campaign on the Rhine has given him military promptness of action, and the girl, though she remembers the plot to take her from his side, for the life of her cannot resist the potent charm of a ride with him—*in his very arms*—and has even sprung towards him, as he has drawn her up to his saddle bow.

CHAPTER XIV.

A FRENCH LOCHINVAR.

FOR one instant surprise stays their pursuers. Then the coach embarrasses them for the moment, for it has stopped just at the entrance of the lane.

A moment after they get round this, and Raymond d'Arnac, his present world in his arms, is speeding on the little by-way, green hedges on both sides, from which comes the perfume of nascent buds and flowers—and behind him, some one hundred and fifty yards in the rear, eight or ten of De Conti's lackeys, bravos, and bullies.

And what a ride it is for them both!

Even with death perchance before him—for the private battles of those days meant little mercy for the vanquished—Raymond feels each drop of his coursing blood glow with happiness. Excitement has driven away thought of everything but the present; her soft round arms are about him, her fair hair is pressing his burning cheek, her sweet voice is whispering in his ear.

As for Hilda, lying upon his breast, her heart beating against his, she forgets all else—save the great passion in her wayward soul.

Glancing back, D'Arnac sees the men are hardly gaining on him. This lane runs straight to the south. He will find a by-path to the east, and so get her he holds so very dear—he acknowledges this to himself now—safely into Mieux.

So they dash on—but not for long!

No by-path comes in sight—BUT BEFORE THEM FLOWS THE MARNE.

The lane only runs to a little corn-mill turned by water power. Beyond is the river, swollen now by a spring freshet. Behind, De Conti's ruffians, who give a yell of triumph.

Raymond has ridden on to a little dock the miller uses for his boat, but there is no boat there!

"Surrender!" comes from behind him.

He mutters hoarsely: "Surrender *you*—NEVER!" Then looking into her eyes very tenderly, and pointing to the raging flood, he whispers: "Will you dare this for me——?"

And she replies: "For you! To any place you go —YES!"

Even as De Conti's horsemen thunder upon the dock, spurring his reluctant charger, he makes leap into the rushing river, as the miller's wife runs out of her little cottage, wringing her hands and crying: "He will be drowned!" and De Conti's ruffians give a yell that is half surprise—half joy; for these Italian bravos like to see a deed bravely done.

One or two of them prepare pistol and musketoon to shoot him as he rises ; but these are dashed hurriedly up by their leader, who cries: "Injure a hair of her head and we are lost ! De Conti will never forgive us."

So, protected by this being who has brought him danger, Raymond rises, still on horseback, and still holding her on his breast, amid the billows of the flood, and carried down by the raging waters, fights his way towards the other bank, though round him are whirling logs and all the other *débris* of a river freshet, sometimes wading if it is shallow enough, sometimes swimming where compelled —the girl hanging round his neck laughing joyously, patting him on the shoulder and whispering : "My brave one ! To risk this for me—HOW I LOVE YOU!" he at last reaches the other bank.

But scrambling up through boulders and loose rocks, just as they reach the shore, a log borne by the freshet strikes his horse heavily in the flank. The noble animal, whinnying with pain, sinks down, his leg broken above the fetlock, as Raymond, with one strong pull, draws Hilda upon the bank.

She cries : "We have escaped !" then bursts into merriment, though she does not say why! for she is thinking of the rage her successful abduction will bring upon the Prince de Conti, old De Moncrief, and that being who is trying to hold her destinies in his hand, Monsieur Lass, at present of Venice.

"Not escaped yet!" gasps young Lochinvar, regaining his breath, for looking backward he sees the two boldest of De Conti's men, encouraged by his successful passage, have leaped their horses into the flood, and are now following after him across the river.

Were his horse uninjured he could be far away before they reach the shore ; as it is he must stay and fight. This he does savagely, vindictively muttering between clenched teeth : "I'll teach these *canaille* to follow a colonel of France !"

Then he turns and his eyes light up with wildest hope as he gives encouragement to his fair companion ; and sees the beautiful picture she makes as she stands on the bank in graceful pose, wringing the water from dripping clothes that drape about and cling to her, showing the exquisite contours of her charming figure.

"Have no fear ! What are two, to me, when I am fighting for *you* ?" he whispers, a cruel, relentless look coming into his dark eyes, as he goes down the bank to meet his enemies at the shore, for he is fighting now, not for friendship, not for his comrade, but for that one great passion which has caused so many of the murders, duels and assassinations of this world—the love of woman !

Though the men who come against him are two, the combat is not so unequal, for Raymond for his journey had armed himself as a soldier; at his side he has replaced the light rapier of the gentleman by a slashing cavalry sabre, from the holsters of his saddle he has just taken two well-tried pistols loaded with numerous slugs.

The first of these firearms places one of his adversaries *hors de combat* as he struggles up the bank. The second, dampened by the flood, fails to explode. Throwing it away with a muttered curse, he stands on foot confronting the man on horseback, who, while Raymond has been attacking the other, has succeeded in making a landing upon firm ground.

Now the combat is unequal! The horse gives the
De Conti ruffian advantage over his opponent.

He is a fellow who knows how to use it, having seen
service under De Villeroy in Italy and D'Asfeld, in Spain,
and charges on D'Arnac, making the movement of his
horse give weight to the stroke of his sword.

This cut is parried by Raymond, who has not time
to avoid his adversary's rush, though the force of the
blow makes his arm tingle to the shoulder.

Then the man, with a frightful curse, turns and
charges full at D'Arnac, to run him down, and crush him
under his horse's hoofs.

But Raymond springs lightly aside.

As this is repeated the second time, D'Arnac changes
his tactics; even as he springs aside he runs after the
horse in its career, and catching the animal just as it
is turning, hamstrings the charger with his sabre,
bringing both it and its rider to the ground.

With sword uplifted and eyes that mean death,
D'Arnac cries: "Yield! Throw away your arms—or
I kill you!"

"Maladetta! Of course I yield," answers the fellow.

"Rescue or no rescue. Quick, or I strike!"

"Then, rescue or no rescue, I am at your orders,
Colonel!"

"Swear it?"

"By our Mother of Christ!"

So, taking his arms from the man and tossing them
over a hedge, he tells the fellow to stand aside.

Then he whispers cheerily to Hilda: "Half an hour's
walk, dear one, and we are in Mieux, where everything
shall be provided for your comfort and safety, and
then—" His eyes have a wistful look.

But she answers him with a hoarse cry: "Too late!
they are landing! We are lost!"

A quick glance at the river and Raymond sees delay
has put further and greater peril upon him. Having
at last secured a boat, four of the men are coming
across to the assistance of their comrades. They are,
of course, unmounted, but it is long odds against him!

He rushes to the bank to prevent their landing, and
the combat takes place half in the water, half on the
land. In it he would be perchance successful, for the

men in the boat are too much huddled together for the free handling of their weapons.

He has already wounded one of them, when Raymond hears Hilda's warning cry.

The ruffian he had disarmed, and whose life he had spared, has regained his weapons, and regardless of his oath, is coming to the assistance of his comrades.

It is the cry to warn him which ruins D'Arnac.

As he turns to see what danger is behind him, one of the men in the boat upraising a heavy oar brings it down with crushing force upon the head of the young man, but still he fights on—for her sake.

Half dazed he staggers up the bank, and meeting the bravo who has broken the faith of both sword and Church, with one last effort, parrying the wretch's thrust, he cuts him down; then darkness comes upon him and he sinks senseless at her feet, and would in an instant be dead under the steel of his pursuers.

But Hilda is standing over him and fighting off their weapons with her fair arms and crying to the ruffians: "Don't kill him—you have me!"

For a moment they pause; then seeing signs of movement in them, her eyes blaze, she threatens: "Raise another hand against him, and I will have your heads from your master, the Prince de Conti! You know how he values me!" and laughs hysterically, jeering herself. "I AM HIS SPECULATION IN BEAUTY."

By this time the leader of the lackeys has sprung from the boat, and is beating up their hands, crying: "Fools! obey her!"

Then turning to the fair object of his pursuit, he says: "Your words are my command, madame! We have our orders to that effect. But you must come with us!"

"Certainly! that is the plan," returns Hilda.

Then she looks at D'Arnac and whispers: "Did he not fight bravely for me! He must live to fight again!" and with her own fair hands bandages his brow, from which the blood is oozing slowly; next commands: "We will take him to Mieux and give him a surgeon's care!"

"You must leave him now!" answers the leader, hurriedly.

"Not till he is under the hands of a doctor!"

"Then in that case, we must use force, Madame!"
replies De Conti's representative politely, but firmly.
"Our orders are explicit to waste no time in this
affair."

"I will not leave him wounded—insensible!" But
though she cries and puts her arms about Raymond, and
even struggles with them, the servants of Monsieur de
Conti are resolute, and drag her from the young man's
side.

At last she sobs: "Promise me by the Virgin that
you will take him to Mieux unharmed, and place him
in the surgeon's hand. Otherwise I will scream out at
every post-house, that you are carrying me away against
my will!"

"I promise!" mutters the leader sulkily.

"On the Virgin?" she ejaculates, taking cross and
rosary from her neck.

"On the Virgin!" says the man, so solemnly that
she knows he will keep his word.

And so she goes away from Raymond, looking back at
the boyish figure, dripping with the water of the river,
the blood coursing slowly from his white forehead, and
sighing: "If they had killed him?" Then she suddenly
mutters: "But no, he will live—*he was born to live for
me!*"

Being placed in the boat, Hilda is rowed across
to the old mill, where the coach has been brought down
to meet her. Stepping into this she is driven off, the
carriage taking a long detour towards the southeast, by
Troyes, Chatellon, and so past Dijon to the Rhone and
the sunny Mediterranean; from thence the passage
into Italy is easy, by Nice and Genoa.

Nestled in the cushions of the coach Madame Hilda
goes into a merry little laugh, thinking to herself:
"Won't my elopement *a la* D'Arnac be a good story for
Uncle Johnny!" as the carriage rolls on towards Italy.
Where, after many days' travel, Hilda reaches Venice,
and Monsieur Law, who is at present playing pharo most
successfully among the nobles of the Grand Canal.
Here she is very safely kept till Louis XIV. will shuffle
off this mortal coil and the time is ripe for De Conti's
grand *coup* and Monsieur Lass and his system.

As for the young Lochinvar of this adventure he wakes up in Mieux the next day with burning head and murmurs faintly: "Hilda!" but seeing she is not beside him turns his eyes to the wall, distressed in mind as well as body, and goes off under the bad surgical treatment of that time into a fever, in which he raves of little save his beautiful companion of that morning's ride and flight.

But after a time youth conquers even unskilful surgery, and Monsieur D'Arnac finds himself well enough to journey back to Paris, where he is met by very cold looks at court, and a pathetic scolding from his sister, Mimi, who has brought back, with her a very sick husband to nurse in Paris, as she whispers to him: "You foolish boy! Every one accuses you here of running away with your friend O'Brien Dillon's wife! What will the Irishman say when he hears of your breaking faith with him?"

"I have already written to him!" replies Raymond, hanging his head, for his sister's words have been so near the truth.

This he has done, but it has not been a letter that told *all* the truth. What gentleman could be so ungallant as to betray a lady's love—unto her husband.

"I shall never see her again!" thinks the young man. "Why should I confess to feelings that would make my comrade despise me—and with good reason!"

For weak from the fever Monsieur d'Arnac has become a good boy again, and conscience has kicked Satan out of him, as it does in most sick men.

Just at this time he is sent for by his old chief, the Duc de Villars, who gives him a very scowling welcome, and growls: "You have not done well, my young colonel! It has cost you your present promotion to a generalship. Monsieur le Duc d'Orleans is very much displeased with you. I do not wish to discuss the affair with you," for Raymond has been about to speak, "because I know—" a little gleam of merriment comes into the old warrior's eyes and he chuckles: "Boys will be boys!" Then his voice grows stern as he says: "I would to Heaven it had been with some one else—but your comrade O'Brien Dillon's wife—you will have to cross swords with the Irish Colonel when he comes to Paris!"

"I think not!" answers D'Arnac. "I was acting in his interest!"

"Acting in his interest by eloping with his wife!" gasps the Maréchal. "*Diable!* Prove that to me and you'll beat old theologian Fénelon himself!"

"Well, then, I make you my father confessor," returns Raymond, who would sooner tell his old chief everything than any one else. And so he does, giving him the whole story of the elopement from first to last.

"Ho, ho! ha, ha!" screams the veteran, the tears of laughter running from his eyes. "On behalf of your comrade you carried off his wife to restore her to him in Vienna; but *parbleu!* Madame was so *naïve,* so alluring, so infernally innocent, that at the last you were going to increase her innocence by carrying her off for yourself *mon Bayard!*"

A moment after he grows serious and adds: "I've more to say. I don't know how, but in this matter you have run against De Conti's interests. Now, that prince is a very hard stone wall for you to butt your young head against. The stories they've told about you are awful—breaking open a convent, sacrilege, and all that! Madame de Maintenon has even spoken to the King about it, and were his Majesty well enough to attend to business, it might go hard with you. D'Argenson has even suggested arresting you, but he is a cur who always growls at the under dog in a fight. As it is, I have done the best I can for you. I want you away from your enemies till they forget you. I want you to be a general soon. I have an order giving you command of a regiment on the Spanish border. There you can gain your step by capturing smugglers and contrabandists. You leave to-morrow."

Under these circumstances D'Arnac deems it wise not to discuss the matter further with his commanding officer, but thanks him for his interest in him, and next day bids his relatives adieu in Paris and takes post for the Pyrenees, traveling through a country that shows the effects of the tax-gatherer grinding down a people; villages that have become depopulated, and large towns half deserted, for France, under the last days of the *Grand Monarch* and his *fermiers généraux,* was the most oppressed and distressed country of Europe.

So Raymond d'Arnac passes out of the life of Paris, and for three years occupies himself in destroying smugglers that are brigands, and contrabandists who are bandits, and in that time changes from the boy of impulsive sword and heart to the man of wit, conduct and experience.

BOOK III.

A Princess of Paris.

CHAPTER XV.

THE BIRTH OF MODERN PARIS.

It is the first day of November of the year 1717 when Raymond d'Arnac returns to the capital of France, riding in at the Port aux Tripes from the South.

His three years of hard service on the Spanish frontier have given him what age always brings to those who learn—experience; not the experience of the courtier, but the experience of the man of action and decision.

His face is but little older, for healthy manhood changes but slightly between twenty and twenty-three. His moustache is a little longer, his eye perchance somewhat sterner, his lips slightly more determined, than when he rode out of Paris that night to carry Madame O'Brien Dillon back to her husband in Vienna; for he has seen that service—the most trying to all officers—the command of mutinous troops.

It is owing to his undaunted courage in putting down an outbreak in his regiment, that he now wears the uniform of a general. On taking his post in the Pyrenees, he had found his command, once veterans of the Spanish war, having done good service in the peninsular, transformed into a band of marauders, foragers, and almost semi-banditti. Having received no pay from the government for years, hardly forage, scarcely rations—they were compelled to subsist upon the country as best they could. They did so after the manner of middle age freebooters.

And this going on for over a year after Raymond had assumed command, one day in the autumn of 1715— Louis XIV. being dead—they had openly mutinied, and swore they would march to Paris to find out what had become of the Commissary General. This *émeute* of the men had been put down by the steady determination of their chief, and in consequence of his conduct, the Regent had given D'Arnac the rank the King had withheld.

Then shortly after, in 1716; their pay arrived—not in driblets, but in a lump—the arrears of years—and half starving men, and officers with uniforms patched, and hungry faces, wondered what had come to make France rich.

Shortly after it became known to the troops that their good fortune was owing to one Monsieur Lass, who had advanced money to the Regent to pay the army.

After that the military swore by Lass, and no man could question or sneer at the new financial power that was rising in France, in the presence of the army, without being asked if he were a common fellow, by one of the privates, how he dared say a word against the good angel of the army; or, if he were of the rank of gentleman, being tapped on the shoulder by some commissioned officer of France and requested to cross swords with him. *Parbleu!* for daring to raise his dirty tongue against the friend and benefactor of all who wore the uniform of France.

This new power coming up behind the Regency has recalled to Raymond the Monsieur Lass of Venice, the guardian of Madame O'Brien Dillon, and though he receives his promotion, he shrewdly thinks it is perhaps owing to that gentleman's kind offices that his requests for leave to visit Paris have never been honored until this time, when they could not well be refused, as he has served for three years on the outposts of the army, and is now called by urgent personal family business to Paris.

For his uncle, the Comte de Crevecœur, has at last concluded that he is too sick to risk his soul by eating meat in Lent, and has made personal interest with

Monsieur le Duc d'Orleans to permit his nephew to visit
Paris, as he wishes to see him before he dies in regard
to the best disposition of his estates, to enable the
family to keep sufficient means together to continue the
grand establishment consonant with its high rank and
prestige.

It is on this business that Raymond d'Arnac is
coming to Paris, though he knows he will have also something to do about his ward, Mademoiselle Jeanne Quinault, who has grown into quite a young lady, his sister
Mimi's letters have told him, and of so wild and head-
strong a disposition that the widowed Marquise de
Chateaubrien finds it very difficult keeping proper control over desires which, Mimi states, are both frivolous
and absurd.

For the little Jeanne has expressed, with tremendous
emotion and emphasis, and frightful stamping of the
feet, her determination to run away from the convent
and go on the stage.

Burdened with the cares of her husband's large estate,
as two years before this Roul de Chateaubrien had
passed away, Mimi has requested her brother's aid
in controlling what she terms "a child of nature and
le diable !"

Occupied with these ideas Raymond d'Arnac, as he
rides along the streets of Paris, would scarce notice the
change in them were it not of so marked an order as to
arouse his wonder—almost his astonishment.

He had left the capital of France filled with the
suffering that always comes with reckless spoliation in
government; the people in want—without occupation
—without hope—even starving. He comes back to find
the city a hive of industry, the populace merry and
happy; well fed, well cared for, and working like bees
in the honey.

Raymond wonders to himself if this is also the work
of Monsieur Lass, who has made the army contented
by regular and sufficient pay and rations, and has
apparently made the provinces that he had ridden
through on his way to the Pyrenees equally prosperous, for
the depopulated villages, on his return, have seemed
full of industry, and the half deserted towns have again
their streets full of busy people, their factories

noisy with the hum of looms, their corn mills grinding away on the plenteous harvest brought in by happy husbandmen. He has said to himself: "*Diable!* who is the author of all of this? Is it Monsieur Lass and his system? (for these were getting to be very much talked about.) "If so, he must be a very great man!"

At this moment this was also the opinion of many at the Court of Versailles and in the City of Paris.

This wondrous change had come about in the years of Raymond's absence, very much after this manner:

When D'Arnac had ridden away from Paris Louis XIV., grown imbecile by age and high living, had for years been under the subjection and rule of that wicked old shrew, Madame de Maintenon, whose religion was a mixture of cant, bigotry, hypocrisy and superstition, and under her domination he had run the Government of France very much as an old woman would run it. He had spent *everything* on himself and his favorite mistress, panders and sycophants, and *nothing* on his country. He had rented out the revenues of France to the *fermiers généraux*, who had despoiled it, grinding the poor to starvation by their taxes, the rich to despair by their exactions.

His foreign policy had been conducted on the personal enmity plan, and he had squandered the lives of his subjects and the revenues of his Kingdom on the war of the Spanish succession because he had taken a dislike to his imperial cousin of Austria.

In the face of common sense, good judgment, and every rational and patriotic consideration, he had continued this war till France was so exhausted, both in men and money, that had it not been that John Churchill, Duke of Marlborough, loved the French gold thrown at his feet by his affrighted Most Christian Majesty Louis XIV. better than he did even glory in war after the battle of Ramillies, the capital of France might have fallen before the Austrian and British bayonets. For Paris in 1706 was more open to the English and Imperialists, under the Duke of Marlborough and Prince Eugene, than it was in 1870 to the Germans, under Bismarck and Von Moltke, after Sedan.

So, under this monarch, who said placidly and believed in his very soul, "I am the State!" France had gone from bad to worse.

What had commenced as a prosperous reign had become an unfortunate one, and a country that had been very rich had become very poor, many of its best population being driven from it for religious belief, and many of its best artisans fleeing to other lands to avoid its tax gatherers; its army unpaid; its ministers and plenipotentiaries without funds for years, so that they almost starved in foreign capitals, and had not money enough even to pay postage on their letters to ask relief from the country that had sent them out as its embassadors.

Filled with that peculiar veneration—that belief of semi-deity—placed around a king who common mortals thought crowned by God—France suffered his rule —and suffered for it—until in the course of time, on Sept. 1st, 1715, "I am the State" died, and the State survived his demise very well and very happily.

His little grandchild, Louis XV., too young to reign came to the crown, but a Regent must be appointed, and that Regent must be Philippe, Duc d'Orleans! At least he had so decreed it, with his following, the Ducs de Condé, de Conti and Saint Simon, and others of his crowd and backing.

So, even before the body of the late King had been placed at rest, they called a meeting of the Parliament, and this Parliament, doing very humbly what it was commanded to do, abolished the will of the late King and promptly took all chances of government from his bastards, who were itching for it, the Duc de Maine and the Count de Toulouse, and placed the Regency in the hands of Philippe, Duc d'Orleans, which Philippe, Duc d'Orleans, made up his mind very promptly, was equivalent to having the full power of a reigning king.

In fact, even before Parliament made him Regent, he had decreed this condition of things, and had three regiments of Gardes, under the command of his crony, the Duc de Guiche, surrounding Parliament at the time they were making him Regent, to bully and browbeat, and whip into shape, and perchance stab and do to death any members of that body who questioned the proposition that Philippe, Duc d'Orleans, was to take the reigns of government in France.

Now, curiously enough, after this statement of affairs, Philippe d'Orleans, Regent of France, was a very good kind of prince, after the manner of the princes of that day. He didn't believe in anybody doing wrong but himself. He ordered all arrested under the *lettres de cachet* of his predecessor to be released from the Bastile.

One, a poor Italian, who had been seized, on the very night of his arrival in Paris, for some reason not one of those who had him in charge could guess, and who had been kept in a solitary *oubliette*, on bread and water, for thirty-five years, on being let out to the light of day, cried in despair that he knew no one in this world—that his relatives in Italy had all thought him dead long ago—that all his property had gone to the winds of heaven—that he did not even know his way through the streets of Paris—that he would starve! For God's sake to put him back in the Bastile and let him die there.

This favor was kindly accorded to him, though he was given a better resting place and better rations, and he thanked his Highness, the Duc d'Orleans, for his kindness to him, and finished up his unfortunate life within the confines of the great fortress that had so long been his prison—his home.

But though Philippe d'Orleans did release all arrested under the *lettres de cachet* of Louis XIV. he did not restrict himself from the proper and polite use of these peculiar engines of despotism, which permitted him to seize, arrest, and confine, without word to relatives, without trial in court—any h man being it pleased his sovereign will to inter, confine, and shut out from the light of day.

Notwithstanding all this, Philippe was of an easygoing, careless, affable disposition, with an unlimited love for pretty ladies, and unlimited conscience in gratifying his love, with an open purse for all his favorites and mistresses, and a most extraordinary wish, for potentates of that day, to pay the debts of his country, which were enormous, as upon the death of Louis le Grand, the Budget of France showed a deficit of twenty-eight hundred million *livres*—an enormous

sum to-day—but one appallingly colossal, judging by
the money value of that time.

But how to pay it?

The troops in arrears for years! The ministers
unpaid for generations!

At first it was proposed to liquidate the public debt
of France in the easy way of that time—by an edict
wiping it out and expunging it from the public ledger.

But easy-going Philippe could not bring himself to this
radical measure, as the capital of many of the favorites
of his court and of many of the country nobility had
been invested in government rents and annuities, and
there came up a great cry from this unfortunate class—
among them the Count de Crevecœur—that made the
angels in Heaven itself hold their ears at their noise,
and, therefore, penetrated the thick walls of the Palais
Royal, in which Monsieur le Duc was very contentedly
basking in his new authority.

Then it was proposed to fall on and despoil the
fermiers généraux, who had been making all the money
out of the collection of taxes ground out of the
country. And this was done until these financial cor-
morants howled for mercy; very much after the manner
that Louis XIV. had treated his *Surintendent* De Foquet,
commanding one day a million *livres*—the next *two*—
the third THREE—until Foquet, though the richest man
in France, became a bankrupt, and was clapped into the
Bastile for having no more money.

But even the *fermiers généraux* were not rich enough
to pay the debts of France.

Then, what to do?

The credit of the country was nothing. *Billets
d'Etat* were worth only twenty-five per cent. of their par
value. Loans could not be obtained. Besides that,
the army threatened to rise *en masse*.

Then one fine day very late in the year 1715, Louis
de Conti, who had been biding his time, proposed to
the Regent, who was now in dire financial straits, to
bring Monsieur Lass, the great gambler—the great
financier—from Italy, and see what he could do with a
bankrupt country.

"He has an infernally great mind!" says De Conti
in his bluff way to the Regent.

"Yes; I have met him before over the pharo table!" laughs D'Orleans. "He was very successful there. He got everybody's money! Don't you think he might get *ours?*" This last nervously.

"Yes, if we had any!" guffaws De Conti.

"As it is, *parbleu!* what can be worse?" laughs the Regent. Then he suddenly turns savagely on De Conti, muttering: "What have you done with HER?"

For during the last six months, engaged in the cares of State, Philippe d'Orleans, who is a fickle man, has forgotten the radiant beauty he had once sworn by all the powers of France and all the gods of the lower regions should be his very own.

"Whom does your Highness mean?" returns De Conti; feigning both innocence and ignorance. "You can't refer to Madame de Paraberè—I saw her in your anteroom as I came in," mentioning the name of the present first favorite in the Regent's crowd of fair ones.

"You know whom I mean!" answers D'Orleans, who is by no means a fool, "that niece of Monsieur Lass. The one I saw but twice—the one whom I would have had by my side now, if——"

"If young D'Arnac had not run away with her!" interjects De Conti, cutting off accusation against himself. "I know to whom you refer now, very well, Sire. She, I believe, was recaptured upon the very night of her elopement, by our friend Lass, who has a longer head than either of us. The lady, I am informed, is at present with him in his Venetian palace."

"Then," replies the Regent, in eager and excited tones, "let Monsieur Lass be sent for!"

"I have already communicated with him!" replies De Conti. "He will come to Paris, provided your Highness gives him safe conduct for his return to Italy in case negotiations do not go to his liking."

"*Parbleu!* that means he will not bring the girl with him!" snarls D'Orleans, savagely.

"That I believe is Monsieur Lass' intention at present!" remarks De Conti, struggling with all his court etiquette to prevent a grin.

So the safe conduct having been given, Monsieur Lass, towards the end of the year 1715, came to Paris, to find the Duc d'Orleans sorely pressed for what is needful, even to princes—ready cash; his unpaid soldiers in a terrible state of semi-mutiny, and the people of France on the verge of incipient revolution.

These facts having been put before the great financier with the hard Scotch brain by the Regent, and his advice being asked, he has answered very promptly: "Pay the army!"

"*Diable!* How, without money?"

"Pay first those troops immediately around Paris. They will be a bulwark to your power against others coming from without."

"*Mon Dieu!* How?"

"*By money advanced by me!* On the conclusion of negotiations here, I will lend to you, as Regent of France, two million *livres*. That will secure you the army in and about Paris. Then on the formation of my bank, I will advance the balance to pay all the other troops in France!"

"Your *bank*?" remarks the Regent. "What BANK?"

"The bank of Monsieur Lass, for which I hope your Highness will see fit to give me letters patent, authorizing me to form such a company as I will describe to you, and issue capital stock and bills of credit, which shall be acceptable as payment throughout France!"

For Lass was a financier in advance of his time, and had discerned his great fact that there was not actual silver and gold enough in the money of the world to do its business; but that paper currency would easily take its place as long as there was credit behind it. That its manufacture was but a matter of printing presses, and that this paper money would be as good as coin as long as people belived in it.

So he hastily explains his system to the Duke, who asks him what the capital of the bank will be.

"Six million *livres!*"

"*Pardi!* You are modest!" returns the Regent.

"Yes, but we may increase the capital afterwards with your Highness' permission," remarks Lass.

"Very well!" answers D'Orleans. "When your bank is organized send me a few of your first bills.

They will be very convenient just at present at the Palais Royal !"

And it was on this insignificant capital began the scheme that was to make France the banking center of Europe, and change it from poverty to unheard of oppulence—while it lasted.

For the plans of Monsieur Lass were so far-reaching that neither he nor De Conti dared spring them on the Regent in a moment, as they embraced not only every colony of France, but France itself, whole and entire, to be made the throne upon which to rear a financial despotism over the world of commerce.

After a few days' negotiations and pros and cons, and "ifs" and "ands" and "buts," the bargain is made, and Monsieur Lass is about to depart for Italy to bring back his establishment and take residence in Paris.

As he takes his leave the Regent remarks to him: ". Don't forget to bring mademoiselle, your niece, with you!"

"If not, your Highness ?" returns Lass, laughing and bowing.

"Then perhaps I shall forget to sign your charter!" guffaws the Regent, for these two understand each other pretty well by this time.

But the financier on his return to Paris does *not* forget to bring Madame Hilda with him, and on the 10th of May, 1716, the bank of Monsieur Lass is commenced on the Rue Vivienne in part of the old Palais Mazarin, almost on the site of the present Bourse of to-day. Paper money flows out very rapidly, and the credit of the bank is really good, for they stipulate to pay their bills not in the value of the *marks* of the time of payment, but in the value of the *marks* when the bill is issued, which in the unstable currency of France, at that time, is a very great consideration, for by this a man knows exactly what he is going to receive even if payment is deferred a year.

The paper money floating about the country has made times at least apparently prosperous. But Law has determined to make them really so, for beyond this bank is a great and grander scheme, by which the colonies of France shall pour the wealth of both the West and East Indies into the lap of the parent nation; as

the Spanish Main and Mexico and Peru had once done,
into the bosom of Spain, making her one century before
this the richest country on the earth.

So things have gone on, until the city that Raymond
rides into this 1st day of November, 1717, has changed
from the old feudal stronghold of the Capets into the
chrysalis that will become, in the course of two centuries, that butterfly of capitals—the Paris of to-day.

It is a change from the middle ages to the world of
modern progress; the arts of war are giving place to the
arts of peace; the boulevards erected as fortifications
are now torn down and made into long broad avenues
and carriage-ways, shaded by trees and beautified by
flowers.

For the time has come when men can breathe the open
air of Heaven and need not to save their lives sleep each
night surrounded by walls and battlements; when men
can take together the good things of life; when the
theatres and the opera and the *cafés* permit the social
intercourse of modern life, and all the *fêtes* and joyance
are not confined to the court of the King and the *chateaux*
of the *noblesse*.

In fact, Paris, as Raymond d'Arnac looks on it, is
beginning to assume the airs of that gay city we of the
modern world know and love; its nobles are already in
hose and doublet instead of armor—its ladies in silks
and satins, the webs of Lyons and Flanders, enjoying
sport, and play, and license, and love—but underneath
the tossing mass of general humanity yet struggles and
strives to better itself and become less of the serf and
more of the man.

But the *fermiers généraux* are still at work—the
serfs still unemancipated.

Their time is to come three generations later, when
amid booming cannons, fire and blood, the Bastile falls,
and with it the heads of king and nobility, and a nation
goes mad for three years, trying in that short time to
right the wrongs of eighteen centuries.

But Paris does not, on the night Raymond d'Arnac
looks at it, anticipate the revolution that came seventy
years afterwards; its streets are full of people, gay and
happy; its equipages more brilliant and numerous than
ever he has seen before; its crowd of mendicants have

given way to chattering hucksters and vivacious peddlers plying **their trades** under the burning oil **lamps** that have doubled in splendor and number.

For **over this** feudal city has come the one great **thing** needed to make it a metropolis — commercial **progress.** From a stronghold and a fortress it has become the banking center of Europe.

CHAPTER XVI.

DE CONTI'S LITTLE JOKE.

SUCH vivacity in the streets raises the spirits of the young man, and he rides up to his Cousin Charlie's very handsome apartments on the Rue de Nevers in high feather.

Here **he is** welcomed effusively by De Moncrief, who cries: " I was expecting you, *mon général.* I am glad **you came to me** first, as I advised you in my letter. A little dinner with me and we will discuss family matters, and then—*voila !* the first *bal de l'Opera !* "

" A ball ? **My uncle** is very sick! "

" Oh, yes, sick—frightened! But he will live six months—a year—perhaps bury us both, though he has given up meat in Lent. To-morrow you can see him. To-night, forget all else but the *bal de l'Opera,* invented by me to give pleasure to the Regent—to bring our people more together.

" Monsieur Lass thinks it well that the heads of commerce and banking should meet the princes of the court, and has suggested that we nobles will be able to borrow more liberally by tapping Monsieurs Bourgeoise and Goldsmith upon the shoulder for one evening in the year. "

Which in truth was the original idea of these entertainments, the masked *bals de l'Opera* for which Paris has long **been** celebrated, and which succeed in no other city as well **as they do** in the one that gave them birth, for it needs French vivacity, French frivolity, French *esprit* and French *diablerie* to make a genuine high-rolling, fun-loving *bal de l'Opera* an emotional success.

"Invented by you!" laughs D'Arnac. "Have you taken to dancing again?"

"I have always danced," replies De Moncrief, stiffly. Then he babbles on: "How do you like my new apartments?"

"Magnificent! Astounding!" answers his cousin, who has just come from camp and bivouac.

As in truth they are, for Monsieur de Moncrief has blossomed out as one of the very great favorites of fortune in this last year.

"How can you afford it?" asks Raymond.

"How? Because, my boy, I am not only the *Procureur du Roy*, but I am a member of the banking company of Monsieur Lass. Lass, who has paid your salary as General for the last year; Lass, who pays everything; Lass, who takes a piece of paper and says: 'Make that into bank notes for one hundred thousand *livres*'—and, presto! it is done."

"You—a banker!" ejaculates Raymond, very much astonished.

But this is the truth, as Monsieur de Moncrief has kept a very tight clutch upon the Prince de Conti's promise to him, and has hung on to the Regent-De Conti-Lass crowd and done their legal work and any little tender matters that required what to-day would be called "a first-class corporation lawyer's advice," *i. e.*, the power of leading his clients as close to the gates of a prison as possible and not letting them get in.

He has performed these various little services for his patrons, with such energy, skill, and general long-headedness, that they have rewarded him with quite a little slice of the stock of the bank of Lass, which having gone up very materially in value, has permitted Monsieur Charles de Moncrief to spend his money so very freely that all the young actresses of the opera and theatre affect to think Charlie has grown very boyish again.

Then boy Charlie and cousin Raymond sit down to a magnificent dinner, magnificently served, with plenty of lackeys in attendance and wax lights innumerable.

During this De Moncrief tells his guest: "I have taken quarters for you near my own on the Rue Christine, not of course, as elaborate as these."

"No, these would be more fitting for a maréchal than a general!" remarks D'Arnac contemplatively.

"Egad! I don't believe old De Villars himself could stand the cost of these—twenty thousand *livres* a year! Yours are only five thousand!" returns De Moncrief, delightedly.

"Five thousand *livres* a year for some beggarly rooms!" cries Raymond aghast.

"*Parbleu!* They are reasonable!" answers Cousin Charlie, for living was fast becoming extravagant in Paris under the influence of increasing money.

Then he goes on contemplatively: "Had I landed property, I would be as great a nabob as any of the comtes and maréchals."

To get estates has been the ambition of De Moncrief's life, and he is determined to have them, and those of Crevecœur are very handsome and extensive ones.

"Do you know, Raymond, my boy!" he says after a minute's musing, "they are going to marry you off to the little Comtesse Julie de Beaumont when she becomes older?"

"Indeed!" laughs D'Arnac. "I have no objection."

"Ah, you remember the child?"

"Yes, as a child. When she was ten, five years ago. She said she hated me, because, I believe, our matrimony was the wish of both families then, and little Julie had already begun to cultivate wifely feelings towards me!" sneers Raymond, so easily and unconcernedly that De Moncrief writhes in his seat.

"Well, that's what Crevecœur wants to see you about!" mutters the old schemer.

Shortly after, dinner being finished, the two sit down together to smoke Virginia tobacco out of long-stemmed clay pipes.

After a puff or two Monsieur de Moncrief, turning matters over in his mind, suggests: "You must see your ward to-morrow, my dear boy! She will astonish you!"

"Ah, the little Quinault! You have noticed her lately?"

"Once at Madame de Chateaubrien's, and then she was so charming that I have visited her often since at the convent. She is no longer the little Quinault—she has grown tall, and of a loveliness that will send you, her guardian, wild with delight."

And the old gentleman babbles on extolling the beauties of this young woman, who is just graduating from childhood, so vividly, that Raymond's eyes begin to sparkle at the charms described to him. So Cousin Charlie chuckles to himself: "Egad! wait till he sees her! Then perhaps he will not be so complaisant in regard to the little Comtesse Julie!"

This brings a very good humor upon his face as he cries: "Now, Raymond, my boy, run around to your quarters on the Rue Christine! You will find them lighted and awaiting you. Your baggage I have already ordered there. Make your toilet *a la général* —prepare to conquer at the *bal de l'Opera*, and I will call for you with my carriage at eleven o'clock. "

Even the first of these *fêtes* was not an early one, though they have become later as the world has rolled on.

"Ah, you have a long toilette to make yourself!" laughs Raymond, perchance maliciously, as the old gentleman is known to devote much time on such occasions in simulating the appearance of boyhood.

"Tut! tut! an affair of half an hour. But you are a little more vain and will require more time, Monsieur Epaulettes," grunts the Procureur.

"Very well," says Raymond heartily, "I'll do my best for the honor of the army," and goes away very gayly and buoyantly, as what young man would not after three years of camp life, to array himself for the *bal de l'Opera*, though at present its brilliance is only in D'Arnac's imagination—the reality is to come, and with it a meeting, which he has said shall never happen, but which he has always looked forward to.

Perhaps it is some presentiment of this that comes to him while he is dressing. He is looking carelessly over his baggage in search of a lace handkerchief and ruffles, fine gentlemen in those days being very vain in these little matters of personal adornment, and wearing as much *Point de Venice* as any court beauty.

In doing so, he comes upon a package of letters that bring back to him the past; they are from O'Brien Dillon and Lanty in Vienna, only three of them, postage being high and couriers seldom in those days.

The first, written by his Irish friend in answer to the one
D'Arnac had sent describing his effort to replace
Madame O'Brien Dillon in his care. He glances over
it and blushes as he reads these words:

"God thank you for what you have done for me! Though
you haven't given her back to me, I imagine she is all right,
as they're keeping her in convents. However, I thank you
from the bottom of my heart for being so true to our comrade-
ship of the sword."

This has been forwarded to him before Dillon's
first campaign against the Turks.

Another and longer one is in Lanty's handwriting,
written on their return to the Austrian capital from
Eugene's glorious campaign of Peterawaradin, in which
he has defeated the Ottoman forces. It runs along in
merry Lanty's light-hearted way, describing the
wondrous plunder they have got. One sentence sets
Raymond laughing. It says:

"As for booty, it is so much that me master speaks of getting
back to Paris to look up Madame O'Brien Dillon. He is a
general now, and, faith, he's so much run after that if it wasn't
that he is already bound by the priest to the woman in France,
I think he might be after marrying a royal duchess, and as for
countesses, he might have a harem of them if he choose, after
the manner of the heathen Turks."

The last letter, but six months before, had met
D'Arnac just before he left the Pyrenees, for epistles
took longer in these days to come from Vienna than
they would to go round the world now, ends:

"One campaign more and I hope to have plunder enough
to come back and clasp your hand and look after the madame,
if the Turks don't get away with your friend.
"O'BRIEN DILLON."

Pondering on this matter, Raymond thinks there
should be an epistle from him even now, for the Turkish
campaign of the year must be ended.

But from this he gets to meditating upon O'Brien
Dillon's wife, and the rare loveliness that had sat
beside him in the carriage in that wild ride out of Paris
the last time he had been in the capital:

"If Lass, her uncle, is here, she should be in Paris also."

His thoughts are broken in upon by the footman of Monsieur le Procureur coming upstairs and announcing that his master is at the door in his carriage, and begs his cousin will not keep him waiting in the cold.

Raymond hurries down to take his place beside his relative, who is cloaked and furred up to his very eyes.

As they drive away, De Moncrief directing his coachman to take the Quai de Conti and to cross the river by the Pont Royal, and so avoid the great crowd of carriages that will be coming from the city proper along the Rue St. Honoré, Raymond suddenly queries: "You are intimate with Monsieur Lass?"

"Certainly; I know him very well. A man of the greatest financial genius—the longest head in the whole world, I think. Egad! money seems to spring from his brain as easily as ideas!" remarks De Moncrief, and means it, for he has been very much impressed with the Scotch financier's genius and tremendous grasp of commercial affairs.

"You are intimate at his house as well as his bank?" suggests Raymond.

"Certainly, as a man of rank I have thought it best to give Lass the countenance of my presence socially," replies the Procureur.

"Then have you ever chanced to meet his niece, Madame O'Brien Dillon?"

At which Cousin Charlie, to Raymond's embarrassment, giggles: "I thought young Wild Blood was coming to that! *Pardieu!* you mean the young lady who got you into all that trouble when you were here last. *Sapristi!* De Conti hates you still; and as for the Regent—" Here he checks himself with a gulp.

"The Regent—what of him?"

"Oh, nothing, but he admires pretty faces as well as you," answers De Moncrief.

"Yes, Madame de Sabran's I have heard," returns Raymond, mentioning the name of a lady about whose beauty Paris was beginning to rave, and to whom was attributed by public rumor the doubtful honor of being the Duc d'Orleans' latest *belle amie.*"

"Madame de Sabran!" ejaculates Cousin Charlie, a kind of unholy glee coming into his sharp eyes.

"Of course, the divine Madame de Sabran; the one every man is charmed by and every woman envious of. Poor De Courcy, of my command, came back to the Pyrenees in love with her, though he had only seen her in her carriage. Perhaps she will be at the ball—point her out to me," gossips Raymond contentedly.

"Madame de Sabran!" mutters De Moncrief, "yes, perchance we'll see her at the ball," then buries his face in his fur cloak as if trying to stifle some hysterical emotion. A moment after he says suddenly and seriously: "I'm sorry my advice got you into that escapade with pretty Madame Dillon; still I would have done the like for a friend myself, though your motives were grossly misunderstood."

After a second's silence, D'Arnac, whose mind has got now to running on his friend, asks suddenly: "Is there any news from the Danube?"

"From Prince Eugene?" says the Procureur "The greatest!" Then he goes on earnestly under his breath: "Not a word of this, for it is being kept very quiet for financial reasons by Monsieur Lass and myself. A courier from Vienna has just brought private intelligence that Prince Eugene has annihilated the Turkish hosts before Belgrade, and captured that city— the greatest victory Christendom has ever had over the Ottoman! They are now suing wildly for peace."

"And my friend, O'Brien Dillon?" asks D'Arnac, hastily.

"There was no further details, save that the Austrian losses were very heavy, as the courier that reached Vienna was nearly a month getting there. The roads were awful and infested by skirmishing parties of light Tartar horse the Turks had thrown out in advance all over the country. Don't say a word of this—it is still private! I doubt even if the Ottoman Ambassador knows of the misfortune of his country. But here we are at the Palais Royal. Put your head out of the carriage—look at the crowds—the excitement—the flambeaux of the footmen—is it not glorious? I and Lass have been the making of Paris!" remarks De Moncrief, with a very self-satisfied air.

Thinking to himself, if Eugene has been victorious, probably O'Brien Dillon is all right, D'Arnac obeys his relative's instructions, and sees a sight the like of which has never been seen in the capital of France before, though many similar ones will come after—the nobles and bourgeoisie mixed in common fête.

They are at the corner of the Rues St. Thomas du Louvre and St. Honoré and are meeting the great string of equipages coming along the latter thoroughfare towards the Palais Royal, the façade of which is illuminated for the occasion.

This Palais Royal is a building of magnificent dimensions, built by the great Richelieu, not only for his own home, but also for the home of dramatic art.

It is an edifice of wonderful extent, but rambling, and of unequal height at different places; over the grand entrance it is but two stories in elevation, but rises three more in the form of a great mansard roof over the theatre that is now used as the home of the opera.

The front of the pile is on the Rue St. Honoré, running the entire distance between the street called Des Bonnes Enfants and the Rue Richelieu. Along these two streets it runs back to magnificent gardens formed for the pleasure of the Cardinal. Like its founder's mind, the building is grandly enormous.

Two theatres—a small one holding but six hundred people, for private representations before the court —a larger one capable of seating over three thousand, for the delectation of the more general public, by his comedians of the Comédie Française, are swallowed up and veritably almost lost in the grand pile of buildings, without apparently intrenching upon their numerous suites of magnificent apartments and great courtyards for sunshine and pleasure, for Armand de Richelieu never did anything meanly, and his great building, called by him the "Palais Cardinal," was worthy of his grandeur and his power.

The great theatre of the building, originally devoted to the *Comédie Française*, is now known as "The Opera." It is to the entrance of this, on the corner of the Rue St. Honoré and the Rue des Bonnes Enfants, to which the carriage of Charles de Moncrief is being driven, though it does not arrive there for some considerable time, as the line of carriages ahead of it is very long.

But Raymond hardly notices the delay, the sight before him is so novel. Dashing equipages of the court are mixed with the humbler carriages of rich silversmiths and bourgeoisie, who now dare to put on the evidences of wealth. These, surrounded by lackeys and flunkeys carrying blazing torches, and the brilliant *feu de joie* in wax lights on the façade of the theatre, all give vivacity, interest and illumination to the scene.

Engaged in looking at this, even as he leaves the carriage, Raymond scarce notices his companion until they arrive in one of the waiting-rooms. Here, surrounded by various others in fancy costumes, who are doffing their wraps and robes, for the night is chilly, D'Arnac first turns his eyes on the old Procureur du Roy, and for the life of him cannot help giving a wild scream of laughter and falling, overcome, into a neighboring chair.

For, as his furs have been taken off, Charles de Moncrief, in all the decrepitude of age, steps out of his wraps, his wig tied up in bows of pink silk ribbons, his toothless mouth grinning with pleasure, his wrinkled cheeks contorted into what he thinks a boyish smile, his senile body attired in flesh-colored tights and shaking a pair of tiny silver wings, and holding up a little bow and arrows, takes infant pose upon the floor and cries: "Behold me, Cupid—God of Youth and Love!" trying to look as cunning as the imp himself.

The effect is enormous and general, the gentlemen standing by fairly shrieking with merriment.

"*Diable!* what amuses you?" mutters the Procureur, his face under its paint and powder assuming so wizened and vindictive an expression that it adds to the merriment, especially as he gives one or two skips of rage, which make his little wings flap fairylike in the air.

"*Mon Dieu!*" shouts De Conti, who has just come in with his pal, the Duc de Guiche and Monsieur d'Argenson, now raised to the office of Keeper of the Seals, behind them.

"By the soul of Bacchus, if this is not little De Moncrief! Cupid—fair Cupid?" he cries, and as wine has

made him forget his rank, and he rejoices in great
animal strength, this prince of the blood takes up little
Charlie, and tossing him on his shoulder, dances round
the room, crying: "Old Cupid and young Venus!"
nursing him after the manner of a baby, and going
through several other grotesque antics, as the crowd of
nobles hold their sides with merriment, and even
Monsieur Peltier, the silversmith, who has come timidly
into the ball, dares to laugh at the joke of one of the
princes of the blood.

A moment after, De Moncrief is let down from the
arms of his tormenter, and he scowls no more, laughing
himself at the Prince de Conti's joke.

But for all that, Louis Armand de Bourbon, prince of
the house of Conti, has danced a very bad *pas seul* for
himself, this evening, though he doesn't know it; and
Monsieur d'Argenson, proud in his new rank, by his
jeers and laughter has done a very bad turn for himself,
and had better—if he but guessed it—as he is yet the
Lieutenant General de Police, abduct, imprison, and
close out from the light of day, Charles de Moncrief,
the Procureur du Roy, for Cupid has no longer love in
his soul—but hate, malignant hate for these two merry
gentlemen—though he will try and forget it in the
bright eyes and playful flatteries of the ladies of the
bal de l'Opéra this evening.

CHAPTER XVII.

THE FIRST BAL DE L'OPERA.

AS IT TAKES some time for Cousin Charlie to re-arrange
his wings and smooth his locks that are tied by delicate pink ribbon, the prince of the blood and most of
the surrounding crowd stroll into the main portion of
the theatre, while Raymond stands waiting for Cupid to
regain his charms.

Then together they enter the great auditorium, which
has been floored over from the stage and made into a
vast ballroom, De Moncrief laughing and passing off
the affair, saying: "*Pardieu!* Cousin, probably I am
the only man in Paris De Conti would feel sufficiently

intimate with to take such liberties. It is not every one a prince of the blood would do duty for as a carrier!" and similar other remarks expressive of his delight at the performance of the wild, boisterous and wine-filled De Conti.

But the sight opening before Raymond makes him hardly heed the words of any one. It is as if he had come into a new and enchanted land.

The two rows of boxes are draped and adorned in various colors and most fanciful designs. The superb ceiling covered with groups of angels and goddesses, by the hand of Monsieur Watteau, is made more brilliant by the flags of France. The whole scene is lighted as if it were day by innumerable wax tapers kept burning brightly by one hundred flunkeys with trays and snuffers.

Underneath this illumination, a sea of figures, costumed perhaps not so correctly as to-day, because even the dress of the theatre proper was at this time incomplete, and sometimes Jupiter or Julius Cæsar were played by gentlemen in knee breeches and perriwigs, while Cleopatra hesitated not to appear arrayed in hoop skirt and demi-train.

For all that, the dashing crowd makes a great show of color, of kaleidoscopic rapidity of movement, but with more than the beauty of the kaleidoscope, because within this sea of changing hues are the bright faces of lovely women and the handsome figures of dashing men.

There is a great display in the costumes of Watteau; shepherdesses with their crooks, and gods and goddesses in silk fleshings and the armor of ancient Greece, Cupid and Venus and Jupiter and Apollo being great favorites in all the ballets of that time.

Most of them are circling in the dance, not the wild can-can of to-day, to the sprightly yet voluptuous music of Offenbach, but in the stately menuet de la cour, to the soft numbers of Luilli and Mouret, from a band that gives forth its melodies with the strings of Cremona, the harps of minstrelsy, the lutes and soft woodwind instruments that belonged to the orchestras of that day.

At first, Raymond's eyes devour this great scene as a whole—then individually and in groups, as the Procureur du Roy, anxious to show his knowledge of every one notable in France, begins to point out celebrities. They have strolled half round the room when he suddenly seizes D'Arnac's arm and says: "There! do you see him?"

"Who?"

"Monsieur Lass!"

"No! where?" whispers Raymond, anxious to see the "Uncle Johnny" of his friend O'Brien Dillon.

"There! The tall distinguished man with the sharp nose and handsome figure and bright eyes. The one standing in the Regent's box alongside of Monsieur d'Orleans!"

Raymond knows the Regent by sight, and looking towards the large box which has the arms of France upon it, he sees standing beside the man who holds the destinies of the country in his hands, the man who is destined to hold the finances of Europe within his grasp.

"Uncle Johnny" is, as De Moncrief has described him, tall, with very handsome eyes, prominent nose, thin but determined lips, and the brow of a mathematician. He has the face of a man who might have invented the binomial theorem or the calculus, were it not the face of a man who would not be contented to starve over pure mathematics in a garret, but rather one who loves the luxuries of life—the excitement of play—and the grand battle of humanity.

He is standing just behind the Regent. Before him, as their rank give them precedence, but at his right, lounge the Princes De Condé and De Conti, cousins of France, but rivals in getting all they can out of France, and both very anxious to make themselves agreeable to Monsieur Lass, whom they have already utilized much to the benefit of their depleted purses.

All the gentlemen are chuckling over De Conti's description of what he has done with little Moncrief the Cupid.

"*Morbleu!*" remarks the Prince. "Even old Peltier, the silversmith, could not refrain from having his grin at Monsieur le Procureur. This is a very fine idea of yours, Monsieur Lass—this mixture of the rabble and the nobles. It may give me a better grip at old Silversmith's purse, if I smack him on the shoulder. He is walking over there." And he strolls off in pursuit of poor old Peltier upon whom he proposes to throw the light of his semi-royal countenance, in order to touch him for as large a loan as possible.

This leaves Monsieur Lass with D'Orleans and De Condé.

His Highness is pleased to be very affable this evening. He says lightly: "Condé, where is Madame la Princess?"

"*Parbleu*, your Highness, she is at home with the children!" replies that Prince. "This is hardly the proper place for my wife."

"Especially," chuckles D'Orleans, "as I see Madame de Prie ogling you from the box opposite."

"Ah, Madeline there! I didn't suppose she was coming so early. Then if your Highness will permit I'll take my leave!"

"Yes, till supper. Don't forget, Condé, bring De Prie with you! You, Monsieur Lass, I hope, will join us also, with any lady you please."

"Thanks, your Highness," replies the financier, "I will bring with me, with your permission, Madame de Locmaria."

"Delighted!" remarks D'Orleans. "There will be but a few more. After supper we will have a little play with the markers you have so kindly invented to save us gamblers the trouble of counting money. I have already invited Madame de Sabran; without her our feast would be indeed a famine!" and the Regent's eyes light up with passion.

"Yes, Hilda told me!" assents Lass. Then he suddenly says: "In regard to that Moncrief matter? This affair will make him surely, if I judge him right, De Conti's enemy—that probably means our enemy—and we want all to be our friends *now*, your Highness!" adds Lass quite seriously.

"Pooh! I'll fix Moncrief!" laughs D'Orleans.

"How?"

"I'll invite him to supper with me to-night. An invitation from the Regent will please his pride more than De Conti's joke hurt it; eh, my financier!"

"It will make our little Moncrief love you as his God!" whispers Lass.

"Better than his God, I hope!" jeers the Duke,
"otherwise I shall be no great favorite of my
Procureur! But come on the floor, Lass, the ladies
and gentlemen down there are all hoping you will make
them rich!"

After one good look Raymond has not paid much
attention to the royal box. Some very pretty young
ladies have intruded themselves on General Epaulettes,
as they call him, and he is at present dancing a minuet
with a sprightly Watteau shepherdess. The young
Comte de Horn, a weary look on his dissipated face,
is at his right with a beautiful, but half nude Venus,
while immediately opposite to him De Moncrief, as
Cupid, is skipping grotesquely in company with the
dashing danseuse *la belle* Prevost.

Everybody is warming to the scene.

The dance goes on, but wilder; flirtations spring up
and champagne changes them to love.

The ball becomes gayer and madder, for wine is now
making bright eyes look brighter, and merry laughs
louder, and dashing steps more audacious, and the
affair is gradually reaching the *élan* and carnival of a
true *bal de l'Opera* when Raymond, bidding adieu to his
partner of the dance, chances to glance at one of the
boxes of the first row and sees a lady who, though she
is masked, brings him recollection.

Perchance it is her glance that has drawn his, for
while he has been dancing this lady, cloaked, hooded,
masked and dominoed, has been gazing at him as if he
were the one man of the ball; perhaps it is something in
her figure—some trick of gesture—but he remembers.

Champagne effaces resolution. He thinks now but
of love and joy. It may not be she, but he does not
care—she is certainly beautiful—the privilege of a mask
—why not take it?

He is at the staircase in a moment jostling his way
through the crowd, but gaining the box, he finds it
empty.

A domino is vanishing into a neighboring *loge*.

After it!

A couple of lackeys attempt to stay him. He
does not note their royal liveries, and, pushing them
aside, steps into the royal box of France, to find himself

confronted by a lady, who, apparently safe from intrusion, has just thrown away her domino and mask.

To her he gasps: " Madame O'Brien Dillon!"

"Hush!" Her taper finger is on her red lips. She whispers: " Not Madame O'Brien Dillon now. Hilda —to *you*. I cannot talk to you *now*—but I remember."

Her words are flashing as her beauty, which dazzles him, for she is in a costume that makes her too lovely for the eyes of man to look on sentiently. She seems to Raymond's fascinated senses a thing that is not of this world—her beauty is too spiritual.

Her dress is white that floats about her yet clings to her and shows that she who was a Hebe has now become a Venus. One little foot in white silken stocking and satin slipper is advanced towards him. One white arm on which are flashing diamonds of purest water and brightest rays is stretched to him. A single ruby red as blood flames on her snowy breast, but it is not as red as lips which speak these words: " I have your address—I have just discovered your arrival in Paris—you have been kept from me by those who have more power than I—a note to-morrow!"

" No, no!" he gasps hoarsely.

"Why not?"

" My friend ——"

" That need not come between us. He no longer lives!"

"O'Brien Dillon *dead ?*"

" Yes. He fell at the battle of Belgrade. I have had sure news from a trusted agent in Vienna. There is no doubt. Don't let the dead efface the living!"

He tries to struggle against her charm, but the wild beauty is the same as that he clasped to his heart three years before as he rode mid the raging torrent of the Marne.

" Don't let the dead efface the living—a note to-morrow! Don't speak of me as Madame O'Brien Dillon. Don't whisper you have seen me, for I am now known." She glides to the entrance and opens a *portière*, leading not to the ballroom, but direct to the Regent's Palace.

The young man steps towards her as if to bar her way, his flaming eyes speaking words his lips cannot bring themselves to utter.

She courtesies to him and whispers: "Yes; do not hate me. They compelled me—ambition dictated it! I am now known as Madame de Sabran. *A note to-morrow!*"

At the word Raymond sinks, overcome in the box, for it is the name of the wondrous beauty who, rumor says, holds France almost in her hand, for she has its Regent's heart. He mutters to himself: "This was what they kept her for. This is why they dare not let O'Brien Dillon come to Paris. This is the bait by which Monsieur Lass has bought the Regent's favor and the right to govern the finances of France."

A moment after these two shocks drive the wine from his brain. He leaves the royal box murmuring: "My God! my friend, dead—killed by the Turks!" brushing past the Procureur du Roy, whom he scarce notices, such is his agitation, but who regards his departing cousin with a cynical and snickering smile.

Then a set look comes on D'Arnac's face as he gazes upon the ballroom floor, and says: "There is an accursed Ottoman now!" for he thinks he sees the Ambassador of the Sublime Porte, as a creature robed in the costume of a Turkish vizier, sparkling with jewels, with scimeter and dagger blazing with diamonds, attended by a gigantic Nubian slave, and followed by a couple of mutes, is passing in triumph up the room, and every one is gazing at his haughty bearing and savage mien.

"Why not pick a quarrel with this representative of the Infidel and avenge my friend?" thinks D'Arnac, impetuously, and hurriedly descends to the floor, there to be astounded, the very soul taken out of him with intense surprise, rapture, astonishment, for as he walks threateningly up to the gorgeous figure, a genuine Irish brogue greets him: "By me soul, Raymond, me boy! Begorra, I've come back both general and count from the Turks!"

And he sees standing before him his old comrade of the Rhine campaign—the man who had saved his life— the husband of the woman who has just said to him: "A note to-morrow!"—O'Brien Dillon, once colonel in the army of France, but now count of the Empire—and general in the Austrian service.

"By me soul, Lanty, me boy, is not this a glorious coming home? First, me friend, and then soon I'll have me wife! These diamonds are genuine, Raymond, me boy—plunder from the Turks! Faith, I captured the Grand Vizier myself—a ransom of eighty thousand ducats, and by Saint Patrick! I've got the Horse-tails—the genuine article—taken in front of the Vizier's pavilion. Wave the Horse-tails, Lanty, ye divil, and show the French they're the real thing."

With wild cries of triumph Lanty waves the five Horse-tails of the Grand Vizier of the Turkish Empire, and these are proved to be genuine, for the Ottoman Ambassador himself, seeing the sacred insignia of the Sublime Porte—the thing only granted to the commanders of the armies of the Allah, comes up, thinking it is some great countryman of his—perhaps some successor sent to take his place; for in those days of long travel, sometimes instructions were not sent in advance to ministers or plenipotentiaries.

Beholding the signal of the power of Mahomet waving in triumph, as he thinks, and not having heard news of the awful fate of the armies of his faith, he cries: "Bishmael! Allah be praised! It means the victory of the Ottoman!"

And forgetting the place, he makes obeisance and does homage before it, until Lanty gives a wild shriek, crying: "Yes, victory of the Christians! Those Horse-tails I seized from the Vizier himself! It means the Turks have lost one hundred thousand men, and have been beaten out of their very harems by Prince Eugene of Savoy, when he captured Belgrade!"

At this sudden and fearful disclosure of his country's downfall and terrible military disaster, the Turkish Ambassador, with a hoarse cry of horror and despair, flies from the room amid the laughter of the gods and goddesses and nymphs and shepherdesses of the *bal de l'Opera*, who now go to dancing a wild *sarabande* that does duty in that day for the can-can of Mabille.

"By Saint Patrick! he's not the first Turk that has fled before us, eh Lanty?" laughs O'Brien.

"Musha! I'm accustomed to seeing the beasts' backs," grins Lanty. "If it were not for the meddling

police outside, I would follow the unbeliever and plunder
him of his diamonds, from very force of habit."

"I've done well, haven't I, my boy?" says .Dillon,
turning to D'Arnac, who is still speechless from
the shock of astonishment caused by the return of this
man, his old friend and comrade, whose wife has but
three minutes before whispered in his ear: "A note
to-morrow!"

"Well?" echoes Raymond, forced to speech, "Enormous!" gazing in admiration at Eastern garments
studded with magnificent jewels, and a turban that
literally blazes with diamonds in the form of a great
crescent and lesser star. Then a sudden thought flies
through him: "Thank God, I can still look my friend
in the face!" and D'Arnac springs forward to seize the
outstretched hand of his comrade of the sword, and
receive his grip of welcome.

"Faith, I captured the Grand Vizier myself, and with
my own hands tore off this magnificent uniform," laughs
O'Brien; and would enter into an extended conversation with his friend did not at this moment a crowd of
pretty young goddesses surge round them, and force
them apart, crying: "Hurrah! for a dance with the
Diamond Pasha!"

"I always accommodate ladies. It's an Irishman's
habit, even in Turkish garb—me little odalisques!"
replies Dillon, and gives each one of the beseeching
fair ones a step or two on his stalwart arm.

But getting away from these, he puts his hand upon
D'Arnac's shoulder in such a brotherly way, that the
young man's conscience pricks him very hard, and says:
"I have got lots to tell you, Raymond, me boy.
Supposing we go home together, so I can do it over a
pipe."

D'Arnac assenting to this, as the ball is now drawing to its close, the two make preparations for
departure, Raymond insisting that his friend and old
comrade shall make his quarters with him in the Rue
Christine.

"Agreed; Lanty will look after getting my baggage
from our inn. We only arrived in town this evening,
just in time to display our fine selves. I thought I'd
find you here, if you were in Paris. Those two fellows

dressed as mutes, following behind me, are a couple of *garçons* I hired for the occasion, to give me greater dignity, and by Saint Patrick! I think Lanty and I have made a sensation!"

As indeed they have, a crowd following them everywhere.

"I will be with you in a moment!" answers Raymond. "Just a word to my cousin," and departs in search of De Moncrief, to find Cupid in most happy mood, the fire of social triumph in his twinkling eyes.

"I am glad you can get home without me," remarks Cousin Charlie, "as I have received a most pressing invitation to sup with the Regent. Royal invitations must be accepted. D'Orleans made it a personal matter with me. That is your friend, Colonel O'Brien Dillon, just returned, rumor says, from Vienna and the battle of Belgrade?" he whispers, inquiringly, fighting down a chuckle as he looks at the Irish officer, who is still strutting about and making great display of himself to the throng that have followed him even to the door of the ball room.

"General Dillon, Comte of the Empire," corrects Raymond, who feels proud of his friend's success.

"Humph! a general and a count—with lots of diamonds and plunder—I observe," returns De Moncrief.

"Any quantity of them. He captured the Grand Vizier himself," cries D'Arnac, proudly, and goes away to take the arm of Comte Dillon of the Imperial service.

Whereupon the two, going out of the theatre, succeed, by Lanty's aid, in getting hold of a carriage, and drive off to Raymond's apartments to finish the night over their pipes, in discussing O'Brien's triumphs and adventures in Vienna and among the Turks.

De Moncrief gazes after them. His cynical mind puts together the interview he knows his cousin has had with the Irish officer's wife in the box, the last words of which he had caught: "A note to-morrow!"

Then, for he has been studying the face of the Count of the Empire, he chuckles to himself: "*Pardieu*, he has the look of one whose sword will defend his honor as a husband. He has come back with a title—and rich enough to make a pretty good fight for his rights over the last *belle amie* of the Regent. Egad! Monsieur

le Comte Dillon's advent into Paris will bring rare joy
to Monsieur d'Orleans, and I doubt not, my dear cousin
Raymond d'Arnac, whose eyes spake love, if eyes ever
spake it, to the woman who fascinates us all," for
Cousin Charlie himself is still captive to the delightful
vivaciousness, the brilliant spirit and the entrancing
loveliness of the lady now called Madame de Sabran.

Occupied with these ideas, Cupid, emitting sarcastic
chuckles and malicious giggles, makes his way to the
royal box, and from there is ushered through the private
passage into the Palais Royal itself, and the private
supper room of the Regent of France.

Here he finds the fun is not all on Cupid's side.

These affairs are very informal, D'Orleans himself tossing away his rank for the time being. They
are regal in nothing save magnificent cuisine and glorious wines, beautiful women and gay men. A kind of
aristocratic bohemianism is thrown over them; every
one doing as he pleases to get every enjoyment of the
senses the devil suggests.

De Conti is one of the party, and has added more wine
during the ball to his bizarre brain. He is telling with
great gusto pretty Madeline de Prie, the Marquis de
Lassa, the sylph-like beauty, De Verue, and Madame
de Sabran, of his joke on senile Cupid, and they are all
laughing very heartily.

As De Moncrief enters crying: "Behold Cupid himself!" De Conti falls upon him and goes through his
previous performance with him, with even more
outrageous gambols; finally dropping the struggling,
writhing, decrepit old imp of love into the lap of the
beauteous De Sabran, screaming: "Who would think
this Venus the mother of *that* Cupid? Mythology is a lie!"

This frightful contrast makes them all very merry,
Hilda laughing till the tears are in her eyes.

Lying thus, his wrinkled head pillowed on her white
bosom, Cousin Charlie concludes to take all the advantage of the situation possible, and throwing himself into
the affair, embraces lovely Hilda, crying: "Mamma's
kisses! mamma's kisses!" and his wizened lips press
the cheek of beauty.

But Venus, not relishing his senile attentions, takes
up the laugh, and crying: "Cupid's naughty! Cupid's

naughty!" boxes his old ears till Charlie writhes with
shame and anguish. At which the whole party burst
into more uproarious laughter; and De Moncrief,
though he loves, in his way, Hilda de Sabran, hates her
also, and makes up his mind for a revenge fantastic.

But this is yet to come.

The Regent is announced, and Monsieur Lass and
Madame de Locmaria entering, they all sit down to
supper, and have a very merry time of it.

Though Cousin Charlie laughs as loudly as any, his
mind is occupied with Cupid's vengeance, of which a
little thing that now happens makes him feel certain.

During the conversation at the table, the Regent
remarks to Monsieur Lass: "Have you heard any
further news from Vienna?"

"No," replies the Scotchman, "though there was a
rumor in the ball, but a few minutes ago, that some
Count of the Austrian Empire had arrived."

"You did not see the gentleman, Monsieur de
Moncrief?" says D'Orleans carelessly?"

"Ma foi! not I!" answers the Procureur. "I was
too much occupied with wood nymphs to bother my
head about Austrians or Turks!"

As he says this, he glances at la Sabran and notes,
though she hears, no uneasiness has come to her, and he
knows her husband's return is still to her unknown.

So after a little he leaves the supper party apparently
in very good spirits, and very proud of having been
invited to the private table of the Regent of France.

But on his way home he is saying to himself: "Here's
a pretty kettle of fish for Monsieur Lass, the Duc
d'Orleans, my Cousin Raymond, the Irish Count, and
Venus who boxed her Cupid's ears—a note to-morrow!—
To-morrow CUPID'S REVENGE!" And the god of love's
fairy wings rustle as he goes into convulsive chuckles of
malignant hate.

CHAPTER XVIII.

"A NOTE TO-MORROW!"

FORTUNATELY for Cousin Charlie, the parties
mentioned in his last remark know nothing of what he
is to bring upon them.

The supper party at the Palais Royal goes on more merrily after he has. left it, D'Orleans basking in the smiles of the beautiful Sabran, until Madame de Parabère, who has joined the company in spite of her sulks, sheds tears of jealous disappointment, which she conceals in a lace handkerchief, saying the pepper on the salad affects her eyes.

De Conti and De Condé, De Guiche and De Lassa dance a wild *sarabande* with impromptu frolics between, to the music of a small orchestra brought in for the occasion, De Conti crying wildly: "Oh, if we only had Cupid here *now!*" Which indicates that it is just as well for Monsieur de Moncrief's dignity that Cupid has left the supper party.

At the same hour that this is going on, Raymond d'Arnac and Count Dillon are seated over their pipes, in the former's apartments on the Rue Christine, talking over what has happened to them since they clasped hands and bid each other adieu in the town of Rastadt, some three years before.

Raymond has but little to tell, save the routine of frontier garrisons on the Pyrenees.

Dillon's stories are those of gay life in Vienna, and two dashing and successful campaigns against the Turks.

"All the time," he says, "I was fighting not only for glory, but for plunder enough to bring me back here.   And thank the Virgin! at last I got it, at Belgrade.   I had had some pretty pickings before, but the booty of that great battle was the making of me. It was like the great siege that learned people tell about in 'Julius Cæsar.'   A town heavily garrisoned.   Round it the army of Prince Eugene—sixty thousand strong. Outside the great host of the Turks—three hundred thousand.   We who besieged, were besieged, and faith! if we had not had the greatest commander of the age (no implication on the old Duc de Villars or Marlborough himself), not a man of us would have lived to get back.   But in the middle of the night, unexpected to the infidels, who thought they surely had us, with a great fog over us, the army, veterans every man of them formed shoulder to shoulder, in darkness so great they went more by touch than by eyesight, and without a sound marched out of our intrenchments, and were on them, and then—God help them!

"But all the time I had one thought—'not only glory but plunder!' And I went straight at the tent of the Grand Vizier, for I had marked it down with my eyes, day after day, and said: 'There's where the finest pickings will be!' But the finest pickings were the best guarded, and we had to cut our way through the Janissaries of the Sultan. At last we got there to find him gone; but I was after him, for the Turks were flying by this time.

"I was bound to have the Vizier, and so I disappeared for a week, chasing him with but one regiment of horse at my back, till finally I captured him seventy miles from the battle ground, and got what has made me able to live like a nabob.

"It was nearly a week before I returned from my expedition—in fact, I was so long gone that the first reports of the battle in Vienna said O'Brien Dillon had left the world along with the Count d'Estrades and many other generals of battalia, slain by the Turks. So my coming to Vienna was such a source of joy to his Majesty, who was about to put the court into mourning for me, that his Imperial Highness said: 'What can I do for you, General Dillon, to celebrate your return?'

"'Faith, your Majesty,' said I, 'you have only one Irish Count in the army now—Count Browne; could you not make it two?'

"'Why, certainly, Count Dillon,' said he, and, by my soul, that is the way I became a noble of the Empire, and when I go back there Countess Dillon will not have to go in behind the oldest baroness in Vienna.

"Lanty, too, has done pretty well for himself, for he took a pasha with his own hands. They would have made him a captain, but a captain could not varnish my boots, and the faithful fellow would not hear of it. Now, tell me if you know anything about the Countess Dillon!"

It is very hard to tell a friend that his wife is the mistress of any man—even a Prince Regent; so Raymond simply says, "That he has no doubt Hilda is in Paris, as her uncle is now known as Monsieur Lass."

"What! my 'Uncle Johnny,' says the Irishman. "Faith, then, I'll hunt him up at his dirty bank. I've got bills on him from Vienna for eighty thousand crowns. He can pay the lady and the money over at the same time. But, Raymond, I've been riding all day, and you have, too, as I understand."

"Yes, we must have both arrived in Paris about the same time."

"Then, as our pipes have gone out, what do you say to bed?"

So the two turn in and sleep the sleep of the soldier, very contentedly.

On awakening late the next morning the first thing that comes into D'Arnac's mind, with a shock of recollection, is: "'A note to-morrow!' and my friend— my old comrade, O'Brien Dillon, sleeping by my side!"

He gets up and dresses himself, and not seeing Lanty about, that worthy being occupied in the transfer of his master's baggage to Raymond's quarters, inquires of his lackey, under his breath, as if he were ashamed of it: "Any letters for me?"

"Yes," says the man promptly, and hands him one, which he is relieved to discover is from his sister.

It says:

If you have arrived, come and see me immediately! Jeanne has grown beyond me. Come and exert your authority over the wild child.

I obtained your address from Cousin Charlie, who told me what apartments he had engaged for you.

This puts other business before him, and he is glad to get away to it. Charging his valet to take careful charge of any letters that may come for him and put them away in his portfolio devoted to his private papers, he leaves his apartments, not even awakening Dillon, who is still sleeping the pleasant slumbers of successful and happy manhood.

Somehow or other he doesn't care to look in his friend's face in the light of day, for conscience is singing in his ear: "A note to-morrow!—a note to-morrow!"

Therefore he goes off to make his breakfast at the café in the Rue de Fosses Saint Germain, which is quite convenient to him, and there chances to meet old Poisson, the comedian.

"Monsieur le Comte d'Arnac, I believe," remarks Paul, coming up and making his best bow. Then he grins: "*Parbleu!* you found the niece of Monsieur Lass, Madame O'Brien Dillon, without me, my young friend," next chuckles: "I did not know it was a love affair, or I would have helped you, young Apollo. It is always the rôle of the comedian to assist eloping Romeos and Juliets."

"Sit down and have breakfast with me," says D'Arnac affably, who wishes any company to keep him from his conscience, and drive "A note to-morrow!" from his brain.

The two make quite a comfortable meal of it, Poisson running on with anecdotes of the stage, and telling of the great success of Lecouvreur, the new star at the Française.

"Perhaps I'll have another pupil for you, Monsieur Poisson," laughs Raymond. "I've a young lady—a WARD"—this very sternly, for the comedian is beginning to grin, "who cherishes aspirations for the boards."

"*Ma foi!* another?" gasps Paul. Then he says, meditatively: "If she is as beautiful as the other, and has the same bizarre disposition, she would make as great a success as I once predicted for the charming young lady Monsieur Lass put under my care. But Lass has become the great banker now and has no more use for the poor comedian, save to laugh from his box, as he sits behind the Regent, at the grimaces and antics of Poisson, the actor."

"Perhaps the young lady I am speaking of has as bizarre a disposition," returns Raymond, "though I doubt if she has anything like the beauty."

"No, that were impossible," says Poisson, decidedly.

"Quite so," replies Raymond, agreeing with him, and rising from his seat, he bids the comedian good-bye, then strolls off to the Hotel de Chateaubrien to find a child who has grown into a young lady during his absence, and who has equal graces and fascinations with even *la* Sabran herself, and a very wild and bizarre disposition, but a much better heart.

He enters the hotel to be embraced by the charming Mimi, who has just thrown off her widow's mourning. She says: "Please don't speak to me of Roul," as Raymond mentions her dead husband; then wipes away some pearly tears. Though Roul de Chateaubrien had been much older than his wife, Mimi has one of those natures who, though brilliant in the world, is domestic at the hearthstone. She has given love and affection to her husband when alive and still has tears and regretful remembrance for him, though he has passed away some two years before.

A moment after she says: "Raymond, let us not discuss family matters," for D'Arnac has mentioned the Count de Crevecœur. To-day I have to lay something before you, about which you must take action at once."

"Ah, *la petite* Quinault ?"

"Yes, *la diable* Quinault!"

"What has she done ?"

"What has she not done ? If it had not been for your strict injunctions, mademoiselle would have been on bread and water in the convent cell. She ran away."

"Where ?"

"Here !"

"Here ! This is a frightful place for a young girl !" jeers Raymond.

"But she ran away to go on the stage."

"What stage ?"

"Any stage. She said she would act in a booth rather than live in a convent any longer. She has been here four days and makes me take her to the theatre every night. The mania is in her blood. If she becomes an actress they will not bury her in consecrated ground."

"*Parbleu !* Mademoiselle Jeanne isn't thinking of death but of life," laughs D'Arnac. Then he asks earnestly : "What is she like ?"

"A riddle and a rhapsody ! A fascinating minx that makes me want to slap her one minute and kiss her the next. But come with me," says Mimi. "She is in the library working herself into a tantrum over Racine or Corneille; she gets herself into emotions over tragedies and into good humor over comedies.

"Just look at her!" whispers Madame la Marquise, as Raymond follows her. She points cautiously into

the library, and D'Arnac, glancing at Jeanne Quinault,
stands in delighted surprise.

Jeanne is sitting in an arm-chair, in careless not-care
attitude, one little foot poked under her, the other lying
on a neighboring ottoman, the short skirt of convent
uniform falling from it to disclose as perfect an ankle as
ever delighted man. A ray of sunshine falls upon a
curly head, with bright blue eyes that gaze upon some
book of the emotions, for her face changes as she reads,
and each expression is one of fascinating beauty.

As D'Arnac looks he knows the bud has blossomed,
the chrysalis has become the butterfly, the little Quinault
of three years ago has grown into a woman of rare beauty
and brilliant mind.

Perchance she has not the unearthly loveliness and
enchanting, erratic graces of Hilda de Sabran, but she
has a beauty that is always potent, for it reflects each
charming emotion of her vivacious mind, each rapid
thought of her bright spirit.

As the two glide into her, Jeanne gives proof of this.

With eyes yet bent upon the book she says sulkily:
" Do I still enjoy your hospitality, Madame la Marquise,
or do I go back to the convent ? " and getting no
answer from Raymond, who gazes, and Mimi, who won't
speak, she goes on :   "If I return to *Des Capucines*
I go back a NUN! I can work up a vocation for
anything in five minutes, and if I endure seclusion I
might as well use it to save my soul. Answer, which
shall it be, nun or actress ? " And working herself
into a rage of the imagination she cries: " Answer,
Madame la Marquise! Take your choice! Answer!
Talk! Do something! Scold me! Kiss me! " and
springs up, raising eyes that have tears, half of rage,
half of laughter. Then, seeing D'Arnac, she gives a
semi-pathetic, semi-startled cry.

" I think I'll kiss you! " laughs Raymond.

But she astonishes him. She says: " No! scold
me, I deserve it! Scold me well, *Mon Seigneur !* "
and suddenly courtesies to him and kisses his hand as she
did when he had left her.

"Not my hand, Jeanne, after three years!" cries
D'Arnac. "As your guardian—" He approaches her
quite reverently and tenderly to salute her.

"Then, if it is your pleasure, *Mon Seigneur*," she returns, courtesying, and holds up a rosy cheek quite complaisantly for his welcome. But just as he is kissing, the cheek turns and his salute falls on lips of dewy coral that burst into a merry laugh, and it is the soldier of the army who blushes and not the maid of the convent school.

This blush of Raymond's helps Jeanne win her battle for the stage. Mimi, looking on, does not like it. She notes the wondrous capabilities the girl gives promise of in that indefinite art—called man killing. She thinks: "On the stage Jeanne will have many admirers, in the convent only my brother. She knows that marriage for a D'Arnac with the girl is as practically impossible as it would be for a Bourbon—the line between the blood of the nobles and the blood of the outside herd is drawn stronger than between white blood and black blood; that it would less offend class prejudice for him to wed a negro *princess* than to marry the daughter of the richest tradesman of the city. The sooner Mademoiselle Quinault is on the boards the better—Raymond will not then have her care. Yet all the time Mimi loves the girl, but the hauteur of the *noblesse* died so hard in France it took the guillotine to kill it, and even then it revived, and still, even at this moment, is gasping.

Acting on this impulse Madame de Chateaubrien says playfully but with rare tact: "Now you have kissed her, Raymond, scold Miss Rebel and send her back to the convent."

"Then what would there be in life for me?" cries Jeanne. "Do you wish to leave me in seclusion forever?"

"Oh," answers D'Arnac, lightly, "a year or two more and we'll bring you out and marry you."

"Impossible—I have no *dot!*"

"Monsieur de Villars and myself will look to that.

"You would marry me—to *whom!*" gasps the girl, a curious light coming into her eyes and wild blushes flying over her bright face—"TO WHOM?" She droops her head, but her eyes give one or two bashful but pathetic glances at Raymond that makes his sister shiver and grow pale—they are so enchanting.

Getting no answer, Mademoiselle electrifies them. She cries in a voice hoarse as Medea over Jason's wrongs: "Coward! you dare not speak—you would marry me to a base tradesman! What would I care for the creature's turns in butter or for the price of Lyons velvet and Venice lace, save to make me prettier? But on the stage!" here she becomes enthused—"There I may not be a princess, but I can play one, and for one night think I am of noble birth, and not—not—an outcast with the pride of Lucifer within my veins!"

"An outcast?" mutters Raymond, moved. "How dare you say that to me?"

"What put that outcast idea into your head, Jeanne?" asks Mimi, who is more used to her rhapsodies than her brother.

"The world!"

"The what?" gasps Raymond.

"The convent school! When I told the girls my mother was an actress, my father an acrobat, they said I was a päriah. Then I proved to them the daughter of an acrobat had the arm of an acrobat!" and mademoiselle holds up in triumph a patrician hand and arm, and says: "Behold! with this I slapped them."

"Then you would prefer the Français to the convent?"

"The Français!" screams Jeanne. "The Français—I shall act there—like Lecouvreur whom I saw last night! Oh, *Diable!* but I'll do you honor! Monsieur le Comte d'Arnac shall say that goddess of the boxes, that pride of the pärtêrre belongs to me—her *seigneur*—and kisses my hand—and I will do so each time you come behind the scenes, and bless you, dear Monsieur Raymond, and kiss your hand as I do now, if you will say 'Jeanne, live the only life that is for you—the life of art,'" and she does so on her knees, putting both tears and kisses on his hand, till D'Arnac mutters: "Have your way; it is not I whose life you saved should refuse you anything!"

To this Mimi remarks: "Perhaps it is the best thing for her after all."

"You—you give consent?" cries Jeanne.

"*Diable!* Yes. It is not much will be refused you in this world if you plead for it in that way," laughs Raymond, gazing at the graceful figure kneeling before him.

But it doesn't kneel long.   As he speaks Jeanne flies up crying: "The *artiste* will no longer be degraded by the school-girl's dress!"

"Don't be in such a hurry!" giggles Mimi. "Dresses must be made, and you'll have to study before you triumph."

"Won't I study? Wait! See! I know the *Phèdre* now! Would you like me to recite it, word by word, scene by scene, act by act?"

"*Mon Dieu!*" gasps D'Arnac, nervously, "It is five hours long!"

"Yes, but you can sit down!" cries Jeanne, and places chairs.

These preparations terrify her guardians.

Raymond announces: "I've got to go back to my quarters. My friend, O'Brien Dillon, has just come from Vienna," and Mimi says: "I'll go and make arrangements for your tutelage, my embryo artiste; I think Mademoiselle Desmares would like a pupil."

"That means you imagine I will not be a *tragedienne*," pouts Miss Quinault.

"Nonsense Fly-away!" laughs Madame la Marquise. "With your bright face and piquant manners, the audience will love you too well to see you suffer!"

"Very well! bring Desmares here, and I'll astonish her!" cries Jeanne, with the true modesty of all great artists.

At which Mimi and Raymond burst into a laugh that makes the *comedienne's* eyes flash all the fires of tragedy, as the two depart on their various errands.

"Do you think," says Madame la Marquise to her brother, as he stands with her in the vestibule of her hotel, awaiting the driving up of her carriage, "that she will make a success, she has such a bizarre disposition?"

"That is one of the things that will do it!" returns Raymond. "I had a talk with old Poisson, of the Français, this morning, and he says uncontrollable emotions generally go with the great triumphs of the stage."

"Then she will be one of the wonders of the theatre!" laughs Mimi. A moment after she says: "You mentioned the return of your friend, the Irish Colonel, the man who saved your life at Friburg. He has come back unscathed from the Turkish war?"

"Yes; a general and a count. Now we are indeed brothers!" remarks D'Arnac. Then his face grows serious as he adds: "I must go back to my quarters at once," and strides rapidly towards the Rue Christine, for "A note to-morrow!" is once more ringing in his brain.

As he walks he meditates, and to one thing definitely makes up his mind; that is, he will burn the letter unread. It is the only way he can put temptation from him; and every sentiment of manhood compels his honor to his old friend. No matter what Hilda may be to other men she shall be nothing to Raymond d'Arnac.

This relieves his mind. He comes up the stairs quite cheerily into his apartments, and, seeing his old comrade seated there with happy face, cries out: "Ah, the world has treated you well to-day!"

Then O'Brien Dillon gives him his answer, and it carries with it one of the greatest *coups de theatre* of his life.

"By my soul!" cries the Irishman, "I'm the happiest man on earth! I went to hunt up my Uncle Johnny at his bank, but could not find him. He was away, busied about that new company he has formed—the India one, they call it—that is to turn all the wealth of the Canadas and Louisiana into Uncle Johnny's capacious maw, though he expresses it, 'into the lap of France.' Not seeing him there Lanty and I engaged a private billiard-room, and had a very pleasant time of it.

"Between ourselves, for this is a great secret, practicing the new stroke in billiards that Lanty has invented. Ah, it's a wonderful one! When first Lanty did it for me, I grabbed him by the throat to strangle the divil out of him, for I thought that old Satan himself was in him, the ball rolled so curious. But he explained it to me when I let him get his breath back, saying it was merely a new law of forces. Something he had discovered kicking cannon balls about when he had nothing better to do, and we were cooped up before Belgrade by the Turks. Faith, it's a stroke a man can win a million on if he plays it properly. It's better

than loaded dice, or Uncle Johnny's pharo combina-
tions.

"And then I came here, my boy, to receive the great
joy of my life. This letter of love from my darling
wife!"

With this, he hands the astounded Raymond a note,
and there are happy tears in the Irishman's eyes as the
Frenchman reads as follows:

My Darling :
    God knows how I have looked for—longed for this—your
return after years of absence—your return in spite of those who
would keep us apart. How I bless your brave heart for daring
to come to Paris for my sake ! But now I think we are strong
enough together to at least brave those who would separate us,
though they tore me from your arms. In my imagination, I
see you now as you fought for me.
    Come at ten o'clock this evening to the Rue des Bonnes
Enfants by the side of the gardens of the Palais Royal. There
my maid will meet you, and bring you to me, and your heart,
as it once did, shall beat against that of
                                    Your loving
                                        Hilda.

With a start, Raymond turns to the envelope, thinking, by some wild mistake, his note has been opened by
his friend. But the address reads plainly:

                    To
                General Comte Dillon,
                        Rue Christine,
Private. Immediate.   Paris.

He knows it is some marvelous error, but blesses
God that every word written to him might apply to
Hilda's husband.

Yet, filled with curiosity and wonder, such are the
vagaries of passion, D'Arnac chews his moustachios
very glumly, as O'Brien descants with excited eyes on
the marvelous beauty of his peer among women—
his heart's darling, who has come once more into his
life.

And so they sit down to dinner, Raymond eating but
little, under the plea of a heavy breakfast. But O'Brien,
pouring down the wine in generous bumpers and shouting every now and again: "A health to the beautiful
goddess of delight! Drink hearty, Raymond, my boy,

to the second honeymoon of General Comte O'Brien Dillon!"

Whereon, Raymond puts the glass to his lips, but the wine seems to him very sour vinegar.

CHAPTER XIX.

THE SECOND HONEYMOON OF O'BRIEN DILLON.

CURIOUSLY enough, this extraordinary complication has been brought about by Cousin Charlie. Monsieur le Procureur du Roy has also had buzzing in his brain· "A note to-morrow!" and has made his preparations accordingly.

Knowing very well the habits of fine ladies, he guesses that Madame de Sabran will rise quite late after the Regent's supper, and determines the note for his cousin will arrive not earlier than one o'clock in the day.

A little before this hour he sends a lackey of his (whom he has used before on similar doubtful errands) with distinct instructions to get hold of D'Arnac's servants and lure them away to a neighboring wine shop.

This is easily done, and shortly after one o'clock Monsieur de Moncrief takes post in Raymond's apartments to receive his mail.

There is no one to hinder him, Dillon and Lanty being out, and the two lackeys of D'Arnac at present engaged in playing dominoes and drinking *Chianti* at a wine shop in the neighboring Rue de Savoye, in company with Cousin Charlie's man, who is very liberally paying the score.

After perchance an hour's uneasy vigil, in comes a little blackamoor servant of Madame de Sabran, ladies of fashion making quite a fad of Ethiopian attachés in 1717.

This creature says in his darkey dialect: "A not-tie for Moussou de Arnack."

"Quite right," returns le Procureur, "these are Monsieur d'Arnac's apartments!" and takes the missive.

Then a wicked twinkle comes into his eyes, as he makes young dark skin happy by giving him a crown with which to buy *bon bons*.

And Blackamoor going off in pursuit of his loved sweets, Charles de Moncrief looks at the address:

To

GENERAL COMTE D'ARNAC,
RUE CHRISTINE,
PARIS.

Private. Immediate.

After a moment's consideration he chuckles to himself: "It will not be difficult to change 'D'Arnac' to 'Dillon!' The Irishman is a soldier and not a scribe, and his deception will be an easy one."

This he does, simulating quite correctly in the few letters he has to make on the envelope the handwriting of the fair De Sabran.

Leaving this note upon the table, in prominent position, where it will catch Dillon's eye when he returns, Cousin Charlie departs, meditating: "I wonder if this will be the quietus of dear boy Raymond!"

But after dinner, being desperately anxious to find out what has been the outcome of the Irish officer's perusal of his wife's note to his bosom friend and comrade, De Moncrief, unable to contain his curiosity, knocks at the door of Raymond's apartments, cogitating: "I doubt not the wild Irishman has killed Cousin Raymond by this time, and gone off to slay that Venus, his wife, who boxed her Cupid's cheeks!"

His eagerness makes his ears alert. The noise of hilarity comes to him through the door. He starts, astonished, but is petrified, as the portal opens to find both gentlemen dining apparently very amicably together.

"Ah! They are doing the thing *en gentlehomme*. They will drink wine with each other to-night, and cross rapiers by to-morrow's morning light," he guesses.

He has heard very good accounts of Dillon's sword-play, and has great hopes that Raymond will not escape the Irishman's vengeance.

So, with his finest bow, De Moncrief begs to be introduced to the celebrated officer, of whom he has heard so much. "*Parbleu*, General," he remarks, on presentation, "D'Arnac has been full of nothing but your conduct on the Rhine, and you have been even more successful among the Turks! I admire your diamonds!"

For Dillon, having rigged himself out for the re-conquest of his blushing bride, is literally ablaze with brilliants he has ravished from the Turkish Vizier.

But now he fairly paralyzes the Procureur with amazement, for he cries out, in his genial Irish brogue: "Sit down and join us! Monsieur de Moncrief, a glass of wine to the health of the fairest woman in France—Madame la Comtesse Dillon!"

At these words the Procureur's knees give way under him. He sinks into a chair and says faintly: "The health of—of Madame la Comtesse Dillon!" for Lanty has filled a goblet for him.

Then, though the wine tastes sour to him, as it does to Raymond, he tries to put on great show of merriment, and attempts a faint joke with the serving Lanty, asking him if Lanty is not the short for Lancelot.

"No, it's Irish for Lanigan!" cries Lanty, at which they all grow merry.

"Faith, I must stop laughing and get on my way," remarks O'Brien. "De Moncrief, I'll tell you the story of my wars with the Turks the next time I see you."

"Indeed! you are in a hurry?" falters Charlie, greatly disappointed, seeing there is no quarrel between the friends.

"Bedad, there's a lady waiting for me," answers the Irish General with a knowing wink.

"Ah," ejaculates the Procureur returning the ogle, "a fair one *so soon?*"

"Yes, and by my soul, MY WIFE! Look at that letter!" cries Dillon, full of wine and joy. "Isn't that a lovely *billet doux* for a man's return to Paris?" And he holds up in triumph the missive Cousin Charlie has prepared for his eyes, to drive him mad for blood with jealous despair, that has brought great joy unto the innocent Irishman's soul of souls.

Gazing at the note De Moncrief is very much tempted to tell the truth of the matter, which would put these two men to flying at each other's throats. But, words that come to him now, make him pause, not daring to give the hint.

As Dillon has risen from the table, Lanty has suddenly brought in sword and pistols to him, saying: "My lord, had I better take mine and follow ye?"

Then he whispers: "Ye know something happened to
ye the last time you saw her!"

"Not a word, Lanty, against the good faith of the
woman who loves me!" cries the General—passion in
his eyes. "Didn't she explain to Raymond here how
old Uncle Johnny had betrayed me, and she was
trying to save me? Do you think I'd ever doubt her
truth to me with this lovely letter in my hand? I'll
take sword and pistol as gentlemen should do when out
at night; but by the soul of Saint Patrick! I have as
much faith in her who is coming to my arms, as I have
in Heaven!"

So he strides off, joy in his honest eyes, leaving D'Arnac smoking his pipe glumly, and the
Procureur du Roy with some very evil curses that
tremble upon his lips, though he does not utter them.

A moment after Raymond rises and says: "You'll
excuse me, Cousin, but I think I'll return to the Hotel
de Chateaubrien, and see what arrangements my sister
has made for placing Mademoiselle Jeanne upon the
stage."

"Ha, you have seen her!" ejaculates De Moncrief.

"Yes," answers D'Arnac, and after a minute goes
on his errand, leaving the Procureur gazing after him
and thinking: "One string to my bow is broken, but
voila! here is another! Egad! Raymond has fallen down
before a new goddess. Even as my cousin now walks
the streets, he is thinking of the charms of Mademoi-.
selle Jeanne."

But as he strides along, Raymond d'Arnac is not thinking of the charms of Mademoiselle Jeanne. The
perspiration of anguish, of disappointment, of regret,
is on his brow. He is sighing over the ineffable loveliness that would have been his had not his friend returned
to claim it.

While this is taking place, the happy victor of this
evening's game of chance, O'Brien Dillon, is slashing
over the streets of Paris whistling a merry air. His
sanguine temperament, once nearly crushed by disappointment and misfortune, under the sun of success
beams on every one who crosses his path.

Even the charlatans of the Pont Neuf receive kind words
and jingling coins from him. He jokes with the venders

of wooden legs, and buys a box of perfumed powder for
Madame la Comtesse Dillon from an imploring
huckster. "Not that she'll need it, for her skin is like
lilies and roses," he laughs; "but it will show her I
thought of her even in battle, I'll inform her I captured
it in the Vizier's tent, for her own beautification, and
that it was much used by the ladies of the harem, to
give them complexions pleasing to the Sultan. Perhaps
the darling would rather have diamonds, though," cogitates the General, looking at the gems that make him
glitter.

In this he is about right, for Hilda will undoubtedly
pounce on the brilliants before the face powder.

So, jostling his way on through the crowds of Paris,
under the lighted oil lamps of the Rue St. Honoré, he
shortly after turns into the Rue des Bonnes Enfants,
and striding down that street comes to its secluded part,
opposite the gardens of the Palais Royal.

Then, after looking about eagerly for some little time,
he steps up to a very pretty maid servant, who is apparently on post at this point, and chucking her under the
chin, laughs : "Rosalie, don't you know your old
master ?"

And the girl turns to him wondering eyes that grow
affrighted, as she gasps : "Major O'Brien Dillon !"

"Faith, I'm glad you remember me, though I'm a
general now !" says O'Brien happily. "But take me
to your mistress, for by my soul I'm as anxious to get
kiss of her as she is of me !"

"My mistress!" gasps the girl.

"Yes, your mistress, who sent me this little note,
telling me to meet you here at ten o'clock, and I would
be taken to her apartments. Your mistress, my wife—
Madame la Comtesse Dillon."

"La Comtesse D—Dillon!" stammers the maid,
who is the one that served Hilda in the Low Countries.

"Don't you understand, ye little addlepate,"
answers the Irishman, for on seeing Dillon's face
Rosalie has grown very stupid, perchance from
fright. "Ah, if I had known you would be here,
I should have brought Mr. Lanty along with me.
Faith, the disappointment of the fellow will be terrible
when I tell him that it was his little Rosalie that met

me here. But Lanty's chance will come afterwards. Quick! run along. Can't you see I'm as impatient a husband as ever came back from war; aye, and the happiest. I think I could love a Turk at this moment."

This rigmarole gives the quick-witted Rosalie time to reflect. He certainly has the note. She knows O'Brien Dillion's impetuous nature. She dare not tell him it is a mistake.

So, with eyes big with astonishment, and a slight snicker that will force itself through Rosalie's pretty lips, she gasps: "This way!"

And he, accompanying her through one or two neighboring streets, Mademoiselle Rosalie taps three times, very cautiously, at the side entrance of a magnificent residence.

Then the door being opened to her, she dashes in, followed by the Irish officer, but being more familiar with the place distances him, and running into a magnificent apartment ablaze with light and decorated and adorned with pictures by the finest artists, and statues of the greatest sculptors, bric-à-brac from Sevres and glass from Bohemia, she cries out loudly and in commanding tone of voice: "I ANNOUNCE GENERAL O'BRIEN DILLON!"

And a lady, fair as Venus rising from the sea, springs up with a wild cry.

But before she can say anything a pair of stalwart arms clasp her to a broad breast, and showering kisses upon lips that grow pale with every emotion under the sun, astonishment predominating, O'Brien Dillon gasps: "God bless you, wife of my heart! Your husband has at last come to you through the dangers of battle—rich and honored—from the land of the Turk!"

And how is he answered?

At first by gasping sighs and trembling shudders and rolling eyes, for astonishment, disappointment, and, above all, astounded fury, would make his new found spouse faint in his arms if he would let her; but O'Brien comes of sterner stuff. "No fainting," he cries, "when there's kissing to do, MADAME LA COMTESSE DILLON!"

This unexpected title gives the lady another shock that partially revives her, though her husband's strong arms still squeeze half the breath from her delicate body, and his impulsive kisses upon her sighing lips consume the other portion.

O'Brien's ardor does the rest.

Under his caresses, she who had grown dazed and clammy with astounded shock and mysterious fear at the sudden substitution of this husband she thought dead on the banks of the Danube, in place of the living man for whose coming she had been waiting anxious as Leda for her swan, grows warm and sentient.

With one great wave the blood flies to limbs that were cold and trembling. The statue that was marble takes glowing life and color. Hilda awakes to the situation in all its embarrassing vivacity.

"It — is — real!" she gasps.

"Is *that* real?" laughs O'Brien. "By my soul, can't ye believe your own happiness? Won't *that* prove it, wife of my heart? Isn't *that* and THAT pleasing and convincing evidence?" These "thats" are all long, strong kisses that have lost no charm or potency by their four years' waiting.

"Y-e-s, I recognize them," gasps Hilda. Then she lisps with most coquettish *moue:* "They— they have the same tobacco flavor."

Under them Hilda throws off the last daze of unreality.

O'Brien can't be dead; never were specter's kisses so vivid, so fascinating.

They are not those she has been longing for, but they are enchanting all the same, not because they are her husband's, for laws of God or man have little to do with this lady's vagaries, but while *he* has been caressing, *she* has been gazing.

Before her stands even a handsomer fellow than the O'Brien Dillon of her Flanders honeymoon.

His mien has grown that of one accustomed to command; his fine, stalwart figure, decked with the full uniform of an Austrian general, and blazing with the diamonds of the Turk, looks imposing, distinguished and dominating to Madame Erratic as she inspects him—in her soul one supreme wonder—how did this occur.

His frankness soon elucidates the affair. " Darling,"
he whispers, " if you are dazed with joy, haven't I been
mad with delight ever since I got your dear little note ? "
and waves the *billet doux* before her rolling eyes.

"You—got—my letter ? " she ejaculates.

Then astonishes herself, as she mutters, "Thank
God!" for his kisses have made Madame Inconstant
love him the most—*for a little while.*

In her first burst of disappointment she could have
slain the unfortunate little blackamoor to whom
she attributes the miscarriage of her letter, but as she
gazes and O'Brien kisses, she could shower young dark
skin with favors and bon bons.

"Look at the darling little love note," runs on Dillon,
thrusting the missive under her eyes.

Thus cajoled she examines the epistle, and finding
that the address has been changed by some deft hand,
knows she owes her unexpected surprise to some other
than her page.

For one instant she thinks perchance it is Raymond, and anathematizes him between her teeth at
this insult to her charms. The next instant Vanity
says, " It can't be he—he loves me now as well as he
did at Mieux. His eyes told me that last night."

But still she goes to questioning: " Did you show
this to any one, *dear* O'Brien ? "

" To only one—my bosom friend—the man who tried
to take you to me in Vienna," answers Dillon. "But
I *told* every one. Faith, do you think a man can have
a joy like this and keep from shouting ? " and he goes
on, with pride and love in his eyes, and gives her an
account of the affair at which she wonders.

But while O'Brien is talking she has been charming
him with little coy, wifely caresses and attentions that
put him in the Seventh Heaven of the Ottoman.

He looks round the room. Its ceiling is frescoed
into gayest cupids and brightest goddesses, and its
pictures and works of art, its statuettes of ivory and
marble, are all of delicate designs; its draperies and
hangings of lightest silks and satins—the fit boudoir for
a goddess, and that goddess *his!*

The place would seem dreamy were it not for the
vivacious loveliness it enshrines.

For Hilda this evening is robed for the conquest of man, and the allurements prepared for Raymond drive Dillon wild with rapture.

He whispers: "You made yourself purty, all for me, ye darling," and sits enthralled, for somehow he knows she must love the man for whom she is arrayed.

Her full evening dress has the suggestions of *tête à tête*. It seems less for the ballroom than for the man she loves—and him ONLY.

It is some coquettish, gauzy texture that drapes over her short, glimmering satin skirt and makes her ethereal but not celestial.

Her neck, arms and bosom gleam above it with ivory effects. In it she is a fairy Cleopatra.

"Tell me," she whispers, as she returns his kisses, "how you slew the Turks, my hero. I saw you fight *once*."

The admiration in her eyes enraptures Dillon. "Which of 'em?" he laughs, "the Vizier or the Pasha or those beasts of Janissaries?"

"*He of the Diamonds!*"

"Ha, trust your roguish little eyes for catching their sparkle," chuckles O'Brien. "Upon my knee, little wifey, and I'll tell ye of the Vizier."

Then a graceful fairy perches herself upon the warrior, and twining her fair fingers into his great red whiskers, laughs, "Tell me, Big General!"

Thus coaxed, he gives her his story of the Danube, explaining how he caught the Vizier all for her, and that his diamonds were worth half a million crowns and his ransom eighty thousand more, "For which, by the bye, I've drafts on me Uncle Johnny," adds Dillon, caustically.

A moment after he mutters: "I suppose I must postpone killing him till after he's paid my checks."

"Of course," murmurs Hilda. Then she grows more serious and suggests that Uncle Johnny has been very kind to her.

"How? By separating you from me?"

"No, but he has made *me* rich; this house is *mine*."

"Is it?" chuckles O'Brien. "Then his giving *me* a palace is one thing in his favor. I may let him off with the loss of an arm or leg."

"Oh," says Madame Hilda, pouting, for this easy assumption of marital rights over her property is not altogether to her liking, "you must do better than that."

"How ?."

"You must forgive Uncle Johnny. He has given me more. I've any quantity of stock in the bank and lots of India securities."

"Then, if the stocks are to my liking, and there's enough of 'em, I may let him live," utters Dillon, growing benign under her blandishments, "though I had sworn to have my Uncle Johnny's blood."

"You will spare him! Brava!" cries Hilda. "Then I ll dance for you in—in—in YOUR DIAMONDS!" and claps her pretty hands at the idea, as if it was a very novel, original and pleasing one.

Next jumping up she whispers: "You remember how you liked to see my twinkling feet, dear O'Brien, in the good old days. I'll dance for you in the diamonds of the Turk."

"Not unless ye let me pin them on yer lovely figure myself!" cries the doting Dillon.

This luxury the lady coquettishly and coyly permits him, and he soon has her sparkling like the stars in Heaven.

The great crescent and its smaller star are blazing upon her fair forehead, and jewels are twinkling from out her hair, and flashing on her rounded arms and gleaming neck and ivory bosom with dazzling luster, though even their radiance adds little to a beauty that is supreme, as she steps before him for the dance.

With one swing, for this lady likes theatrical effects, she tosses the gauzes of her overdress all sparkling with jewels about her, waving it as a scarf, and tucking up her shining white satin petticoat, makes her fascinating feet trip the measure of a dashing little *sarabande* till the enthusiastic Dillon cries: "Brava!" and stops her with enraptured kisses.

"Faith, you're like the Goddess Terpsichore herself!" he laughs. "You look so beauteous in those diamonds ye shall *always* wear them!"

An idea that has entered Hilda's brain before his.

"Sure, I'm happy enough to dance an Irish jig to-night, myself," cries the general, "in my own house with my own wife, after my return from all the dangers of battle."

"Yes, we must take good care of our valuables now," suggests Hilda; "though, of course, they are safe in your own house, *dear* O'Brien."

"My valuables! sure, haven't I them all in my arms! What more do I have?"

"Your drafts on Uncle Johnny!" laughs his adored.

And at her suggestion the doting Dillon entrusts to her all his orders upon the bank of Monsieur Lass, obtained from the ransom of the Turkish Vizier, as he has already given her his diamonds. Locking these documents up in a little safe Madame Hilda has for her jewelry and trinkets, the lady presently suggests supper.

"Ah, bedad, you haven't forgotten my weakness, Hilda!" laughs O'Brien. "When I'm not making love or fighting I'm eating or drinking."

So putting a strong arm round her fairy waist the Irish officer escorts his spouse to the dining-room, where a delightful *petit souper* has been prepared—but *not* for him: O'Brien drinking libation after libation to the Comtesse Dillon.

During this fête a little comedy scene takes place.

Rosalie is in attendance upon them—a mass of wondering eyes and suppressed giggles.

"Sure, any one would know this little banquet was got up for the man you love, my darling!" says the General, attacking a *pâté de Strassburg.* "You've even remembered my favorite champagne."

On this unexpected announcement Mademoiselle Rosalie, unable to contain herself, flits out of the room and goes into hysterics in the neighboring pantry.

But an awful contretemps follows after—one that might in a breath have become a tragedy.

The general making himself at home, seeing the little blackamoor in an adjoining apartment, cries: "Come here!" And the boy entering, he addresses him with the ease of the master of the house: "Sambo, what's your name?"

"Apollo!"

"Well then, Apollo, my shoes at nine in the morning, and don't forget to burnish my silver buckles. You know me?"

"Yes, Moussou," returns Apollo, "you'se the gen'leman I brought de nottie to—you'se Moussou the Comte D——"

But Rosalie is behind the boy and her quick fingers grip his neck destroying utterance and the latter part of the name is destroyed, as she whirls Blackamoor away, crying: "Remember your master's boots at nine, lazy Apollo!"

"Faith, he knows me," laughs the general, and turning eyes upon Hilda, he exclaims: "Darling of me heart, what's the matter?"

She is trembling and her face is white, for she thinks: "If he discovers now—he'll kill me!" As indeed he would.

"Only my—my sudden happiness," she gasps. "I —I thought if the Turks had slain you."

"Be Saint Patrick! you need have no more fears, my shivering lamb!" replies O'Brien, "now that thy lord and master has come home."

"My master?" says Cleopatra looking at him with open eyes.

"Aye! thy master!" returns Dillon, taking playfully her fairy ear between his great thumb and finger. "The master who'll love you and RULE you, Madame la Comtesse Dillon."

And this turn though it astonishes her, pleases her; her volatile spirit has grown tired of adulation and deference from sycophantic courtiers and even the Regent of France.

"Then I am my lord's obedient handmaid!" she whispers, and gives him a mocking courtesy of deference, but all the time she looks up at her big Irish warrior as Cleopatra looked at Julius Cæsar when she was his slave and did his bidding—not as Cleopatra gazed at Antony whom she commanded and destroyed.

The Marc Antony business came afterwards!

And in this attitude, as she drapes her robes about her to give grace to her movement of obeisance, she looks perchance more alluring than the Eastern queen.   One little hand is extended to her conqueror, the other drawing back the glistening skirt from a foot sandaled with pale blue satin and an ankle gleaming like pinkest coral through its weblike silken hose.   Her lips parted with a little sigh of delight, her blue eyes beaming, her arms and shoulders gleaming in the light, and over all the charm of ineffable but indescribable coquetry.

Looking at this, her Irish lord whispers: "By Venus and the Muses, I'd go through a hundred battles of Belgrade for such a SECOND HONEYMOON!"

At his words, this fairy Cleopatra becomes a blushing Goddess of Love.

CHAPTER XX.

O'BRIEN DILLON AT HOME.

THUS it comes about that early in the next forenoon, pretty little Rosalie Lutin trips up to D'Arnac's apartments, to the joy of Lanty, who gives wild yells of delight on seeing her, and promptly inflicts kisses upon her, by way of punishment, for not notifying him she was still with her old mistress.

"By all the powers of the other world, if I had known ye were the little darling that was going to meet the general, and take him to Paradise, faix I'd have been knocking at the gates behind him, my darling. Did ye come here to bring me a kiss? Yer mistress knew me master was in town yesterday; why couldn't ye have been of an equally inquiring disposition?"

"My mistress knew of your master's being in town yesterday?" giggles the girl.

"'Deed an' she did.   Didn't she send him the prettiest little note in the world, to bid him to come to her? Bedad! you ought to have seen him showing it in triumph to his friend, the Count d'Arnac."

At this announcement, little Rosalie cannot refrain from shrieks of uncontrollable laughter. Finally checking this, though she still holds her sides, she says: "I have been sent over to bid you follow me to your master's new home, with all his baggage and belongings He says his wife has a house fit for a prince, and it's a long time since he's been under his own roof, and he'll stay there."

"Fortunately it is not much baggage we have!" remarks Lanty, "only two hand valises and this little belt I carry strapped round my waist. We military gentlemen travel light."

Seeing a look of disdain upon Rosalie's face at this paucity of *impedimenta*, the Irishman adds: "Sure there's many a duke would like to travel with this little belt of mine. Bedad, it contains half a million ducats' worth of diamonds when the general is not wearing them."

"Yours?" cries Rosalie, matrimony beaming in her eye.

"No, the general's!"

"Oh!" quite disappointedly. Then a moment after she laughs: "Won't my mistress be delighted!"

"Divil doubt she will when she sees 'em! Many's the duchess would have liked to have *married* our plunder when we came back from Belgrade!" mutters Lanty, making his preparations. Then giving word of his master's orders to D'Arnac, he departs, followed by a couple of serving men he has picked up, carrying the luggage, and with little Rosalie trotting complacently by his side.

But on the walk over, apparently the secret in her pretty mind is so amusing, so side-splitting, that she cannot keep it entirely to herself, for Lanty all this day, on seeing D'Arnac or his master, looks at them with very curious eyes, and sometimes unable to contain himself, walks out of the room, and indulges in tremendous guffaws, whistles, and such irreverent and ambiguous remarks as: "Wirra! was there iver known the like of it?" "By me soul, it must have been the divil's own surprise to that enchantress!" "What will become of us?" "Good Lord! if the general iver knows, they'll be butcherin' each other!"

But O'Brien Dillon's advent into Paris produces new and curious effects upon other people than his servant.

Monsieur Lass, desiring to see Madame Hilda, to ask her to use her influence to gain an additional concession from the Regent for his India Company that he

. and De Conti have organized shortly before this, and which embodies the main scheme of this gentleman, to ultimately get control of the finances of France, his bank being merely a stepping stone to this, drives to Madame de Sabran's residence to receive a shock that makes even his cool brain reel.

Entering this lady's house, perchance a little unceremoniously, he is received by Madame Hilda, who comes to greet him in most enchanting morning *négligé*, her eyes very bright, her cheeks perchance a little blushing but wonderfully radiant and fair, as she astounds him with these impulsive words: "'Uncle Johnny,' congratulate me! I am once more a happy bride."

"What do you mean?" says Lass hurriedly, for her appearance indicates a curious change has come over this volatile lady.

"What do I mean? I mean he who called you 'Uncle Johnny,' has arrived."

"*Diable!*" mutters Lass, growing pale, for no man on this earth, save the Irish Major, had ever applied such a term to him. Then after a moment he steadies himself and laughs: "This is some joke of yours, Miss Badinage—you don't mean it!"

"I mean O'Brien Dillon has come back to me a general in the Austrian service and Count of the Empire. And, furthermore, he has brought back the plunder of the Grand Vizier and his harem with him, and blazes with diamonds worth half a million ducats. In fact," continues Hilda, perchance a little maliciously, "I think he would be just the person to subscribe for the stock of the new India Company that we are getting up —my husband and I will make investment!"

"Your husband?"

"Yes!" Here she astounds him. "The husband who has come back to my arms—*the husband that I love!*"

"The husband that you *love!* You love too many," sneers Lass savagely.

"But this one I ADORE. This one I have determined to KEEP."

"For how long?" mutters the financier sulkily. Then he goes on, affecting lightness: "Pooh! it is some little *jeu d'esprit* of yours. *Ma belle*—you are telling me a fairy tale."

" Is that a fairy tale ? " laughs Hilda, throwing open a portière.

And "Uncle Johnny's" knees knock together and tremble under him as he sees, seated in the most comfortable armchair in the house, the one devoted to the use of the Regent himself, in all the domestic content of home, the wild Irishman, who, he knows, has sworn to kill him, taking his ease in dressing-gown and slippers, and enjoying with that comfort peculiar to a man's own hearthstone a long pipe made fragrant with the fumes of smoking Virginia tobacco.

"Come in, my Uncle Johnny!" cries O'Brien affably. "All's well that ends well! And faith I've forgiven you, though it was hard work; but the dear creature pleaded for you, and told me of the great things you had done for her, and how you had made her rich by bank stock, and were giving her a great chance in your India scheme.   Bedad! What is hers is mine, so I thank you for it. *Sapristi!* as your treachery to me only drove me to the Turks to capture a vizier loaded down with diamonds, and get a ransom from him of eighty thousand ducats, by my soul! you need not be frightened of me!"

For at the sight the financier has started back astounded and aghast.

"Come in, and have a bite with us," continues the General hospitably.   "We're just finishing breakfast, and the Comtesse Dillon will be happy to receive you and do the honors."

He waves the astounded financier to a seat, for like most Irishmen, O'Brien Dillon has that peculiar faculty of accepting the good things the gods have given to him, very much as if he deserved it, and along with his wife he has taken possession of the grand mansion (given to this lady by the Regent, though he does not know it, and furnished with all the taste, and splendor, and lavishness of the Royal Exchequer) as easily as if he had earned it by the sweat of his brow, or the blows of his sword.

But the gentleman he speaks to is a man of equal presence of mind and resources.

Monsieur Lass comes in, claps O'Brien lightly on the shoulder and says: "I'm happy to see you. As you suggest—let bygones be bygones. I did what I thought best for my niece's interests; but as you have won a title, and she accepts you again, I have nothing more to say."

Then he runs on, a twinkle in his keen grey eyes: "We had supposed you dead. News had come that you had fallen at the battle of Belgrade!" And there is an attempted sigh in his voice as he murmurs: "Hilda, this will be hard news for the young Duke."

"Oh, divil doubt it!" laughs O'Brien. "There will always be plenty of moths after such a flaming light as this!" and he points to Hilda, who is even more charming in the *négligé* of the morning, with its alluring laces, lawns, and broideries, and flowaway sleeves and float away train, to give ruffled petticoat and delicate hosiery and petite slippers a chance, than she had been in the full dress of the evening before.

So they all sit down together, Monsieur Lass kindly taking a pipe to accompany the Comte of the Empire.

Soon they are a merry party.

For on hearing O'Brien's account of his darling's note that had come to him telling him of a waiting wife, and how he had popped into the house to find himself just as much at home as if he had been born there, Monsieur Lass gives one or two piercing glances at Hilda that bring color to her cheeks, and though he strives to fight them down, for the life of him cannot help tears of merriment.

On this, the newly made Comtesse covers her confusion by bursts of laughter at Dillon's story, and O'Brien joins with her from very pride and joy.

"Yes, your return home must have been a delight to Madame Hilda!" giggles the financier, his eyes twinkling and his thin lips smiling the cold smile of the man who discerns.

A little after, however, the Irish benedict puts this doting spouse in a pet and makes Monsieur Lass very meditative. Chancing to have no lighter convenient for his pipe, O'Brien, after the easy manner of a man in his own house, picks up a sheet of paper lying upon a neighboring table, and is about to make use of it.

"Not that!" cries Hilda, suddenly. "It's a poem —a great poem in manuscript!"

"Faith, I always loved the muses!" remarks Dillon, easily, and commences to peruse the document; but soon bursts out very much after the manner of a man who is determined to be the head of his own household. "What's this I see?" he says. "A poem to the beauteous Madame de Sabran, by Poinsinet?"

"Yes," remarks Monsieur Lass. "He is one of the foremost *littérateurs* of the day; he wrote the celebrated poem called 'The Circle.'"

"Then he could put his pen to better use than writing up, with so much ardor, the beauties of that baggage Sabran! I have heard of her. Bedad! in Vienna they call her 'The Princess of Paris.' She's the Regent's jade." And Dillon coolly crumples up in his big hand the verses Monsieur d'Orleans had paid Poinsinet to write to the charms of his adored, and uses them to ignite his tobacco.

"Take a light yourself, Uncle Johnny!" he says, complacently. "Up go the charms of the naughty minx in smoke!"

At this Lass gives two horrible suppressed gasps of laughter, and remarks: "Don't you know that Madame de Sabran is the most beautiful woman in Paris?"

"No, she's not," cries O'Brien, stoutly "the most beautiful woman in Paris is *there!*" and he points to Hilda, who is blushing, yet biting her lips till they bleed. "I will defend the charms of the Comtesse Dillon against those of any other woman in the world, with sword and pistol. Faith, who should be a better judge of her beauty than her husband?"

"Quite true!" replies Lass. "Though they say that Madame de Sabran looks very much like the Comtesse Dillon."

"Yes, and the nearer she comes to her, the more lovely the baggage will be!" answers the uxurious Irishman, turning admiring eyes upon the beautiful face that is opposite him, which is now a mass of blushes mingled with uneasy laughter.

A moment after O'Brien goes on quite dictatorially, for he has been used to command in camp, and does not propose to give up his epaulettes when in his own house: "Comtesse Dillon, I have a slight suspicion that you know this Madame de Sabran. Do you?"

"Yes," stammers Hilda, "s-s-slightly."

At which Uncle Johnny gives a hideous chuckle under his breath.

"Now I think of it," cries Dillon, "as I was poking about one of your bureaux this morning looking for a place to store my extra uniform, I ran across an envelope addressed to her. Are you intimate with this Madame de Sabran?" -

"Y-e-es!" This is a half sigh from the lady addressed.

"Great powers! Mayhap she visits you."

"Sometimes!" giggles Lass, the smoke from his pipe seeming to get into his throat and stifle him about this time.

"Then, Hilda, you have my commands," continues Dillon, "Madame de Sabran is never to put her naughty foot in this house again. I'll not have the Comtesse Dillon associating with the likes of her. You hear me?" for Hilda has given a half gesture of dissent at his words. "THAT SETTLES IT!"

And Comte Dillon goes on smoking placidly, and believes it does settle it, though a hasty glance that passes between Hilda and Monsieur Lass, means that IT SETTLES HIM!

For the financier's look is very serious, and the Comtesse Dillon's eyes are blazing, her face crimson, and her little foot in its silken stocking and petite slipper is beating a devil's tattoo on the rug beneath it. She has not been accustomed to being dictated to by the Regent of France, and does not take it very kindly from her new found lord and master.

A few remarks of the latter tend to precipitate his fate.

He casually insinuates that in a day or two he'll take his wife's fortune under his protection—women are better on an allowance.

"Not that I'll stint ye, my darling—but home is the place for ladies who love their lords, and they think all the more of their husbands if they have to ask them when they want extra folderols," he generously adds.

This makes Madame Hilda pout and bite her red lips at a great rate.

In tne next breath, the doting husband announces after a month or two of the delights of Paris he shall take the Comtesse Dillon back with him to Vienna, to show her beauty at the Imperial court. "*Parbleu!*" he remarks, "that will be a hint to a certain archduchess, of the reason that O'Brien Dillon never had eyes for her entreating glances."

A little of this makes the conversation lag, for Hilda seems to have gone into a brown study, and Uncle Johnny's pipe goes out very often as he smokes it meditatively.

The Irishman finds he is doing all the talking himself, and very shortly suggests: "Comtesse Dillon, my darling, run and get your doting husband's coat. I'm bursting to tell my good fortune to my friend D'Arnac! Egad! you should have seen the fellow look at me when I showed him your letter. He seemed more surprised than even I."

"Very well, darling," replies his spouse, whom his last sally has nearly driven in confusion from the room. "Here is your coat. Am I not obedience? I'm more than that. Go off and make a night of it with your old comrade. When you return," here she turns roguish eyes on him, "you will find in your home the wife who loves you!"

Then giving him one or two very sweet caresses, and calling him her wild Irish boy, she sends O'Brien Dillon, Comte of the Empire, out into the streets of Paris, with very proud and haughty stride.

As soon as he has gone, Hilda, taking a quick look around the room, falters: "What shall we do? If he hears I am Madame de Sabran—*Mon Dieu!* What may he not do to *me!*" and she wrings her hands.

"Do you love him *now?*" laughs Lass.

"Not well enough to be taken to Vienna by him—not well enough to be called a jade and forbidden to put foot in my own house—not well enough to have *my* property coolly taken as *his*—not well enough to be the slave of an Irish general, when I have the Regent of France at my feet!" cries Hilda with blazing eyes and crimson cheeks.

"I had supposed that would be your determination. In fact it is the only one of common sense! If

D'Orleans hears of this—good-bye the Regent of France—good-bye Madame's dream of glory and wealth and power! That would not suit you, eh?" sneers the financier.

"No! but what to do?"

"Oh, leave that to Uncle Johnny!" remarks Monsieur Lass complacently. "And now to other matters. You must see D'Orleans immediately! The next concession that I have proposed for the India Company, we must have at once. Your words will help us?"

"Don't I know that very well?" laughs Hilda, who seems to have regained confidence and spirit at the Scotchman's words. Then she says coaxingly, yet imperiously: "My twelve hundred shares of the new stock?"

"Yes, when it is issued."

"Don't forget! or perhaps you had better make it fifteen hundred.".

"Fifteen hundred it shall be, *ma belle* financier!" remarks Lass. "But you must give up O'Brien Dillon into my hands!"

"That I will, with pleasure, with *delight*, with JOY!" cries the changeable beauty.

"Perchance Monsieur d'Arnac, the young gentleman who escorted you on that wild night ride, may console you for the loss of husband? A letter reached the wrong man—eh, *ma belle?*"

And with these words, and a cool, sinister smile, Monsieur Lass steps hurriedly out of Madame de Sabran's house, and going to his bank with clouded brow, sends for the Prince de Conti.

CHAPTER XXI.

THE FIRST MASSE SHOT AT BILLIARDS.

AT HIS message De Conti, who is very much interested in most of the schemes of Monsieur Lass, comes hurriedly to the Palais Mazarin.

In the private office of the bank the two hold earnest conference.

After hearing the banker's story, De Conti remarks: "Little Cupid de Moncrief helped me with the other man who was in our way. Supposing we get the advice of Monsieur le Procureur du Roy ? This matter should be done legally."

A messenger being sent, half an hour afterwards Charles de Moncrief is shown in. He listens placidly to De Conti's advice, and Lass' description of the affair —a great deal of which he knows much better than the gentlemen who tell it.

Then after meditation he replies slowly: "If you will leave the matter to me, I think this Irish general from Vienna will trouble you and his pretty wife no more."

"But this must be done *legally !*" argues De Conti.

"And you, Monsieur le Prince, would come to the Procureur du Roy," says Cupid, drawing himself up, with stern dignity, "to suggest anything outside the law ? This affair shall be accomplished legally. But I am to have fifteen hundred shares of the new stock!"

"Fifteen hundred!" groans De Conti. "*Ma foi !* what will be left for me ?"

But Lass is a greater man than De Conti. He knows, though the price asked is high, the service is worth it. He says hurriedly: "There will be plenty for you, Monsieur le Prince, and for all of us before long. The fifteen hundred shares of the new stock, when issued, shall be yours, Monsieur de Moncrief. Only you must do as you promised, legally and *at once*—for speed is *vital !* The Regent must give us a further concession. Then we will have a whole hemisphere to draw upon— THE NEW WORLD !

"France is four thousand miles away from it; we can throw around Louisiana the fable of romance. We can have gold mines there and none can say us nay. We can talk silver mines and none can say we lie. The diamonds of Golconda will come to us—and who shall say *where* they come from, but above all, behind this proposition, we have the great undeveloped, exhaustless wealth of a new land that some day will be greater than any country of the globe. I have had reports from trusted agents in Quebec and Canada. I have also the secret report of the Chevalier La Salle, who explored the Mississippi, from those great inland fresh water seas to the Gulf of Mexico, and it states the land is grander and will be more productive than all of the colonies that once made old Spain the richest country ever known!"

With this he expands into a scheme of glorious colonization and development that, had it been carried out, would have caused a French civilization to come to both America and the East Indies, instead of the Anglo-Saxon one that triumphed forty years after, because France ran away with a prosperity that came to it too unexpectedly and too suddenly, and went crazy in its impulsive Gallic way, because in six years Monsieur Lass raised it from utter poverty to a prosperity until that time unheard of.

At him with open mouths and watering lips both his co-adjutors gaze. They are both greedy to the hearts' core, and such visions of boundless wealth as he predicts makes them drunk with love of money.

De Conti whispers, with rolling eyes and trembling lips, to De Moncrief as they depart together : "*Morbleu!* if he can do what he says, what a pie for us to pick, my little Cupid." For in this Prince's ignoble, yet bizarre brain, has come a scheme not only of picking the pie, but of picking every one connected with it, and picking them clean as ever starving dog picked unexpected beef-bone.

But this makes Cousin Charlie work very hard for his fifteen hundred shares of new stock.

De Moncrief goes to cogitating, and thinks it is just as well that he should see the whereabouts of the gentleman on whom he is to put his evil eye; concluding, from what Monsieur Lass has told him, D'Arnac's quarters will be as likely a place as any in Paris to find O'Brien Dillon.

Strolling over by the Bridge Au Change, he marches straight through the broad Boulevard de Palais, over the Ile de la Cité, and crossing by the Pont St. Michel, soon finds himself at the Rue Christine, just in time to take part in a very jovial dinner.

At the table O'Brien Dillon is enthusing over his new found happiness, and announcing his Hilda is more beautiful than ever, though a little wayward. "Bedad! though, I soon showed her that I was the cock who

would crow in that barnyard. I burned up a poem
written to that jade De Sabran's eyebrows, and ordered
the Comtesse Dillon never to let the trollop in my
house again." Then his eyes grow severe. "What
the divil are you giggling for, Lanty?" he cries.
"Divil take you! I don't know what's come into ye.
For the last three hours you've done nothing but
grimace. It's that little Rosalie has made you too
happy, but it's not nice for a servant standing behind
a man's chair to take part in the amusement of the
company. Where are your manners?"

At which Lanty exits, though they can hear his
merriment through the open door.

To his greeting Dillon says affably: "I'm right glad
to see ye, Charlie de Moncrief. We'll have some great
nights of it in Paris together and I'll show you my new
stroke at billiards. I'm going to astonish Paris with it
to-night. Raymond, I think I can win a thousand
crowns at least this evening. Lanty has picked out the
place. It's a billiard café on the Quai des Augustines;
there's quite a little sprinkling of the high-betting nobility in the place each evening.

"The stroke is a peculiar one?" asks Cousin Charlie.

"Faith, it's the most wonderful punch with the stick
ever invented. It's like the work of a wizard or a
sorcerer. I've me stick which Lanty made me for the
purpose, with a piece of leather stuck on the end of it.
Come and see me do the stroke to-night, Monsieur
le Procureur. Raymond is too much interested in the
young girl who saved both our lives to come with me. By
the blessing of God some day we'll make her an actress."

For Raymond has used Mademoiselle Quinault as an
excuse to get away from his friend, whose eternal babbling of the beauties of Madame Hilda drives him to
despair.

After a little, O'Brien gets to explaining his wonderful
shot to them more definitely, finally illustrating it by
making coins spin and telling them it will perhaps
frighten ignorant lookers-on. "Devil take me," he
laughs, "perhaps they'll think me a magician!"

On hearing this a bright yet sinister gleam twinkles in
Cousin Charlie's eyes. He says· "When do you do
the shot?"

"This evening. You can see me if you'll come to the Café St. Michel, near the bridge of that name, on the Quai des Augustines, about nine o'clock."

"Thank you," replies Cousin Charlie; "your explanation of the stroke has very much interested me. I will try and witness your triumph."

A little after he takes his leave, for De Moncrief has a good deal of work to do this afternoon and now thinks he sees his way to doing it.

Then Raymond departs for the Hotel de Chateaubrien.

So, a little before nine, on this bright evening, which, though dark, seems very pleasant to the happy and contented soldier of fortune, O'Brien Dillon, attended by Lanty carrying his "magic wand," as he calls it, steps into the Café St. Michel from the Quai des Augustines.

The Seine is flowing dark and silent beside the street that is almost deserted now, though a few people passing from the Ile de la Cité across the St. Michel Bridge move along the street.

But if it is dark without, the café inside is bright with many burning candles and a few oil lamps. Its two billiard tables are made with board beds and solid wooden cushions, and have some holes upon their surface, into which the players of that day sometimes drove their balls, very much as boys play marbles at the present time.

These are surrounded by a crowd of excited players, among them several of the young bloods of the court, who have just taken up this amusement.

With these gentlemen Dillon soon makes himself conspicuous; announcing himself, in his easy Irish manner, as count of the Empire, and a general in the Austrian service, "and the best billiard player that ever put mace to a ball!"

"Indeed, I doubt that, with your permission, Monsieur le Comte!" says a young gentleman, standing by. "Permit me to introduce myself—the Baron de Pontineux! I shall be proud to uphold the honor of my country in any game of skill you may suggest!"

"Very well, hazards and cannons!" remarks O'Brien, "for one hundred *livres !*"

"Agreed!" replies the young gentleman.

And the two take off their coats, as the stake is
rather high; O'Brien Dillon removing also his cavalry
sabre that clanks at his heels, and his pair of trusted
pistols, to give greater freedom to his arm and movement of his body about the table.

The two go to playing, and find themselves quite
evenly matched.   After a game or two, the stakes grow
higher, and the crowd leaving the other table gather
about to witness the more exciting game.

During this time the café has been filling up rapidly,
and not by any means with gentlemen of station or
rank.   A number of more commonly dressed people
surround the table, a few of these almost disreputable
as to their clothes, bearing and odor.

"*Parbleu!*" remarks the young baron, "Mine host, your
company have a greasy smell about them this evening!"

This   makes   a   few   of   those   standing   around
growl, but O'Brien laughs nonchalantly: "Pay attention to your game, my dear Baron.   Don't bother yourself with the *canaille*.   Let the poor creatures look at
gentlemen at play."

So the game goes on, with varying fortune, the
stakes always growing higher, until they have wagered
one thousand *livres* on the result.

And now O'Brien Dillon, with the true soul of the
gamester who will win or lose all at the hazard of a die,
remarks carelessly: "By Saint Patrick! you seem to
doubt my skill, my young friend.   Perhaps you do not
think I can make this shot—the carom from the red to
white!"

"That is impossible for mortal man!" answers his
opponent decidedly; for the stroke, a very simple one
to the players of to-day, was unheard of, unthought of,
and absolutely impossible to the implements and skill
of the experts of that time.

"Very well; look on me and see me do it!"

"Not for five thousand *livres!*" cries the Baron.
Then he examines the shot and remarks; "Your ball
would have to run forward and then run back.   IT WOULD
BE CONTRARY TO THE LAWS OF GOD!"

"Then see me break the laws of God!—I take that
bet, and I'll double it, if you've got the stomach for me
skill!" chaffs the general lightly.

"Take it? Of course I do! Never was ten thousand *livres* gained so easily!" replies the young man.

And numerous other bets are offered to this Irish general, whom those surrounding him think insane to offer such a wild proposition.

One or two, however, shudder and say: "It is wicked to bet, for if he wins it will be the black art."

Taking all these wagers very rapidly, until there are no more to bet against him, O'Brien Dillon, who likes the *coup de theatre*, says: "Behold me! Now Lanty bring me MY MAGIC WAND!"

This remark is indiscreet, for half the people of that day believed in magic—the other half feared it.

"Coming, your Honor!" cries Lanty, bringing the weapon demanded.

"This is the *magic* of it!" cries O'Brien, and taps the leather, at which some of them look upon him with frightened eyes.

Then he cocks the stick on high, and in a bungling manner, but still effectively, strikes straight down upon the ball, the leather tip catching the sphere and giving it what is now called reverse English.

With gaping lips and open eyes the crowd watch. The rolling ball flies along the table and strikes the red, then of course it must go forward on its path.

It stops!—Horror! *It is coming back!* Horror! Horror!—It takes a wondrous and mysterious curve and caroms on the white. *Horror!* MAGIC! HORROR!

"I'll take your money, my young friend," cries O'Brien Dillon, delighted at his stroke, though it would have been no great performance to-day—and grins in triumph at the shuddering crowd.

BUT NOT FOR LONG!

There is a cry of horrified terror from the assemblage, and shouts of: "The wizard! the wizard of *Notre Dame* has come back! The sorcerer! Burn him! Into the Seine with him! Drown him or he'll murder us with the black art!" "Demon!" "Magician!" "*Asteroth!*" "BEELZEBUB!" and other wild and awful screams.

And with this shriek the crowd are upon him, and before O'Brien, taken by surprise at this tremendous and unexpected rush, can grab sabre or pistols, he is seized by a hundred superstitious arms and tossed in the air and dashed to the earth.

In scarce a second he has no clothes on his back and *is naked as when born:* some thieves purloining one or two very fine diamonds the sorcerer has upon him.

In a flash and a yell they are out upon the Quai, and have dragged him over the stones, banging him about till he is nearly insensible; but all the time rushing the fainting Irish Asmodius rapidly along.

Lanty, who is fighting with arms and feet, sees his master disappear in the distance, but can't make after him, being even now engaged with a couple of billiard markers and three or four *garçons* of the street.

A minute after with one billiard marker left for dead, and the breath almost out of the other, he breaks from them and reaches the Quai des Augustines.

O'Brien Dillon and the crowd have vanished.

He thinks he sees them on the Bridge St. Michel, and rushes after, but in the darkness and the narrow streets of the oldest part of Paris, he misses them. Then he wanders searching for half an hour, and finally thinks he must have aid.

Though his own coat has been torn from him, he goes wildly over into the main portion of the town, and flying to the Rue St. Honoré has pointed out to him the Hotel de Chateaubrien.

There, after some confab with the flunkeys, and piteously begging to have a word with the Comte d'Arnac, he is finally admitted.

His appearance is more that of a drunken man, or a maniac, than of a being of common sense; but Raymond, seeing that his face is very serious, cries: "Come in!" and drags him into a bright room where pretty Mimi and a lovely girl who has just been giving some recitation, or reading, look at him with startled eyes.

To them he tells his story.

"Pooh! it's nothing—only a riot! Trust O'Brien Dillon to get out of that!" remarks D'Arnac.

"But they said 'BURN HIM!' they yelled 'INTO THE SEINE WITH HIM?'" answers Lanty.

"Then I'm with you in a minute," replies Raymond, and they leave the two wondering women in the great hotel, and coming out upon the street get conveyance, and drive down to the Cité. They patrol its streets, and make inquiry of the archers standing on duty about the various bridges, but can hear no word of the missing man.

Then they drive back along the Pont St. Michel and still do not come upon him, and finally return to the café. Here they can get no information from the proprietor, who is going about half crazy, for in the mêlée one of his billiard tables has been broken, his fine oil lamps have been destroyed, and half the fixtures of his establishment have been made into kindling wood. He gabbles: "*Mon Dieu!* if I could find him—the sorcerer—the black art—Asmodeus himself has been here! One of my billiard markers lying half dead, the other disabled for life! God knows what will happen! If the police come upon me I am a ruined man!" and wrings his hands piteously.

For the *gendarmes* of France of that day had very much the same ideas of justice as the police of the present time. They must have a guilty man, and when they could not find the guilty, generally took the innocent, if he were worth the plucking.

Here D'Arnac says: "I must have further advice!" and, suddenly, thinking of De Moncrief, cries: "Cousin Charlie will help me!"

They go to the rooms of the Procureur du Roy, but Cousin Charlie is not in, and after waiting for him for two hours the old gentleman saunters in and cries: "Hallo, Raymond, my boy—what's the matter? You look serious."

"Yes—Count Dillon! He played his great shot with his magic stick, and the crowd seized him and cried: 'Sorcerer! into the river.'"

"And divil a one of the spalpeens paid their bets," adds Lanty ruefully.

"Did they put him in the river?" asks Cousin Charlie hurriedly.

"No; I think not. We can't tell what's become of him."

"Then let us go to the Lieutenant of Police. My name will gain us instant admission even at this time of night," remarks De Moncrief, who apparently is anxious about the Irish General's fate himself.

They drive rapidly to the bureau: But the head of the office is not in, and a gentleman who represents him named Celestin, with mild eyes and placid face, does not know anything about it, and cannot tell, though he makes inquiries with apparent great care among his officials.

But none know anything of Count O'Brien Dillon, and none ever do know anything of Count O'Brien Dillon, for though D'Arnac tries both police and municipal authorities, and even goes to the court, and then to his old chief, the Duc de Villars, and Prince Eugene of Savoy writes a letter to the Regent of France, asking what has become of his officer, it is almost as if this earth had never known O'Brien Dillon, General in the Army of Austria, and Count of the Empire, after he made his magic shot in the Café St. Michel on the Quai des Augustines.

Doubtless he is dead!

At least his two-honeymoons bride thinks so. For after a very little time she produces his drafts upon Uncle Johnny's bank, and makes Monsieur Lass liquidate them to the last *livre*, and takes possession of plunder of the Turk—for the beautiful Hilda de Sabran has all the diamonds of the Ottoman Vizier, and the great crescent and its star blazes on her fair brow at many a court festival and many a theatre *fête* and many a Regent's supper party.

CHAPTER XXII.

A NIGHT AT THE FRANÇAIS.

BUT though others give up the search for O'Brien Dillon, Raymond does not.

"A general and a count," this young gentleman reasons, with all his pride of rank, "was not born to conquer the Turk and then be slain by the scum of a billiard café."

He continues his inquiries and investigations, and finally offers a reward of five thousand *livres* to any one who can give him information tending to elucidate the mystery of his friend's apparent disappearance from the face of the earth.

"You're very foolish, my dear boy," remarks Cousin Charlie on hearing of this step. "If the police cannot find him, how can any one else?"

"I do not trust the police," replies D'Arnac hastily.

"Not trust them!" ejaculates De Moncrief, apparently very much shocked at this lack of respect for the powers that be. "Why not? The Bureau de Sûreté have made every effort."

"Yes, apparently," rejoins Raymond, "but Celestin has never even taken the trouble to have the morgue watched for Dillon's body. Therefore I argue Celestin knows where my friend is. If the head of the bureau knows, some of his underlings also do, and it is to their avaricious souls my reward is offered."

"*Mon Dieu!* five thousand *livres* won't tempt anybody NOW!" sneers De Moncrief. "They can make ten times that amount gambling on the Rue Quincampoix in Monsieur Lass' Mississippi securities."

For it was now the year 1718, in which commenced the first little wave of that gigantic stock speculation which was ultimately to make Paris crazy.

"*Pardieu!* but some of them have no money to make a beginning. That one may come my way! But I have other affairs on my mind!" returns D'Arnac, rising.

"Oh, of the theatre—La Quinault's *début* is arranged for June 14th?" queries De Moncrief.

"Certainly!"

"Then what troubles you?" laughs Cousin Charlie, noting concern on the young man's face. "Will little Jeanne not pay attention to La Desmares' elocution, or does she refuse to practice her steps with Mademoiselle Prevost?"

"Sometimes one and sometimes the other," snarls Raymond. "She has a *diable* of a will of her own."

Then drawing himself up he continues: "I now go to exercise my authority as guardian. She—she has an admirer!" This last in a kind of half sigh.

"An admirer? Ha! ha! Ho! ho! Who?"

"A reptile of an actor, whose head I will break!" cries D'Arnac, and goes away, leaving Monsieur le Procureur with wildest hopes in his subtile brain that

the fascinations of the *débutante* at Le Français will
give him another chance at the Crevecœur estates; for
it is land he wants most now.

He has already made a million with his India stock,
and hopes to make four or five more in the big game
just commencing on the Rue Quincampoix, the little
street in which the first great scheme of stockbroking to
remove money from the pockets of the general public
and place it in the hands of promotors of finance had its
origin—the place in which began the Paris Bourse,
and to which we owe the London Stock Exchange and
Wall Street, with all their achievements for human
greed and human woe.

With his efforts to discover the fate of his friend,
D'Arnac has now upon his hands, perchance, a more
difficult duty, that of controlling the budding beauties,
the bizarre mind and the electric art of the young lady,
who, rumor has commenced to say, will make a great
triumph on the Parisian stage.

"Egad! she's sure to enchant him," chuckles Cousin
Charlie, who has seen and approved of this young lady's
powers of fascination. Already he forgets la Sabran
for Quinault's witcheries.

And this is really so, for Jeanne is becoming an
enchantress to every one about her, though perhaps
more to others than to this gentleman she playfully calls
her soldier guardian.

A strange bashfulness seems to overcome this young
lady, who is archness itself, whenever Monsieur
d'Arnac strolls into the theatre or sees her at his
sister's hotel, where la Quinault is living, greatly to the
envy of her brother and sister artists of the Français,
who reside in much less elegant and aristocratic
luxury.

On arriving at the Hotel de Chateaubrien, D'Arnac
gets some of this mixed with a little tantrum that
astounds him.

Madame Mimi comes to him and says pathetically:
"I'm so glad you're here. She is in hysterics in her
room."

"Why?"

"Your aunt has made me a visit."

"Clothilde?"

"Yes; Jeanne chanced to return from her rehearsal before the countess left and they had a fearful combat."

"Wheugh! With their hands?" laughs Raymond.

"Oh, don't jeer—it was terrible! Madame de Crevecœur doesn't like Jeanne, and remarked sneeringly to her that she was sorry she had forgotten her convent teachings."

"'What does Madame la Marquise insinuate?' asked Mademoiselle Jeanne very haughty and freezing.

"'Why,' answered Clothilde, 'did not the nuns teach you that if you went on the stage you would be defiled? That no actress can be buried in consecrated ground?'"

"*Diable!* then there was a tragedy."

"More," answers Mimi, though she can't help smiling, "there was a scene from the Inferno. *Mon Dieu!* what a success that child will make upon the stage! She grew two feet taller, and then—WENT CRAZY! Clothilde fled from her as she would from a pythoness possessed, and I slipped out of the room on tiptoe. At present the *tragedienne* is upstairs in her room doing the grand act before a mirror, I imagine"

"At present the pythoness is at your elbows!" is whispered in so weird a voice that Raymond turns with a start, and starts again as he sees a figure in which comedy and tragedy are strangely blended.

Miss Jeanne has great red exaggerated eyes, from weeping. She is garbed again in convent uniform, but catching Raymond's eye, she gives him the wink of a soubrette.

"*Diable!*" cries the young man. "What is the meaning of this masquerade?"

"I put it on," answers Jeanne, grandly, "to go back to the convent again to do penance to remove from me the sin of *rehearsal.*" This last is said with an awful, vivacious, vicious sneer.

"Then," she goes on pathetically, "I changed my mind, and concluded to be a lost soul for my art's sake. But hearing your voice, my young guardian general, I ran down to get scolded and punished, so I —I could be naughty again." With this last idea she gives the astonished but admiring Raymond a wicked, but most enchanting pout.

" Yes, you have been a very bad girl," says D'Arnac,
assuming a grand and martial manner.

" Of course; that's my normal state; isn't it, Mimi?"
jeers the *comedienne*. " Look at him—he is putting on
the airs of an officer. He'll treat me as if I were one
of his soldiers, and beat me with a cane," and making a
mocking military salute she stands before him in the
attitude of attention.

" Bah!" laughs Raymond, " You could soften even
the heart of a provost marshal."

" But not that of your aunt, Madame la Comtesse de
Crevecœur," sneers the young lady. Then she suddenly bursts out laughing. " What have I really done?
I know you came here to scold me for *something*." Next
pouts at him: " That's what you always do *now*."

"It is because I take an interest in you," mutters
D'Arnac quite tenderly.

" Ah, that's what makes me take your scoldings so
nicely," says the young lady playfully.

"But if it is to be a long one," interjects Mimi,
"suppose we all go into dinner. You can be severe,
Raymond, between courses."

Over the table they have quite a little discussion. Monsieur d'Arnac produces two letters and says
sternly: " Jeanne, attention!"

" Yes, General! Just one more piece of lobster, and
I am under your guardian thumb."

" This is a serious matter. I have a note here from
Mademoiselle Desmares, who threatens to give up
teaching you. You will not follow the old reading of
Phèdre's lines."

" Of course not! That's how I am going to get
my effects!" cries Jeanne. " And between ourselves, I'm going to make a lot of them—new ones—
revolutionizers!"

" You think you will make a success?" queries Mimi
anxiously.

" *I'm sure of it!*"

" Why?"

" Because all the other actresses hate me already,
and la Desmares cries: ' *Mon Dieu!* What will become
of the traditions of the stage? Where Duclos made
them shudder, this chit is going to make them cry for

her and pity her!' and I will, too!" says Jeanne
savagely: "I'll torture their hearts!"

"This second letter, Mademoiselle Heart-twister,"
remarks D'Arnac sententiously, "is from the celebrated
Prevost, who, notwithstanding her great fame, kindly
consented to teach you stage dancing."

"Yes, I supposed she would write to you," laughs la
Quinault, playing with a truffle daintily. "She wants me
to dance like a ballet dancer. I prefer to put emotions
into my skips like a *comedienne*. I contrive to get some
of my brains even in my heels."

She emphasizes the last with a sarcastic dash of her
fork into the truffle, which she transfers to her pretty
mouth; then laughs: "What's the *real* matter? Why
don't you come to your subject?"

"Very well," says Raymond, sternly, "you have an
admirer."

"A dozen, I hope. Already Monsieur le Duc de Villars
has been to see me twice, at rehearsal, and has patted
my cheek, and kissed it—what do you say to that?"

"I am not referring to Monsieur de Villars, or any
other *old* gentleman of the army, who may take an
interest in you on account of what you did for the
regiment of my poor friend Dillon, at Friburg," says
Raymond. "The man I refer to is that cursed serpent
of an actor, young Arnoul Poisson."

"Oh, the *ugly* one!"

"Yes," replies D'Arnac, trying to be stern. "Did
you deliver my message to him?"

"Word for word!" answers Jeanne. "I said to
him: '*Mon Seigneur*, to whom I do homage, General
le Comte d'Arnac has asked me, Monsieur Arnoul
Poisson, to present his compliments to you, and to say
if you ever dare to speak to me again off the stage of
the theatre, he will break your infernal head!' That
was word for word, I believe," laughs the young lady.
"If I had put it in more polite language, he might not
have believed that it really came from a *noble* to an
actor. Then I went on, and told him—" here she
rises and courtesies to Mimi, ceremoniously,—"that
Madame la Marquise de Chateaubrien had kindly
suggested that if I ever walked home from the theatre
with young Poisson again, she would like to box my ears."

"Oh," cries Mimi, "I never said that!"

"No, but you *looked* it."

"Did I?" laughs Madame la Marquise. "Then forget it," and taking Jeanne into her arms, she gives her many tender kisses.

This vivacious young creature has grown into the generous heart of her patroness, and has gained from her love and affection, and gives it back again with interest, for she returns Mimi's kisses, and purrs: "I'll never be naughty again!"

"Whenever you are," laughs D'Arnac, "I shall have you dressed *a la* convent again; it is very becoming."

At which Jeanne goes to blushing, for she has grown out of the garb, and it would make her look gawky were not her figure admirable in its proportions, and her small feet and beautiful ankles, of which it makes liberal display, in piquant bottines and faultless hosiery.

"If you threaten me with this dress I am obedience itself, tyrant," she babbles.

"Then beware! No more of Monsieur Poisson, the younger!"

"Very well, make your commands and I obey," she says, half mockingly, half seriously, and coming before him, gives him her most humble courtesy, and murmurs, "*Mon Seigneur.*"

Then as Raymond goes away her eyes grow tender, and she whispers to herself, "What's the matter with him? Why does he hate that ugly little Poisson?" Here suddenly a great wave of blushes flies over her face and she puts her little hand upon her heart to stay its wild beating. But all this day Jeanne Quinault's laugh is lighter and her spirits seem to be in clouds which are gilded by the brightest sun.

"I should not wonder," cogitates D'Arnac to himself as he leaves the hotel, "if little Jeanne astounded the Parisians. She'll give 'em a performance of *la Phèdre*, the like of which they have never seen before."

He is confirmed in this opinion a moment after.

De Villars, meeting him on the Rue St. Honoré, as Raymond salutes him, suddenly turns, and putting his arm within that of the "boy general," whispers in his ear: "We're going to give a great actress to the public, eh, *mon ami?*"

" I hope so," returns Raymond.

"*Diable!* Monsieur Faintheart. I tell you yes," cries the Maréchal. "Doesn't she make me weep at rehearsal every day and the next minute go wild with admiration at her graces incomparable!"

"Now," continues the genial old warrior, "I have determined to make *our* protégée's debut a great one. The Regiment of Alsace is stationed only twelve miles out of Paris. I have engaged the whole gallery for myself. I shall *order* the Regiment of Alsace to occupy it. Who should give greater plaudits to little Jeanne Quinault on her *entrée* to the stage than the brave men whose lives she saved when she was a child ? What do you think of the idea ?"

"Immense!" answers Raymond, "It is as big as your kind heart, my chief."

"And my brilliant brain," chuckles De Villars. "There are only two hundred and fifty men alive that she personally saved, but every recruit in the regiment knows the story, and his bravas will be the loudest, because he will think that will prove him one of the heroes of Friburg. The officers, of course, have seats below. When Sergeant Le Bœuf waves the banner of the regiment with Jeanne Quinault's name upon its folds, every man of them will yell as if they were charging a battery. Then where will Monsieur les Critiques be, eh, *mon garçon ?*"

"Nowhere!" cries Raymond.

"Precisely," remarks De Villars; then sighs: "What a night it would have been for poor O'Brien Dillon, their old Colonel! What a curious fate—to return rich, titled, and a general, to be wiped from the face of the earth in a row in an ordinary billiard café! There's more behind this than either you or I know, D'Arnac," continues the Maréchal, who has been very much exercised over the disappearance of one of his favorite officers of the Army of the Rhine.

"Yes, but I mean to solve it," replies Raymond as De Villars squeezes his hand and dismisses him.

But his hopes grow gradually smaller and smaller, day by day, and though he still keeps his reward before the public, no clue comes to him.

But even this is finally driven from his mind by the approaching début of Mademoiselle Quinault at the Français.

Assisted by Mr. Lanty, who has been acting as Raynold's attaché since his master's disappearance, the young officer finds himself engaged in an affair of which he knows practically nothing, but is desperately anxious as to the result. Finally he makes the wise course of giving over all the details of the début to Monsieur Michel Baron, telling him to do everything to make it a success, and as to money he can have a *carte blanche*.

"With my experience and your protégée's abilities, I think you need have no fear," remarks the veteran of the stage, pocketing a check for a goodly amount.

"You think she has talent?" questions Raymond, anxiously.

"Talent?" replies Baron. "*Talent!*" Then he shrugs his shoulders and laughs. "She's brushed fifty years' cobwebs out of the Français *at rehearsal!* What won't she do at night!"

But notwithstanding this prognostication, as the evening of June 14, 1718, draws on, D'Arnac finds himself more nervous than he has ever been at any stage of his life.

At two in the afternoon of the day, he wanders past the Theatre Français. At half-past two he finds himself in the Rue des Fosses Saint Germain again. At three he strolls into the *Café Procopé*, opposite the theatre.

Then he suddenly bolts for the Rue St. Honoré, for a quick and awful thought has come to him: "Perchance Jeanne is sick!" he sees so little signs of movement about the theatre.

On arriving at the Hotel de Chateaubrien he is encountered at the door by Mimi, who whispers: "Hush! you'll disturb her—you'll make her nervous." Then she falters: "Raymond, if it should not be a success—if little Jeanne should fail—it would break my heart."

"Do you think it is as bad as that?" mutters Raymond gloomily.

"No, I don't," cries his sister. "I know she'll be a great hit. Her dresses are divine!" With this, she turns on D'Arnac and says viciously: "Why do you come here, to make me nervous? Leave the house this instant' The child might see you and have a fit. She gave me this note for you, but don't come on the stage until the performance is over."

With this missive in his hand, Raymond finds himself expelled.

On the doorstep he tears it open and reads:

Mon Seigneur :
Mimi won't let me see you because she says I'm nervous—but I'm not—I've only cold shivers.
The dresses! Ough! the dresses!
God bless you for what you've done for me! **Come to-night** and see a butterfly die, but don't fear for your
PHEDRE.

Turning this extraordinary effusion over in his mind, D'Arnac goes back to his apartments to get more cold comfort there.

Seeing Mr. Lanty, he asks him what he thinks of the chances for the night.

" Faix, I think we're in a very bad way," chuckles the Irishman. Then he goes off and mutters to himself: "He's gone! He's getting the same crazy fever that came over my poor master, when he was ruined by that beast who will give me back none of my diamonds, though I have been after her with prayers and imprecations every day."

For Lanty has been beseeching la Sabran for some of the jewels of the Turk with very indifferent results.

"Any way, you'll be there to applaud, Lanty," calls Raymond after him.

"Bedad! Did I ever refuse free tickets?" returns his servitor.

At this assurance, D'Arnac, taking out his watch, suddenly thinks: "Just time for dinner before the performance."

Bolting off to the Armenian Café in the Foire Saint Germain, he meets Achille de Soubise, and the two make their meal together, D'Arnac continually taking out his timepiece and thinking: " In an hour— in half an hour—in a quarter of an hour more!"

Finally the two march for the Theatre Français, and arriving near the entrance see an immense audience surging into the old theatre, and brilliant equipages

dashing up and delivering their loads of beautiful
women and distinguished men—lots of them, for Paris
under Monsieur Lass has been growing very rich.

A moment after, he and his friend elbow their way
through the foyer to find the Français nearly filled.

It is quite a military audience. Raymond sees
many of his old comrades of the Rhine campaign, their
gold lace flashing among the beautiful toilettes of
court beauties and the more flaming colors of the wives
of city magnates.

So they come crowding in till the boxes are now all
filled save one reserved for the Regent.

Though excitement makes almost a blur before
Raymond's eyes, he notes the man he had distrusted
four years ago—Gaston Lenoir—chatting to one or
two court ladies in De Conti's *loge*.

Beside him sits Cousin Charlie taking snuff nervously,
for just now Monsieur le Procureur is praying with all
his little soul la Quinault will make a mighty hit, not
only on the audience, but upon a certain young gentleman who seems so anxious this evening.

Presently De Villars strolls into Raymond's box,
attended by two or three of his staff, and chuckles to
the young man: " Look at the gallery!   A little surprise
for Mademoiselle!"

Gazing upwards, D'Arnac whispers: " The Regiment
of Alsace ?"

"Yes, every man primed and loaded.   They are to
make only a little noise till I give the signal—then
Sergeant Le Bœuf waves the banner and then, *Voila!*
Though they'll be quiet till the time comes, God
help the critic who utters a word against their savior.
I would not hiss in that gallery for the spoils of a captured city!"

A moment after the Regent enters; with him Monsieur
Lass and two ladies.

But Raymond does not notice them.   The curtain is
going up.

The opening scenes come hazily to him.   He is only
conscious of waiting, though the cast is a tremendous
one.

He has, by means of influence and money, induced
Baron to volunteer to play the part of *Hippolyte*, though

he had retired from the stage nearly twenty years before.

But he comes on with all his old youthful fire, gallant mien and dashing bearing. He is, as he was of yore, the first *jeune premier* of the stage, and above all, France's greatest tragic actor.

The audience enthuse to him *en masse*.

But though Raymond follows his speeches to *Théramène*, he is always waiting—waiting—waiting for *Phèdre*.

So it runs on to the third scene, when Jeanne will make her first *entrée*. That grand entrance where the Grecian queen appears, sick with the awful longing of a love she dare not gratify—the unholy passion for her stepson *Hippolyte*, for which she curses herself, yet lets her imagination revel in.

As *Phèdre* falters on, half supported by her women, Raymond fears Jeanne is sick almost to death with agitation, for the queen is like a lily bud, crushed to the earth by love. But, as the scene goes on, the recollection of that love revives her; the lily expands upon its stalk; and, made glorious by the subtleties of remembered sensuous passion, changes to a full blown rose, glowing with dazzling color.

Then she commences to sway her audience, and give them passion ALSO.

They gasp at her astounded—Raymond and the public as well.

This rôle that had always been to them a stilted tragic declamation, becomes in her that of a loving, despairing woman, and that woman not only Queen of Greece, but queen of her auditors' hearts—whom she begins to charm by her exquisite tricks of manner and *naïve* ways of doing the little things of the play to make these fascinating.

To *Ænone's* denunciation and abuse of *Hippolyte* all former *Phèdres* had *screamed* "Ah, Gods!" This one *sighs* it forth, and makes the audience sigh with her, for she is causing them to love her and suffer for her.

In this she has one potent ally to all her art—her beauty! which she has made pathetic in its very unpretense, for her costume is a revelation of modest simplicity.

Before, other *Phèdres* had appeared in fashionable gowns, and had even sported Watteau plaits, balloon hoops, and other modiste fads of court costume.

This one has only the white robes of ancient Greece, that give full play to the graceful beauty of her limbs, as from beneath its classic folds peep forth two tiny feet, bare as when Raymond first saw them on that Friburg night, and gleaming pink and dimpled, under Grecian sandals.

Above all, she has that personal magnetism—that divine fire, without which even great dramatic art is puny, *uneffective*, DEAD!—for every eye pursue her as she walks, and every ear drinks in the ripple of her voice.

So she comes on to that great speech that tells the actions, fears, and guilty blushes of a woman who has in her soul a love she dare not reveal to other eyes. As she speaks these lines she seems to blush and burn with shame; she seems to tremble with the hidden fire, and her eyes scintillate and glow, illumined by some new and strange emotion that seems to frighten her.

Is it *Phèdre*, or Jeanne Quinault who speaks, blushes, and suffers this night in the Theatre Français?

A lady sitting in the semi-regal box, on her right, the Duchesse de Prie, on her left hand the Duc d'Orleans, and behind her Monsieur Lass, noticing this pathetic fire in the young actress' eyes, and following their gaze, sees that they light on Raymond; and trembles herself, and pants with burning rage, and mutters with pale, quivering lips: "At last my RIVAL!"

For De Sabran, since her husband's disappearance, has wondered with tortured pride, why Raymond came not. For he has avoided her. Some half-suspicion in his mind that she may guess the reason of his friend's taking off, has kept him from her. For with all his soul Raymond d'Arnac knows if he looks upon Hilda's glorious eyes, or hears her voice, he will be hers forevermore!

Noting the wondrous beauty of this being on the stage, the glories of her voice, the grace of her gestures, the loveliness of her form, De Sabran suddenly remembers.

"It is the chit at *Des Capucines*, who had the childish admiration for D'Arnac, whose life she had saved;" she moans in her mind. "This is the budding beauty that has kept him from me!" The ivory sticks of her lace fan snap with one vicious grip of her gloved hand, and with all her unbridled soul la Sabran, court beauty, and Regent's favorite, hates la Quinault, the budding actress of Le Français.

Just as she breaks her fan, the house breaks forth, for the curtain is descending on the first act of the play, and the audience has gone into a French hysterical emotion—but it is nothing to what is to come.

"We are just warming ourselves for our work," whispers old De Villars to Raymond. "I have not given the signal yet," and goes off, with tears of pride and triumph in his eyes, to the green-room to kiss and congratulate the young lady in whom he takes so much interest.

D'Arnac, remembering his sister's injunction, hesitates to follow him, and an instant after is seized upon by De Rohan, De Soubise, and several of his friends, and dragged off to the café Procopé, opposite, to drink the health of the coming goddess of the stage.

"*Pardieu!* he is her guardian!" is the whisper among the young officers of the army and the nobles of the court. "THE GUARDIAN OF LA QUINAULT!" And they look at him with envious eyes.

Cousin Charlie, who has come over with the boys, cries: "*Sapristi!* Are we not all jealous of you!"

Monsieur Gaston Lenoir remarks, with his polished bow and Spanish smile: "*Per Bacco!* D'Arnac, who would think you had such an eye for beauty in the street fight that night at Friburg?"

On the stage Baron says to Mademoiselle Jeanne, as she finishes bowing her acknowledgments to the audience, "In the green-room, you will have your choice!"

"Of what?" whispers la Quinault.

"Of a caress and congratulation from the Regent of France, or from Le Duc de Villars, or some advice as to making your fortune from Monsieur Lass. I see they are all leaving their boxes to come on the stage."

"Then," laughs Jeanne, "I shall choose grandpapa's caress *first!*"

In this prognostication the great actor is right.

D'Orleans, as the curtain descends, whispers to Lass: "She is the prettiest actress I ever saw!"

"Yes," replies the Scotchman, "and the most natural."

"Come! I will give her the kiss of royal approbation," laughs D'Orleans, "and you, my financier, will give her a hit how to make a fortune."

Overhearing this, as the two leave the box, a fear as to her own loveliness—the first she has ever had in her life—comes to De Sabran.

But little Jeanne does not know she is making any enemies this night. She is unaffectedly happy.

In the greenroom she walks up to old De Villars and receives his paternal kiss, and her eyes grow triumphant, as he whispers: "I am proud of you! Permit me to present you to his Highness, the Duc d'Orleans!"

Then Jeanne, making profound courtesy, receives the congratulations of the first gentleman in France.

A moment after the Regent says: "*Ma petite*, permit me to introduce to you Monsieur Lass, a gentleman who will kindly give you hints as to making a fortune *off* the stage, as well as *on* it."

On this suggestion the financier is delighted to offer his assistance to the young lady in speculations in the India stock upon the street; for this has now become the prevailing rage, and duchesses and comtesses would give much for the few words the comptroller of finance whispers to the actress of the Français.

Then the play goes on again, and little Jeanne produces a new and peculiar effect in the piece.

Having made the audience *adore* her she makes them *hate* those who do not love her on the stage.

"*Mon Dieu!*" whispers De Villars into Raymond's ear, tears of rage in his honest old eyes, "that villain *Hippolyte* does not love her! He is going to break her heart—damn him!"

And the audience, agreeing with De Villars, curse Baron, for all his noble speeches of indignation at the love of his stepmother, until that actor, after the curtain falls upon the second act, goes off with tears in his eyes, and says: "*Morbleu!* she is a witch! The more virtuous and noble I am upon the stage, the more they hate me, because this *Phèdre* has made them adore her and sympathize with her, and think *Hippolyte* a cursed scoundrel for loving *Aricie*, the other woman."

So she goes on, producing peculiar effects—not those of a *tragedienne*, but those of a *comedienne* of the highest class, bringing tears where horror had come with other actresses, until at last, in the fifth act, as Raymond gazes at her, he understands what she has meant in her note, by "seeing the butterfly die!"

In this poison scene, that *tragediennes* make horrible and awful, little Quinault comes on to die in a robe that makes her look a fluttering fairy, and gives to it the suffering pathos of a beautiful soul that sighs out its death of passion—its death of love—in its death of body. Like the butterfly, she becomes more beautiful in color and effect as she dies.

The audience cry and sob and weep for her, and as *Parope* ejaculates, "She expires, Seigneur!" there is a sigh of sorrow—the being they love is dead.

Then, unheard of before in the *Français*, the speech of *Thésée* is not heard.

De Villars waves his hand and cries "NOW!"

And Lanty, in the upper balcony, opens the action with a wild blood-curdling Irish yell.

The big sergeant of the Regiment of Alsace upwaves its banner, torn with Austrian shot and shell, and bearing upon it the name of Jeanne Quinault.

And the Regiment of Alsace, with the same wild howl with which they have charged many a German battery, drown the more feeble plaudits of the boxes and the pit—though they are tremendous.

Carried away, the audience go into that emotional, ecstatic, hysterical Gallic enthusiasm, such as only Frenchmen have, and a captain of the Regiment of Alsace shouts from below: "Throw me the banner!"

The sergeant tosses the battle-flag to him, and he runs up on the stage and drapes the bowing actress with it.

Then pandemonium reigns! The pandemonium of la Quinault's triumph; for the story has got noised about of her heroism when a little girl—for France.

It is not an affair of the theatre now—it is a triumph of the army—a triumph of France.

One of the critics, who is muttering to himself: "*Diable!* what are we coming to? She cut a line in her last scene! She has turned Racine upside down for her own effects!" is suddenly tapped upon the shoulder by a dashing lieutenant, who whispers in his ear: "If you want to live—shut your vile mouth!"

Another, who has remarked: "She is pretty, but not a *tragedienne!*" receives these words in his ear, from a ferocious applauding major: "Repeat that slander against the heroine of the army, and to-morrow I'll cleave you to your lying jaws!"

So the curtain falls upon Mademoiselle Jeanne Quinault, until this evening unknown to the world, now one of the greatest stars in the constellation of art.

CHAPTER XXIII.

THE FRIEND OF THE ARMY.

But this night, which is Jeanne's triumph, is not all Jeanne's happiness. Towards the last she has commenced to whisper to herself with trembling lips: "He does not come. Why not? Does he think I am not worthy his praise?"

Turning from the last plaudits of the vast audience she thinks, "At last! Now he must come,"—but finds him not.

Others congratulate her and go away; others praise her and take their departure, and still no Raymond.

Madame la Marquise de Chateaubrien, who has been with her off and on during the evening, and who has even now tears of joy in her eyes over the triumph of her loved protégé, keeps gazing about for her brother and wondering why he of all men is not here to say one kind word to Jeanne.

Finally the two stand alone together in the green-room—the auditorium of the theatre, judging from the sounds that come to them, is empty also. The vast audience have gone away, the place becomes as other theatres when deserted, gloomy and bare and desolate.

The lights are being put out, but still no Raymond.

"I am unable to understand this," remarks Mimi, a flicker of rage upon her face. "My brother promised to come to supper with us."

"I—I presume he—he has forgotten," stammers Jeanne. Her lips tremble and she droops her head like a wounded bird.

But only one moment; then the pride of a haughty spirit comes to her. She laughs, "I—I presume there are *other* ladies than us in Paris this evening. Besides, sisters don't count." This is a stab at Mimi, who sympathizes with her, but Jeanne, in her agony of wounded pride, hardly knows what she says.

"Come, let us go home; your tremendous triumph has been too great for you, *dear* Jeanne," whispers her protectress, who sees tears upon the face of this night's victor.

As they step out of the green-room towards the stage entrance, in front of which Madame la Marquise's carriage is drawn up, Lanty brushes past them with glowing eyes and excited mien, followed by two or three men.

"Lanty, why is my brother not here?" calls Mimi to him imperiously.

"Faix," answers Lanty, with jovial ease, "it's because I'm afeard Monsieur d'Arnac has got work that's more to his liking this night," and goes hurriedly away to the property room, where they can hear him in great dispute with the guardian of the theatre's stock of weapons for stage warfare.

"Work *better* to his liking this night," thinks Jeanne, and her steps become the stalk of a *tragedienne* as she accompanies Madame la Marquise to her carriage and enters the equipage in haughty silence.

"Home," mutters Mimi to her footman, and the carriage drives off, Madame de Chateaubrien very savage at the slight her brother has put upon this young lady who sits with quivering lips and restless feet at her side.

But as the equipage turns on to the Rue des Fosses Saint Germain, Mimi suddenly screams: "They are fighting in front of the theatre!" for the noise of desperate combat is wafted to her ears.

But she has no chance to look. Just as she says this, little Jeanne, with a cry soft as a swan's dying note, drops limp and helpless upon her in sudden swoon.

Looking at the pale face and drawn lips of the great artiste who is suffering in her lap Madame la Marquise mutters to herself: "This brother of mine has a very careless—yes, a very cruel heart!"

But Raymond is not so bad a fellow as Mimi credits him with being.

D'Arnac, elbowing his way in the great crowd to get near the stage entrance, after the fall of the curtain, has been stopped by military discipline.

He has nearly reached the door leading to the stage; in another moment he will be upon it, greeting and making happy little Jeanne Quinault, when Lanty, forcing his way through the throng, gets alongside of him and whispers in his ear: "The Maréchal wants to see ye in his box again."

"Tell Monsieur de Villars I'll be back in a moment."

"He wants to see ye NOW. He said 'order him to report to me on the instant!' Faix I think from the appearance of the old gintleman, it's a matter of life and death. He looked like he did at the fight at Denain."

"Very well! come with me," returns D'Arnac, guessing the matter must be very serious from Lanty's excited manner.

"I'd like to, but I've other duties to do," whispers his servant. "I'm ordered to get together, as quickly as possible, all the Regiment of Alsace I can gather up, and any officers I may put me hands on."

With this Lanty forces his way out of the foyer, trampling upon the trains of the few ladies now going out, with reckless disregard of silks and laces, for the last of the audience is just leaving the theatre.

A moment after, Raymond is in the box of Monsieur de Villars, who is seated alone, a little tremble of excitement in his old hands, but the fire of battle in his eyes.

"Would you like another little brush with the enemy, my boy general?" whispers the Maréchal of France.

"Anything that you order, my chief," answers Raymond, saluting.

"Well then, to you I confide the safety, this evening, of Monsieur Lass, the friend of the army—the friend of the Regent."

"*Sapristi!* what do you mean?" asks D'Arnac astounded.

"It is a delicate little affair. Therefore I have given it into your hands. I have learned within the last five minutes, by this note just given to me, and signed "A Friend of the Army," that Monsieur Lass, as he drives home alone in his carriage, is to be arrested by order of the Parliament, and that they intend to hang him within ten minutes after he gets into their hands."

"*Diable!*" mutters D'Arnac. "But the Regent?"

"The Regent has gone away. Monsieur Lass is there alone in his box. I have warned him not to leave it for the present, until Lanty can get some of the men together. Lass has seen that our soldiers received pay, when no one else would look to their interests. We must look to our financier's safety now that this infernal Parliament (which is ready to take away the privileges of royalty) has decided that its first blow shall fall upon the man who has given France prosperity under the Regent. This note states that there are three details of Exempts and Police to make the arrest. Twenty immediately outside the theatre, twenty on the Pont Neuf and twenty stationed outside Lass' house in the Place Louis le Grand. You must get Monsieur Lass safely to the Palais Royal. They will not dare to enter the palace of the Regent. These are my orders! The details I leave to you."

"You may depend on me! Monsieur Lass shall not be arrested," replies Raymond.

"Come—I will introduce you to him," whispers De Villars.

So they step over through the empty theatre, and for the first time D'Arnac meets Uncle Johnny face to face.

"You have made the arrangements?" he says to the Duke, a slight tremble in his thin lips, for he knows once in the prison of the Conciergerie, he will be hung up like a dog within five minutes, long before the troops of the Duc d'Orleans can batter down its massive gates.

This combat had been coming on between Parliament and the Regent for some months, but this *coup d'etat* is an unexpected step in the contest. It is the plan of De Mesme, their chief president, and it has all the greater chance of success for Parliament will not be in full session for two more days—consequently it is unlooked for.

"I entrust your safety to Monsieur le General d'Arnac," remarks De Villars. "With him I know you are safe, if courage and conduct can save you."

"I am pleased to meet you, General," replies the financier, though he opens his eyes a little at the name, and looks searchingly, almost doubtingly, for one moment, at the young man.

"I'll have everything safe for you in three minutes," replies Raymond, "as soon as Lanty gets the men."

A moment after the Irishman comes in upon them. He stares horribly at the financier, and his appearance does not seem to make that gentleman over-confident, as De Villars says: "Into the hands of these men, whom you can trust, I place you!"

"Tare-an-ages! It's Uncle Johnny!" mutters Lanty, looking with evil eyes upon the gentleman confided to his charge.

But Raymond whispers to him: "Military duty—obey me! Are the men ready?"

And Lanty, from force of military habit, saluting, says: "Yes, General."

"How many?"

"Thirty."

"Good fighters?"

"Veterans, every one. I picked 'em up fighting drunk in the wine shop around the corner."

"Are they sober enough to obey orders?"

"Yes, and God help the men opposed to them!"

"Are they armed?"

"Only with bayonets, but we broke open the property room of the theatre, and I have given out all the Grecian spears I could find, and be jabbers I've got the sword of Theseus to fight with meself!" mutters Lanty with a grin. "Here's a blunderbuss for you, which ain't been loaded since Richelieu, but it will do to frighten 'em with. Its bark is worse than its bite!"

"Did you find any officers?"

"Yes, De Soubise, De Rohan and Lenoir are waiting outside for you. I told them the Maréchal commanded it."

"Do you think we could get him out by the stage entrance without their knowing?"

"No. They've two spies there to give the alarm!"

"Very well!" replies Raymond, and turning to Monsieur Lass, he says: "If you will step into the foyer so you can enter the carriage quickly, I think I can arrange the affair."

"What are your plans?" asks De Villars.

"First, to bring on a fight with the police in front of the theatre. Whip them before they can obtain reinforcements. Then put Monsieur Lass in his carriage, myself riding by the coachman, and drive, avoiding the Pont Neuf and his house, straight to the Palais Royal. It is merely a matter of time; if we can dispose of the police outside before they receive reinforcements."

But to succeed in this he must act quickly.

Hurriedly telling Lanty to get his forces and attack the police in the rear, as soon as he sees them engaged in front, Raymond comes quickly down to the entrance of the theatre, and there finds the three young officers to whom he explains the affair, and who are very eager to draw swords in defense of Monsieur Lass, who has given them their pay, and the Regent, who will give them their promotion.

Then Raymond steps out upon the street.

In front of the theatre are lounging about twenty *agents de Ville*—some in uniform—others in citizens' clothes—but all apparently armed.

Monsieur Lass' equipage, which is immediately in front of that of the Duc de Villars, is drawn up some ten steps away from the entrance of the theatre, its coachman apparently asleep on the box, and its footmen lounging about the entrance.

The *gendarmes* will evidently not move till Lass comes out to his carriage.

The combat must be brought on at once.

Raymond does so. He steps up to the foremost *sergeant de Ville* (one whom he thinks the leader) and promptly, without a word of warning, knocks him down with his fist.

Then, as the man lies groveling, he hisses: "*Canaille*, clear the way for an officer of the army!"

But the *canaille* do not clear the way!

With an awful curse, the *gendarme* springs up and cries to his men to arrest this ruffian!

But that is not so easy. D'Arnac's blade has flashed from its scabbard, and De Soubise, De Rohan and Lenoir have run out beside him, drawing their swords as they come on.

The four form, as if on parade, barring the entrance of the theatre.

"That's the scoundrel who struck me!" cries the leader of the *gendarmes*, pain making him oblivious of the fact that the blow was simply to bring on attack. "Arrest him!"

Then the fight commences.

The police think they will have an easy matter of it, but they do not; for there are three good swordsmen opposed to them, and one a master of every art of fence, the finest swordsman in France, perchance in Europe—Gaston Lenoir!

Even as he fights, Raymond can't help noticing the beautiful play of this gentleman, as he stands by his side, keeping two *exempts* armed with sabres, and a sergeant of police with his partisan, not only at bay but *very* busy.

"*Pardi!*" laughs Lenoir, as he springs at and spits the sergeant, "I have had no real play for my Toledo now for months!"

But this combat will not last long. De Soubise, though he has wounded one of the police, has received a blow that has dazed him; Raymond has a slight scratch on his left arm, and numbers would conquer in the end.

But just at this moment, with a wild, half drunken yell, the thirty veterans of the Regiment of Alsace come into the street, from around the corner, headed by Lanty, and fall upon the rear of the amazed and astonished *officiers de Ville*.

"God forgive the police, for we won't!" shouts Lanty. And though his sword of Theseus is dull, he uses it as a club, flooring an unfortunate *gendarme*.

With this they make very short work of the police, driving them up and down the street, and scattering them everywhere.

"Now is our time!" says Raymond, and orders up the carriage of Monsieur Lass, but the coachman seems to be dazed.

"Wake up, or I'll blow your brains out!" cries D'Arnac, and the sight of his blunderbuss arouses the coachman.

The carriage is drawn up, and wringing Monsieur de Villars' hand, and thanking him, the financier is put into it, D'Arnac mounts the box alongside of the coachman, Lanty and the big Sergeant Le Bœuf of the regiment (who is still waving its banner with little Quinault's name upon it) take the place of the footmen, Lenoir and De Rohan spring into the carriage, and off they drive.

"Fast!" whispers D'Arnac to the coachman.

"*Pardieu!* do you want to kill the beasts?"

"Faster!" cries Raymond, and they fly along the Rue Dauphin, towards the Pont Neuf; but arriving there Raymond says: "Along the Quai Conti, cross by the Pont Royal!"

"The other is the easiest and quickest bridge!" mutters the man.

"Obey me, or out go your brains, and I drive myself!" and Raymond has the property blunderbuss of the Theatre Français at the head of the affrighted *cocher*.

He remembers there are twenty policemen in waiting for Monsieur Lass upon the bridge the man would drive across, and altogether from the conduct of the coachman, suspects him.

The property blunderbuss is potent. They fly along the Quai Conti, and cross the river by the Pont Royal, and so on, by one or two roundabout streets, till they reach the Palace of the Regent.

So Monsieur Lass, arriving at the Palais Royal, comes in with his peculiar body of attendants, and brings astonishment to the potentate of France.

As the financier is announced the Regent sends word by one of his gentlemen in waiting to admit him, and before selection can be made of his attendants they all crowd into the supper room of Monsieur d'Orleans.

For these entertainments are of so promiscuous a character that the lackeys having orders to admit the party do not feel sure in refusing any one.

So Raymond comes in because he has promised the Duc de Villars to deliver Monsieur Lass safe to the Regent; Lenoir and De Rohan because they want Monsieur d'Orleans to know that they are his very good friends and zealous officers; Le Bœuf because he thinks there may be drink money for him in the affair, and Lanty, because he has made up his mind to make personal appeal to Uncle Johnny for some of Dillon's diamonds of the Turk.

On seeing this heterogeneous following of his financier D'Orleans springs up from the supper table, crying: "*Diable!* What have we here?"

And one or two of the fair ones at his board arise with little cries of fear, for the appearance of the whole party gives evidence of savage fray.

"Only my friends, and I believe your obedient servants, who have saved me from the police of Parliament to return me safe to your Highness!" replies Lass, and, telling his story, he introduces the three officers to the Regent, "Uncle Johnny" having made the acquaintance of De Rohan and Lenoir as they have driven along.

"My duty both to your Highness and the Maréchal de Villars being accomplished, if you will permit me I'll take my leave," remarks Raymond.

"I see you have a scratch that needs looking after," returns D'Orleans heartily, "so you have my permission. But I shall not forget you, General d'Arnac!"

As Raymond goes out he hears the Regent thanking Lenoir and De Rohan for their action.

"And you, my fine fellows," laughs the Prince looking at Lanty and the sergeant, "you did your share of the fighting, I presume?"

"Yes, your Highness, if killing a policeman is what you mean," says Le Bœuf bluntly; at which the fair ones about the table who have regained their spirits, go into giggles of glee.

"That's your duty. Sergeant, always remember killing policemen is your duty!" guffaws De Conti, "Monsieur Lass has a generous purse. What's your head rate for dead *sergeants de Ville, mon cher* Jean?"

"A thousand *livres!*" laughs the financier who has a very open pocket-book for those who serve him, and he hands a bank bill to the soldier that makes his martial eyes open. Then Lass continues: "Here are ten thousand more for the common soldiers who aided me. Will you be my almoner, Monsieur Lenoir?" passing the money to that gentleman.

But as he does this the banker grows pale, for he hears the too well remembered voice of Lanty speaking to the Regent of France, who is screaming with laughter at the Irishman's account of fighting the *gendarmes* with the property weapons of the *Comédie Française*.

Mr. Lanty is also proudly exhibiting to his Highness the sword of Theseus.

"Bedad!" he remarks, "I did as much damage with it as if it had been the real thing!"

"Here is your thousand *livres*, my good fellow!" cries Lass, interposing quickly, for he fears Lanty's glib tongue may make some awful confidence about la Sabran.

"Yes, that's very good in its way," replies the Irishman, "but it's the diamonds of the gineral I came to ask you about, Uncle Johnny."

"The diamonds—of the general! What's this—a new story?" laughs D'Orleans.

"Yes, and a divilish intertaining one!" answers Lanty.

But he doesn't get farther for the financier suddenly ejaculates:

"Oh yes—those in my charge—I understand—To-morrow at my bank!" and fairly hustles Lanty to the door, whispering: "To-morrow at twelve, remember."

"Divil doubt I'll forget!" jeers the Irishman, and goes away cogitating: "If I had told the Regent I'd have made an awful mess, but got nothing but hate and curses from any of them. Now as I've still the secret, I think I'll make Uncle Johnny come down handsome."

The sudden entry of the Prince de Condé and Monsieur le Marquis d'Argenson fortunately keeps his Highness from asking Lass inconvenient questions, for ever since he has heard the news of this step of Parliament, the Regent has been making his arrangements, and his friends and confidantes have been summoned and a company of *Musquetaires Noirs* are on guard in front of the palace.

A moment after the supper party breaks up, Monsieur d'Orleans and his confederates go into council—for the attitude of the deputies of the people is a very serious question for them to consider.

Going over the matter as they sit about him, the Regent concludes: "We must make very short work of this *canaille* Parliament, and their backer, that bastard, the Duc du Maine!"

"It's that accursed president of their's, that villain, Jean Antoine de Mesme!" growls Conti, savagely, "who's doing his bidding!"

"Let me at them!" whispers D'Argenson, who remembers the insults they have put upon him as Lieutenant de Police. "Let me at them with the seals of France in my hands, and the King upon his throne, and we'll crush them to the earth."

And so they do!

And in the course of the next two months, Monsieur Law remaining under the protection of D'Orleans in the Palais Royal itself, the Regent and his gang fall upon the representatives of the people.

Though on June 27th, Parliament sends a remonstrance, and on July 2d, the deputies go to D'Orleans in person, and on August 12th, issue a decree declaring that the administration of finance is to be in the hands of Parliament, taking from the Regent and Monsieur Law all power over the taxes of France, and demanding an accounting of all the *billets d'etat* issued and given to the Mississippi and Western companies, as well as those taken to the mint to be exchanged for specie,—all these come to naught!

The Regent and his clique, De Conti, De Condé, Saint-Simon, D'Argenson and all his backing, fall upon Parliament, threaten them with *lettres de cachet* and to lock them up in the Bastille. Finally, bringing the child, Louis XV., into their session, D'Argenson, as Keeper of the Seals, tells them the King wants to be obeyed, and to be obeyed quickly!

Then D'Orleans kindly informs the deputies what are the King's commands, and though their chief president gnashes his teeth, they obey very quickly, and rescind their bill taking from the Regent financial power, and acquiesce in his appointment of Law as comptroller-general of all the finances of France, and he becomes a grandee of the Kingdom, and is addressed humbly as *Monseigneur.*

Then the country grows apparently more prosperous and richer than ever, and the people cry with wild huzzas: "Long live the King and Monseigneur Lass!"

The Duc du Maine has his titles taken from him and is imprisoned, and Lass and his system reigns supreme.

The stockbrokers in the Rue Quincampoix cry louder and louder, and the shares of the India Company become more and more valuable, until finally they reach par about the middle of the year 1719.

CHAPTER XXIV.

THE WATER FÊTE AT MARSEILLES.

BUT Raymond does not remain in Paris to see all this.

Coming back from his interview with the Regent, he makes his way to the Hotel de Chateaubrien, and there is received for a moment but indifferently well.

Madame la Marquise strides up to him as he enters the salon and whispers: "You cruel one! You have stabbed her to the heart!"

"How?"

"By indifference."

"Does this look like indifference?" remarks Raymond glumly, exhibiting his wounded arm, and showing his battered uniform.

"You were wounded for *her!*" gasps Mimi excitedly. "Some fight with those awful critics?"

"*Sapristi!*" answers D'Arnac, with a mocking laugh. "Though critics' pens cut deep, this is not exactly a wound of their making," and gives his sister a rapid history of the affair. Then he suddenly says: "Where's Jeanne?"

"In her room. She wouldn't—" but Mimi checks herself. She does not care for her brother to know how deeply her young *protégée* has been affected. She goes on suddenly: "I will run up and tell her. I'm sure she'll be happy to understand she did not miss your congratulations by willful neglect."

"Very well," says Raymond, "while you make my apologies to *la Phèdre*, I'll help myself to supper. By-the-bye," he calls after Mimi, "if you have some old linen in the house, bring it back with you. I think a bandage would rather improve my arm."

With this he walks into the dining-room, to find the supper table decorated *en fête*, and undisturbed in all its flowers and menu.

"*Diable!* What delicate appetites we ladies have," he laughs, not guessing that Jeanne, from wounded pride, and Mimi, from intense indignation, had forgotten to eat.

Sitting down to this, and making himself, with the assistance of butler and attendant flunkeys, very comfortable and happy, Monsieur d'Arnac in five minutes finds two ministering angels at his side.

For Mimi has made his peace with Jeanne, and the two have come bounding down to him, bearing armfuls of softest linen to save the wounded warrior's life.

Little Quinault is a sylph as she flutters around him with pathetic hands. In her haste to come to the assistance of the dying hero, she has hastily thrown on an exquisite *négligé* that is all lace, furbelows and ribbons, and makes her look as ethereal as the butterfly *Phèdre*, that had died upon the stage an hour before.

"To think, Mimi," cries the girl, "while we were saying he neglected us, he was fighting one hundred awful policemen, under the orders of grandpapa De Villars, and saving the life of Monsieur Lass, who has made every one in France so rich and happy, and who has hinted he would make my fortune, if I would put my salary upon the Bourse. By-the-bye, what is my salary, Monsieur Raymond?"

"Nothing!" remarks that young gentleman hurriedly.

"Nothing?" scream both the ladies in commercial horror.

"To tell you the truth, Jeanne, when I made the arrangement for you, I forgot about it. No sum was mentioned," mutters Raymond sheepishly.

"Brava!" ejaculates Mimi, who has been forced to become a business woman in the management of her estate. "Brava! no contract—name what you please—they'll have to pay it *now!* Raymond, they must not have her cheap!"

"No," answers the young man, "for little Jeanne I will become as greedy as a contractor."

But business is soon forgotten in bandaging the wounded warrior's arm. They make it almost a caressing business. With two such nurses the young general revives sufficiently to eat a very pleasant meal, and curiously enough, appetite has also come to little Quinault and Madame la Marquise.

There is no happier trio in Paris this night, as they sit together and talk over their plans for the coming star in the great dramatic world.

"You must have your own *salon* and establishment, Jeanne; a great actress should always have a *salon*. Raymond will arrange for a handsome suite of apartments for you, and I will furnish you a duenna."

"Do with me what you like," remarks la Quinault, "only don't—don't turn your backs upon me." Here tears come into her eyes and she begs: "Don't think I am strong enough to fight my own battle without your love, your friendship, Mimi—and your far-seeing brain, guardian general, to guide me!" This last a little archly.

Then, as the young man is taking his leave, she suddenly courtesies to him, takes his hand and kisses it as she did when a child, and whispers: "*Mon Seigneur*, this triumph of mine has made no difference between us—I am *still* your vassal!"

This kind of thing makes Mimi tremble. She breaks in, saying: "Nonsense, Jeanne! You have now a great career before you!"

"But I am still under vassalage to the man who has placed it before me by his kindness, his influence, and his generosity. The higher I am, the humbler I shall make obeisance to Monsieur le Comte d'Arnac—*Mon Seigneur!*"

And the coming great star in the dramatic firmament gives the young general a glance that sends him away very proud and very important and very protecting to this beautiful creature who places herself so much under his wing.

But Raymond is fated to see very little of the immediate glories of la Quinault.

The day after her début he receives notice of his appointment to the command of the great port of Marseilles.

This is a tremendous step for a young officer, for it practically gives him the rank of a lieutenant-general with emoluments and fees that produce a very fine professional income.

This sudden luck has been owing to Uncle Johnny, who, wishing to do the young man a favor, yet fearing to have him in Paris on account of various matters connected with the volatile mistress of the Regent, thinks this is the best way to settle the affair, and has petitioned the Duc d'Orleans to that effect.

It would be madness to refuse. Raymond accepts at once, and four days after departs for Marseilles.

In doing this he leaves Lanty behind him, for that gentleman has made his bargain with the financier and has received as compromise for the diamonds of the Turk (of which the avaricious la Sabran will not yield a single one) a piece of property which is now quite valuable, and as real estate is rising rapidly, promises to make him very comfortable in the world.

With the title deeds to this in his pocket, Lanty decides to give up soldiering and turn innkeeper.

"Faix, I'm tired of taking plunder and playing the game of 'light come—quick go!'" he remarks to Raymond. "If ye will honor me by sending any friends of yours from Marseilles to the tavern of 'The Turk's Head,' at the corner of the Rue de Petit Lion and Rue St. Denis, I'll pray for you whenever I go on my knees."

Which will not be often, as Lanty, after the manner of most soldiers, is a very bad churchman.

But before D'Arnac departs, one little interview with la Quinault takes place, and impresses itself upon his memory.

She is already in her own apartments on the Rue de Condé quite near the theatre. She has had another appearance and an equally great triumph, and D'Arnac has made a very good arrangement for her with the

management of the *Comedie Française*. In a few months
she will become a *societaire*.

She says pathetically: "You have your walk in life
—I have mine now—this separates us, but not for long,
I hope. But here—here is something by which you can
remember the little Quinault, the naughty girl for whom
you have done so much!"

This something is a miniature of her own fair face on
ivory set round with pearls; not perhaps as gorgeously
beautiful as the one he still has of la Sabran, with its
flashing diamonds—but oh, how much sweeter womanhood there is in it!

"When you hear of my triumphs, if I ever have any
more," she murmurs, "look at this picture, and think it
is all owing to your goodness to me! And so, good-bye,
Mon Seigneur!"

Then says, hysterically: "I—I must not sob, for I am
studying a—a comedy rôle," and cries, vivaciously:
"What do you think of that? I am to make people
laugh! Do you hear me? Laugh! Ha! ha! Ho! ho! He!
he!" and, with a giggle on her dear little mouth and a tear
in her bright, blue eyes, Mademoiselle Jeanne bids
her guardian good-bye.

"It is the best thing in the world for him," thinks Mimi,
as she gives Raymond her adieu kiss, for la Marquise is
growing fearful of Mademoiselle Quinault's praise, which
is being sung everywhere, and imagines it just as well that
her brother should not have too much of it.

So Raymond takes his departure for Marseilles, leaving behind him Paris, which is growing greater and
richer every day, with its increasing commerce, its
excited stock market, and the tremendous financial
operations of Monseigneur Law, that seem to scatter
paper money all over the land, making it rich.

For now gradually developing itself, his great
commercial schemes of colonization and settlement
in both the Indies and the new world comes to the
fore.

Early in 1719 a decree goes forth from the Regent
giving the India Company the sole right of trading
in all seas beyond the Cape of Good Hope, which means
all the East Indies, the islands of Madagascar and
France, and the Archipelago of the Indian Ocean.

In addition to this, the bank of Monseigneur Law is reorganized and made the Royal Bank of France, with one hundred and ten million *livres* of capital, and that great financier puts out his lines to draw into his companies and schemes all the great trading interests of France.

It is with these great views of interesting the general public of France and impressing upon them the grandeur of his scheme of colonial settlement and development that Monseigneur Law, under the sanction and by the aid of the Regent, proposes the great water fête at Marseilles.

It is to be the welcome of the grand fleet bearing the first great shipment for the year of the products of Louisiana to France. It has been heralded through the country by word of mouth and by official announcement, and Paris is all agog for the wonders of the New World that the India Company is opening to it.

It is rumored on the Rue Quincampoix among the brokers, who are already becoming very rich in dealing in this new stock that Monseigneur Law is touching with the hand of Midas, that there is to be gold from the mines of Louisiana among the shipments. The grand dames of Versailles and the Faubourgs St. Honoré and Saint Germain are all eagerly petitioning the financier for promises of handsome little pickaninny Indians, to be decked out with their armorial bearings and serve as pages, carrying their trains and fans and parasols, and, by contrasting bronze, make the lilies of the fair ones' cheeks seem doubly beauteous, for it is whispered there is a whole tribe of the savages of the Mississippi on board the coming squadron.

This fleet is expected about the first of June of the year 1719, and preparations are being made to receive it in a way that shall impress not only France, but Europe itself, with the grandeur and immensity of the riches the New World is about to throw into the lap of the India Company.

This is the idea of Monsiegneur Law, who, in some things, is quite theatrical.

The necessary orders having been issued, Raymond d'Arnac, as commandant of the port of Marseilles, finds himself very busy in carrying them out and making the necessary local arrangements, for a couple of extra regiments have been ordered to the place to give additional military grandeur to the scene, and a squadron of galleys and frigates have come from the great naval arsenal of Toulon.

Deputations from the merchants of Lyons, and even Havre, have come to meet this first shipment of the products of the new land, whose distance gives it a fabled wealth.

Now, Monseigneur Lass has altogether too long a head to make any mistakes of time, even in a theatrical fête.

He has received news by quick felucca that the squadron of ships bearing the products of Louisiana has passed the Straits of Gibraltar, and has made his arrangements as to date of reception accordingly.

He is journeying to the Mediterranean by quick relays of post horses, followed by a goodly number of the court of France and leading financiers of the city of Paris, for he has put money into the pockets of many of them—both nobles and commoners. In his personal party, even De Conti does not hesitate, notwithstanding his pride of rank, to travel. The Prince de Condé and the Maréchal de Noailles are with him, and among the beauties in their company are the pretty Marquise de Prie, the sylph-like Madame de Verue, and the vivacious Locmaria; but the loveliness of none is to be compared with that of la Princess de Paris.

Monsieur d'Orleans, being of too easy-going and lazy a disposition to trouble himself with any such long journey, has delegated the Prince de Condé to represent him, and has given permission, grudgingly perchance, to the beautiful De Sabran to grace with her presence this fête that is to be semi-royal at least in magnificence.

Cousin Charlie would make one of the party, for his avaricious soul is glowing with the thought of all the money that will come to him from the success of their grand enterprise, but his rickety old bones cannot endure a journey to the Mediterranean by post chaise. "Five hundred miles," he sighs; "*pardieu!* that is too much for even a boy like me, to view the wonders of the West. *Sapristi!* but it is at this end, in Paris, that the money will flow in!"

On this journey, the second day after they have passed Arles on the river Rhone, a courier, riding for his life, reaches Monseigneur Lass and his party, bringing news that the fleet have already been sighted from Cape Morgion.

Plying whip and spur, on this joyful communication, they reach Marseilles, to find that the fleet have anchored outside the islands of Ratoneau and Pomègue; they having been boarded by the orders of Monseigneur Law and told not to enter the harbor until everything was prepared for their reception.

So the sailors on their decks, after their six months' voyage, sit waiting for the next day and whistling for a breeze to put them once more on the shore of their native France, and in the arms of their friends and sweethearts, who are awaiting them on the platform of the Fort St. John and gazing at them from the more distant Cape Corisande.

The town of Marseilles is wildly excited over the coming fortunes that this new commerce from Louisiana will bring to their docks to make them rich, for at the suggestion of Monseigneur Lass, the Regent is about to make the city a *free port*.

Entering the town rather late in the evening, the great financier finds most of the nobility have arrived before him.

He is received, in company with the Prince de Condé and his party, by General d'Arnac as commandant of the garrison, the Mayor of the city and various local officials.

He gives Raymond his hand warmly, for this Scotchman is a great diplomatist, and believes in making every one he can his friend. Besides, Uncle Johnny, remembering D'Arnac had practically saved his neck that night at the Français, forgets for one short moment the part this dashing general of twenty-six has played in the life of Madame de Sabran.

He is reminded of this, however, by the beauty's greeting to the handsome young officer.

She has *not* forgotten, and as she looks on Raymond's distinguished face and easy martial bearing, she has said to herself: "The cup that has been twice dashed from my lips shall be at last placed there. This man, from whose arms fortune has twice stolen me, shall yet be mine!"

She forgets the slight of the theatre—she remembers only the boy who swam the flooded river for her sake—who said: "Will you dare it for me?"—whose heart her's has once beaten against so wildly—who she had seen fight for her, one to six, that day near Mieux.

If Raymond has grown more handsome, she perchance has become more fascinating, for her experience in the social world has made her bright intellect even more vivacious. Perhaps this meeting with the man she has often said to herself is still the man of her heart, adds to her arch loveliness.

The other ladies of this gay company look worn, pale and dusty, after their long drive of over five hundred miles from Paris But she, shaking coquettishly the dust of the Rhone Valley from her pretty traveling costume, and displaying a foot and ankle that poor O Brien Dillon used to rave about, is fresh and radiant, and apparently untired.

This evening Hilda finds chance for very few words with D'Arnac, but these are to the point.

She says lightly: "Oh, if I had known you were here, Monsieur Raymond, I should have put on a new toilette after my ride; but to-morrow I hope to do honor to the fête. To-morrow, I am told, we have a very beautiful pavilion prepared for us on the Isle Pomègue I presume music and a dance. You, I hope, will be one of our guests."

" If my official duties permit," answers the young man, dubiously, struggling with all his might against the fascination of her manner, and something in his heart that makes it beat again as it did at the *bal de l'Opéra.*

" Official duty will compel you to be there, as General Commandant," she says haughtily. Then her tone suddenly changes, for she notes that though his words are curt, perhaps harsh, his eyes are speaking very tenderly. She says pathetically: "Not as commandant of the forces but as Raymond d'Arnac, who has hardly been kind to me since he was once so very kind—that morning at Mieux. Let us forget the four years that have passed between that time and

this.   They are no more! To-morrow morning let it
be as if Mieux was to-day."

This, emphasized with beauteous eyes and an entreating hand that is extended to him—patrician in its deli-
cacy of outline—makes her irresistible.

Raymond remembers also that morning at Mieux, and
says eagerly: "Then to-morrow we commence as if
Monsieur de Conti's ruffians—" he glares savagely
at that Prince, who is pompously addressing the Mayor
of the town—"had not stolen you from me!"

It is a daring speech, but De Sabran likes ardor and
audacity.   She whispers one word into his ear, that
makes the young man tremble with a sudden passion—and
as he turns to go upon his official duties, Raymond d'Arnac
would not exchange places with any man in France.

It is just as well he leaves her, for at this moment,
Uncle Johnny, who has been watching them surrepti-
tiously out of one of his eyes, the other being devoted
to a deputation of the Marseilles merchants, succeeds
in breaking away from his surroundings, and is edging
towards naughty De Sabran with the intention of cutting short her *tête-à-tête* with General d'Arnac, whom he
recollects now—TOO WELL!

Until early morning Raymond is occupied in making
the necessary dispositions—civil, military and naval—for
the celebration of which he has supreme command.

These being finished, he gets a few hours' sleep,
and arises, refreshed, vigorous, and as he thinks of the
word whispered in his ear the evening before—elated
and exultant. He says to himself, his eyes lighting up
the fires of passion: "To-day—to-day—she whom I
love is mine!"

For like most young men D'Arnac called passion,
love and fleeting desire undying devotion.

CHAPTER XXV.

"TOGETHER!"

AFTER a hasty breakfast the young commandant,
whistling one of Lulli's happiest airs, saunters down to
the main port or basin, and walks along the Quai,
looking at the shipping decked with bunting in honor

of the occasion, more elated than Monseigneur Lass himself.

The day is warm and sultry even for Marseilles in June, surrounding hills keeping away all breezes that might give comfort under the blazing sun. The white walls glare, unmitigated by the green of the vineyards on the hillside, for the vine leaves are covered over with their summer dust. There is no sea breeze; all is quiet and placid and burning on the harbor of Marseilles.

Floating upon the waters of the tideless Mediterranean that scarcely ripples, are five galleys in the King's service that have come from Toulon, rowed hither by the wretched slaves they call *forçats*. These, decked with bunting, and two or three frigates of France, made also picturesque by the flags of all nations displayed from lofty masts and tapering yards, make the naval portion of the pageant.

The heavy frigates, driven only by the winds of heaven, cannot move in the still air. The light galleys, propelled by the arms of men, must do all the work of conveying the semi-regal party to the Isle of Pom gue, and towing thereafter the ships from Louisiana into the basin of the port.

Soon word is brought Raymond by his orderly that Monseigneur Lass and the Prince de Condé are anxious to proceed with the affair.

They are desirous of getting through the ceremony of the reception as soon as possible, so as to journey to the little island that looks so cool, surrounded by the blue sea, where pavilions have been erected, and a fête fit for the gods will be held.

On this isle the semi-regal party will spend the night, sleeping apartments having been erected and decorated especially for their accommodation by the order of Monseigneur Lass.

The military are drawn up, the Mayor reads the proclamation of the Regent making the port free of duties, from the steps of the Hotel de Ville, right opposite the Quai. The populace, decked in the light costumes of summer, make all the borders of the basin of Marseilles brilliant with moving life. The cannons thunder from the Forts St. Michel and St. John and the frigates and galleys in the harbor.

The frigates remain motionless. No breeze is rippling the water to permit their spreading sail.

The galleys, propelled by human force—the steamboats of that day—dash about from quai to quai, picking up the various divisions of the guests assigned to them to take them first to the Isle Pomègue; then to escort and, if necessary, tow the ships from the New World in triumph past that island and into the basin of the harbor.

One of these galleys, *La Sylphide*, is detailed for the personal use of Monseigneur Law and his semiregal party.

It has been especially decorated for the occasion, and floats the water graceful as a beautiful bird. Its two short masts, with their long lateen yards, are made bright with the colors of all nations. Its high forecastle, on which are mounted several culverins and short light cannons for salute and offense, and its prow ornamented by some dragon's head, the work of that great naval designer, Le Puget, have been freshly gilded for the occasion.

Its poop cabins have been decorated in blue and gold, and over them waves a canopy of tapestries woven in the looms of Lyons, with the arms of France. Above this floats a great white silken banner, bearing the royal *fleur de lys*.

In the eyes of the admiring multitude she looks fair enough to have come from fairyland; but between this gilded forecastle and this high poop decorated with delicate silks and satins that make awnings under which beautiful women will lounge in softly cushioned chairs, bent over by gallant men, happy, triumphant, prosperous—is the long low waist, ONE HUNDRED FEET OF LIVING HELL; peopled by wretches that have no hope in this world, nor the next—the galley slaves!

Driven by fifty oars, twenty-five on each side, she skims the basin like a thing of life—but oh, the agony of flesh and blood that produces this graceful velocity—this birdlike agility. Three hundred *forçats*, red caps and camisoles upon them, but practically *almost as nude as the day they were born*—curse and sweat under the lashes of the stalwart boatswain and his cruel mates.

Through the dead center of the craft, extending from decorated poop to gilded forecastle, is a plank some two feet wide occupied generally by the *comité*, or boatswain, and his agile assistants, who use it for their convenience in running about and urging with swishing lash the naked shoulders of the slaves—to greater toil and harder exercise.

Each of the ponderous oars, fifty feet long, thirteen feet of which is inboard, is driven by the exertions of six wretches, whose sinews have become of steel, and whose muscles have become of iron, under the relentless toil of the galley.

Each individual wretch is chained to his bench, on which he toils till he dies and is thrown overboard, by one iron circlet round the waist, another round an ankle.

Thus they row, sleep and *die;* in winter covered, if the night is cold and the galley is at anchor, by a few rugs to keep them from freezing to death.

Three work sitting, the other half of them nearer the extremity of the spar, toil standing; all pushing the oar forward, its blade out of water, to the length of their tether, and then throwing themselves backward upon the seat, which rebounds with their concussion—the work of giants given to the bodies of wretches whose rations are but poor, scant and irregular.

Moved by this force of agony, *La Sylphide*, her guns booming, her one hundred and twenty-five free soldiers and sailors cheering, her officers laughing and saluting, her boatswain's lashes hissing merrily, dashes up to the Quai to receive the Princes De Conti and De Condé, Monseigneur Lass, Financier-General of the Kingdom of France, and their surrounding sycophants and beauties.

Among them is Hilda de Sabran, more lovely perchance than ever she has been in her life, for the costume of summer suits her graceful, willowy form, and she has been decked by the greatest milliner in France for this *fête* and pageant.

She is laughing, happy, triumphant, radiant—for is *he* not here, standing by the side of the gang plank, and offering gallant hand to pass her on to the galley's poop? And she is whispering in his ear: " Raymond, the *fête!*

Remember—THIS NIGHT NAUGHT SHALL STAND BETWEEN
THY HEART AND MINE."

They are all on board.   Her delicate hand, decked in
lightest glove, is waving D'Arnac adieu, and surrounding
her in attitudes of grace are the fair women and brave
men of France, laughing and chatting and loving.

The captain of the galley, the dashing Comte de
Chateau Rouge, gives signal to the *comité*, and cries:
"Speed there!   Give the slaves the measure!"

The boatswain's pipe whistles cheerily, and his savage
mates, anxious to show their skill, ply rattan and whip
over the bending backs of the sweating *forçats* that
struggle with the oars to make the galley fly over the
harbor of Marseilles.

Outside on the blue sea, the vessels from Louisiana,
favored by a little wind, are now coming up.   So *La
Sylphide* heads straight for the temporary landing
place that has been erected and beautified upon the fair
shores of the island Pomègue.

But as they dance over the waves one of the other
galleys, which has an ambitious captain, nearly overtak-
ing them, the volatile little Marquise de Prie cries, clap-
ping tiny hands together: " Oh, we shall have a race!
Captain—a race—a race if you love me!"

And the Comte de Chateau Rouge, wishing to find
favor in the eyes of his fair guests, and proud that *La
Sylphide* is the swiftest in the fleet, commands the *comité*:
" More speed! *Tonn..de Dieu!* the *forçats* lag to-day!"

With this the boatswain quickens the stroke, whips
are plied on laggard backs, and moans come up from
the *forçats*.

The other galley increases her velocity as well, and is
now nearly alongside.

"O–o–ugh—Captain! don't let them beat us!" cries
la Sabran, who has grown interested in the affair.
" Haven't you the quickest galley of them all ?"

These words from the favorite of the Regent and the
beauty of France excite De Chateau Rouge to greater
efforts.   He goes forward and orders: "Increase the
measure, quick!"

Which the boatswain does, *till the stroke is that of a
galley in action*, when slaves drop dead from horrible
exertion.

The ladies clap their hands and cry joyously: "We're gaining!" "Row, Captain, row!" "We've gloves wagered!" and other little ejaculations of feminine delight.

De Chateau Rouge says to the *comité* again: "Increase the measure!"

And now the foam is flying from the galley's beak, and the great panting breaths of the struggling *forçats* in the waist, come up in heaves, and the lash is plied by ambitious boatswain's mates, till groans and curses and screams roll up as if from *Tartarus*.

"Oh, we're doing beautifully *now*, Captain!" cries De Sabran, springing from her seat. "We're gaining—we're gaining—we're winning!"

And tripping forward with two light steps, she takes stand on the foremost plank of the poop deck.

Her pretty little hat sits jauntily upon her delicate head, her blue eyes are blue as the sea on which she looks. Her fair hair is gilded by the sun; her lips are red as the coral that is coming from the Indies. Her dress, light as the gossamer of fairyland, is studded with sparkling jewels. Upon her head blazes the great crescent of the Ottoman, with its lesser star. One perfect foot is perched in silken hose and dainty slipper upon the low rail, and gathering from it with one deft hand her shimmering skirts, the other waving an excited parasol all lace and ribbons, she stands—the goddess of beauty triumphant over Hades.

And just at this moment the sunbeams light the great crescent of the Ottoman Vizier, with its lesser star, and the diamonds of the Turk gleam and flash in the very faces of the struggling galley slaves.

Suddenly over the moans of suffering toil and the quick gasps for mighty breath taken in their awful travail, over the swift swish of the flying lash, over the screams of writhing wretches whose shoulders drip with blood—comes up one shriek more potent than the rest —one scream so shrill, wierd and unearthly that it seems the first shriek of a lost soul let loose in hell.

With a shudder, for Hilda has feminine nerves, the beauty of the Regent puts both little hands to her ears and runs back to the stern, where she sinks upon a lounge and tries to forget this awful cry, meditating on

the coming night, and Raymond; though De
Guiche is whispering in her fair ears the latest *bons mots*
of Paris, and trying very gallantly to entertain the
goddess of the *fête*.

This scream is little thought of by the others,
ladies or gentlemen, officers or sailors; though the
boatswain whispers to one of his mates: "To-day has
given us another maniac at the oar!"

But this is a common occurrence. Creatures go mad
upon their benches, and row as madmen till death
comes to them, for they are not released. The
maniac's strength is even greater than that of the
despairing wretches who work beside him.

So naught answers this awful cry, save that the
lashes fall quicker as the *comité* gives increased speed
to the measure that each oar must keep in perfect time
and cadence, no matter how quick the stroke, for one
oar out of time, the rest become disorganized—disabled.
Dead men must row when the galley is in motion.

Monseigneur Lass, the gentlemen and ladies on the
poopdeck and in the cabin, are all chatting very
merrily.

The financier remarks to the Prince de Conti: "The
scene is beautiful, and the sun is not so very hot!"

For there is an awning over his head, and he is in
quite an affable humor.

Even now they are rowing past the vessels of the
Mississippi fleet.

The ladies clap their hands as these sail past them,
making quite a theatrical effect, for their captains have
had instructions, and parrots are perched upon their
rigging, and monkeys play among the shrouds, and
there are Indians in feathers, wampum, and war paint,
dancing on their decks; and strange animals from the
New World call forth cries of astonishment and admiration from the wondering lips of lookers on.

One vessel has its rigging tufted with the cotton of
the new colony, and another her mast'heads surrounded
with the sugar cane of Louisiana.

The sailors are cheering, and the pageant looks very
bright, beautiful, and happy, as *La Sylphide*, after
inspecting the fleet, dashes for the pretty isle of
Pomègue.

But now the wind fails the ships, and the galleys, after delivering the guests at the island, dash out, take these great vessels in tow, and the slaves must again toil at the oar, for their day's work is as merciless and hard as the fête is successful and grand.

So the vessels swinging into the harbor, past the Fort St. John, come up to the Quai to be received by Raymond d'Arnac. There is great cheering from the crowd, for part of the cargo of one of the ships is gold and silver bullion, which did not come from Louisiana, though the throng do not know it, and, perchance, was taken on board when the vessel stopped at Cuba—the products of mines in Mexico or Peru.

The sacks of coffee that they display to eager sight-seers probably come from the Brazils, though all is credited to this new land that is to make France rich, and the India Company's stock goes very high in the financial firmament.

Though D'Arnac has a good deal to do, he is General Commandant of the Port of Marseilles, and promptly getting through his more important duties, details the rest to subordinates.

Consequently about seven in the evening, as the great band of musicians, brought from Paris for the occasion, are playing the sweetest melodies of the ballet entitled "The Loves of Jupiter," Raymond arrives, on one of the galleys plying between the Quai of Marseilles and the Isle Pomègue, at the fête of Monseigneur Lass.

Not having had anything to eat since the morning, he makes a hasty but delightful supper in one of the pavilions of refreshment.

The end of the meal is even more pleasant than its beginning, for, with the instinct of love, Hilda de Sabran has found him, and with fluttering eyes and blushing cheeks, has seated herself at his side, whispering: "At last you are here!"

Then the young man grows blushing also, for she has purred in his ear: "Raymond, my love!"

Perchance as he looks in her eyes, the blue eyes of another woman, who is at this moment making the Français ring with plaudits at her piquant graces and fascinating emotions, on the stage of that great theatre, come to him—but these eyes he looks upon are the *nearest*.

But now the present goddess goes to plying her arts of fascination and becomes curiously trembling and bashful, which makes her doubly enchanting, as she pathetically questions: "You have forgiven me?"

"Forgiven YOU?"

"Yes," she whispers, "that awful note received by O'Brien Dillon. You knew; in your heart of hearts you must have known it was addressed to YOU."

"Was it for ME?" asks Raymond, who likes to hear her supplicate, though he is very well aware she tells the truth. Then he gives a little sigh, not altogether of disappointment, for he is thinking of his lost comrade.

"Oh, cruel one!" falters Hilda, who, gazing on her handsome companion, now loves him with her very soul *for the present*. Then she breaks hoarsely forth: "Who changed the direction of that note? What traitor kept us apart and made you doubt me?"

"I have thought of the matter many times," replies D'Arnac, "but I cannot guess."

"Well, I can!" she mutters savagely.

"Who do you think?"

"Your Cousin Charlie."

"Impossible! Why do you think that?"

"Because Apollo, my negro page, confessed to my riding whip that he had given that letter I wrote you, my heart in each pen stroke, to a gentleman; and compelled by me he pointed out Monsieur de Moncrief as the man."

"What reason could he have?"

"That I do not know, but some day—" whispers Hilda, and her eyes say that "some day" will not be a pleasant one to Charles de Moncrief. But suddenly, as if afraid of her own rage, she turns the conversation, and her glance grows tender as her words as she murmurs: "To-night let us forget everything but *ourselves!*—you and I—my Raymond."

"Yes—all but ourselves. You tyrant of my heart," returns D'Arnac, who is romantic now, as what man would not be with supreme beauty by his side—that this night will be—HIS VERY OWN! the blue waves of the Mediterranean sighing at their feet—the soft moon lighting the eyes of his adored—the tender music of Lulli giving cadence to their heart beats.

At this moment even the memory of O'Brien Dillon stands not between. Why should the dead destroy a living love?

Into this reverie Hilda breaks with happy laugh—she whispers: "We must not linger here too long."

"Why not?"

"Uncle Johnny!" replies the beauty, tapping her little foot playfully. "Beware of Uncle Johnny!"

"You dance this evening?" whispers Raymond, looking at his prize, who is now gleaming under the blazing lights of the *pavillion de bal.*

"With you, if you wish."

"Come!"

The music is still playing, the minuet is being danced, and no more graceful couple move over the smooth floor, and no happier faces are under its bright lights, than that of Raymond d'Arnac and Hilda de Sabran, for one has thrown away conscience, and the other has no conscience to throw away—and both mean to be very happy in the love that lights their eyes this evening.

"BUT!"

This "but" is Monseigneur Lass.

Uncle Johnny, notwithstanding he has many engagements with fair women for the dance, and many bits of diplomatic social intercourse to make his standing stronger with the nobility, sees a good deal of what is going on.

And taking his opportunity, he gets chance word with Raymond, welcoming him to his fête, but saying to him: "My dear young officer, I am sorry to put an end to your pleasure this evening, especially as I am your host, but there is a meeting at the Prefecture to-night, in the city. The Regent gave me this address," he produces a paper, "charging me to request the officer in command, as his representative, to read it to the people of Marseilles. It speaks chiefly of the new fortifications that are to be erected to make the city stronger, as it is now to become such a great commercial port. It is especially appropriate for you, as general of the garrison, to read it. I know that was his Highness' intention when he gave it to me at Paris.   The meeting takes place at nine o'clock.   You will have plenty of time."

Under these circumstances, all Raymond can do is to accept the commission, though he does so with by no means the best grace.

But as he is going Hilda is beside him.   She says: "I saw my Uncle Johnny say something to you.   It was some commission that requires you to return to the city ?"

"Yes!   Confound his tricky soul," mutters D'Arnac in the agony of awful disappointment, gazing upon the fair being of whom he is despoiled.

"Oh, I guessed as much.   But we may balk Uncle Johnny after all.   What is your duty in Marseilles ?"

Then Raymond telling her of the commission given to him, she whispers: "The meeting takes place at nine.   It will be ended by ten.   At eleven o'clock the ball will still be going on.   By that time the revelry will be at its height, and Bacchus and Venus reign supreme.   The others will be too occupied in themselves to miss my presence!   If you love me, as I adore you, my Raymond," she goes on with entreating eyes, "meet me in front of pavilion number five at eleven o'clock.   That one—the one with the blue silk hangings.   Remember the time is vital. Be sure the place."

"At eleven o'clock—by that pavilion our hearts beat together," answers D'Arnac, his soul aflame.   Then he whispers words into the shell she calls her ear that make her very happy, but make her blush and run away.

And Raymond, taking one of the galleys that is still plying between the island and Marseilles, arrives at the Prefecture in time, and there makes a very glum and surly representative of complaisant royalty to the good citizens of the town, reading the Regent's letter in a haughty, hard and hasty voice, and not caring very much whether any of it is understood.

At last this is over, and he flies down to the Quai to utter the imprecations of disappointed eagerness.

Not one of the galleys is there.   They are all at the Isle Pomègue.

How to get back to the island in time, where the woman he longs for is awaiting him!

"If I disappoint her now, she will never forgive me," he moans, scanning with anxious eyes the port.

Suddenly hope springs up in him again. *La Sylphide* is coming into the basin with sturdy strokes, for fatigue is not permitted to interfere with its human machinery.

As soon as she puts off her passengers, among whom is the Prince de Conti, who has some engagement in town, Raymond steps aboard.

The Captain de Chateau Rouge is at the fête on the island, his Lieutenant Polignac in command, a man who is more of the sailor than the courtier.

D'Arnac says hurriedly to him: "Drive the galley back to la Pomègue as fast as possible!"

"*Morbleu!*" dissents the tar, "we were about to drop anchor. We have rowed from six o'clock this morning and now it is ten at night, towing vessels and taking passengers. The labor has been enormous, two or three of the *forçats* have died. Not one of them has had a bite to eat. They have been toiling continuously."

"I must go back to the island—it is imperative!" returns D'Arnac.

What are galley slaves to him, to delay his assignation with impatient beauty.

"Give the orders, Monsieur Lieutenant," he says, "and to-morrow afternoon, if you will dine with me, I will try to recompense you for your trouble by a very excellent meal!"

"Oh, we officers have had plenty to eat," laughs Polignac. "Besides, if we anchor at the island, De Chateau Rouge can come on board in the morning, and I will have an hour or two at the dance to-night." He orders: "*Comité!* give the measure." "Quartermaster, head for la Pomègue once more!"

"*Tonn de Dieu!*" growls the boatswain, "how many slaves will live with another five miles to their credit and nothing to eat?"

"Blow the *forçats!* Give them the measure quick!" answers Polignac.

This is done; the pipe rings out again, and the boatswain's mates have now double lashing to do, for the slaves are so faint from fatigue.

As they pass the Fort St. John, Raymond looks at his watch.

He has but half an hour, and falters to Polignac:
"*Mon Dieu!* I shall be late!"

"You are in a hurry?"

"Very much! I must get there at eleven."

"Order the *comité* to quicken the measure!" cries
the lieutenant, anxious to please the general commanding.

Again the slaves increase their toil, and now many of
them commence to lag and droop under the heartbreak-
ing, unceasing toil of all that long, burning day.

During its hours no wretch of them has tasted food.
But the plying lash is on them. They must row on—
or die, or both.

The moon coming up, sheds a soft radiance upon this
scene; on the toiling flesh and blood below, on the
officers on watch, on eager Comte d'Arnac, who sits
on the poop staying his impetuosity by a friendly pipe
and Virginia tobacco, and gazing at the far-off glimmering lights across the sea, that tell where she is
waiting.

As the oars swish to and fro unceasingly, the groans
of their wretched rowers come up into the soft air of
night, and their haggard faces, and bare, sinewy arms,
gleam and flash under the moonlight.

In one of these sighs that come up to Heaven, part
of despair, part of exertion, Raymond thinks he hears,
mingled with its breath, one little word, "*Together!*"

It may be but a groan.

At first he does not heed it, and goes smoking on.

Then, as the oars flash once again in the moonlight,
he hears floating up on the sigh of the slaves,
"TOGETHER!"

Something in the tone startles him. His pipe drops
to the deck.

The boatswain and some of the sailors are now going
about putting between open, panting lips, as they move
in the cadence of the swing, pieces of bread moistened
with sour wine; a custom not born of humanity, but
simply of convenience. If too many slaves die, the
galley is disabled.

And still at each swing of the oar, and each gasping
sigh of the slaves, there floats up to D'Arnac's astonished
ears, "TOGETHER!"

He springs to the *comité* and cries: "Some bread and wine quick—I'll help you!"

Then he passes tremblingly along the first bank of oars.

He finds not what he seeks, but shivers as he looks, for it is louder now and *nearer*—this word of the night that takes him back to Flanders and battle, and puts a kind of desperate hope within him.

Thus coming to the second bank, before the sturdiest of its crew, who pulls untired, standing up with each stroke, and swinging back with a crash upon the bench, he sees a haggard face, lighted by eyes that gleam with what appears insanity, but is *hope!*

As Raymond presses the moistened bread upon this wretches' tongue that hangs out black and parched between the panting lips, tones come to him that make him start with shock and horror—with pity and amaze—with agony and joy—for it whispers: "TOGETHER! OH, GOD OF HEAVEN! SAVE ME!"

With one bound, D'Arnac is on the poop, screaming: "Stop rowing! For God's sake, *stop!*"

"What do you mean? You'll miss your appointment."

"*Stop rowing!*"

"Is there a bark ahead of us?"

"Stop rowing! I order it—I, Commandant of the Port! STOP ROWING!"

His words make the officers jump! The vessel stops.

"Take number one of the second oar out of his chains!"

"A galley slave—A *forçat?*"

"Quick! What's one more galley slave to you? You have three hundred! I need one for shore duty at the hospital for infectious diseases. The last one died to-day. Take number one of the second oar out of the irons!"

"But what the devil will I say to the captain? He's the strongest wretch in the boat!" replies Polignac.

"I'll explain to Chateau Rouge. BESIDES, I ORDER IT!"

"Then it must be done! Boatswain, order the armorer knock off the irons on number one of the second oar!" directs Polignac.

Even while they are doing it, O'Brien Dillon, no more the dashing soldier of fortune, but a wretch broken by toil, staggering and faint, is in the arms of his friend, and as the shackles fall from him, he is crying like a child and wringing his hands, and panting.

As he is lifted to the poop, and clothes thrown over his nakedness, he is chattering as one insane: "I didn't dare to cry my name to you—if you had not heard— to-morrow morning the bastinado!" Then he shrieks out: "I heard her voice—they called her ' La Sabran.' Now I know why they made me a galley slave."

"Who did this awful thing?" shudders Raymond.

"The whole gang of them, your Cousin Charlie, the Procureur du Roy."

"Impossible! For what crime?" gasps D'Arnac.

"For being a wizard! Lanty's infernal shot of the billiard table!" moans Dillon. "They swore I had the black art."

And he goes into wild imprecations on such high names that D'Arnac fears he will be overheard and gets him into the cabin.

Then, for the galley is near the island, Raymond says to Polignac: "Stop rowing! Back to the harbor!"

"Why?"

"To get a thousand crowns at my office to-morrow morning," whispers D'Arnac, who sees he must have the lieutenant's aid.

"Good!" replies that officer, and the vessel swings round on water illumined by the *feu de joie* right in the lights of the festival, the music of which comes faintly over the waves in happy cadence, and there are shouts of "A health to the King and Monseigneur Lass!"

At this, on the deck of the galley a half crazed creature who has just come back from hades, screams: "I know him—my Uncle Johnny—I know her—the mistress of the Regent—the De Sabran! It was for this they have made me the wretch I am! High though they are, God help them both when the galley slave takes the revenge of a devil that is all they have left him in life!"

Next he moans: "Let me sleep! Raymond—let me sleep—but for God's sake don't let me DREAM; for if I dream—I shall DREAM I am again at the oar—and in hell!" then goes into a slumber that is almost as strong as death itself.

So D'Arnac sits sighing over—weeping over—this man, whom other men have degraded to the brute.

And this man's wife standing draping about her beauty the folds of the blue curtains of the pavilion number five of Monseigneur Lass' fête of triumph, waits—waits till even morn has come again, for a lover who does not return, and listens for a voice she pants for, yet never hears. And finally, turning to the rising sun eyes that burn with disappointed longing and unquenched desire, mutters: "It is la Quinault! He has remembered *her*, he has forgotten *me*. She shall repent in tears and blood the insult this night for love of her, Raymond—*my* Raymond—has put upon the Princess of Paris!"

FINIS.

THE SEQUEL TO THIS NOVEL IS

THE KING'S STOCKBROKER

JUST OUT

A Complication

in Hearts

A NOVEL

BY

EDMUND PENDLETON

AUTHOR OF

"A Conventional Bohemian," "A Virginia
Inheritance," "One Woman's Way"
etc., etc., etc.

THE HOME PUBLISHING COMPANY

3 East 14th Street, New York

ANOTHER GREAT SUCCESS.

Miss Nobody

of Nowhere.

BY

ARCHIBALD C. GUNTER.

"Full of incident and excitement."—*New York Herald.*

"The popularity of Mr. Gunter will now be greater than ever."—*Tacoma Globe.*

"A story that will keep a man away from his meals."—*Omaha Bee.*

"There is not a dull page in this volume."
—*Daily Chronicle*, London, Jan. 14, 1891.

"Gunter scores another success."
—*Morning Advertiser*, London, Dec. 16, 1890.

"Well worth reading."
—*Galignani*, Paris, Nov. 24, 1890.

"Nothing could exceed its thrilling interest."
—*Glasgow Herald*, Dec. 25, 1890.

"Gunter's latest remarkable story will not disappoint his numerous admirers."
—*Newcastle Chronicle*, Dec. 4, 1890.